THE

Dear

ian. An art-
words. Other
ist, m
ersuade and
time
conv

n all you can
rite a thank-

about how to improve your writing you letter, an essay, a resume, or that article for the newspaper about your garden club's upcoming annual fundraiser—I believe you'll find something in these pages that will help.

Writing, like anything else worthwhile in life, takes discipline, instruction, and most of all, confidence in your ability to do a good job. You gain that all-important confidence through practice—and by studying samples of other works. That's why you'll find so many examples in this book. I include lots of information about what goes into tackling specific writing chores and then provide examples of how it's done: examples that you can then use and adapt to help you complete your own writing projects or chores, whatever the case may be.

Never be afraid to express yourself on paper. The days of the woolly mammoth era when words were chiseled in stone are no longer a part of the human experience. Today you have an eraser on your pencil or, even easier to use, delete and backspace keys on your keyboard. Write, delete, and copy and paste (what was once known as editing), and then write some more.

Whether you read this book cover to cover, or only peruse those pages that answer whatever writing questions that might arise from time to time, please keep in mind that to become a good writer you must not only learn from example, you also need to write. Regardless of how you approach this book, it's my sincere hope that you have as much fun reading it as I had writing it.

Pamela Rice Hahn

Welcome to the EVERYTHING® Series!

These handy, accessible books give you all you need to tackle a difficult project, gain a new hobby, comprehend a fascinating topic, prepare for an exam, or even brush up on something you learned back in school but have since forgotten.

You can choose to read an *Everything*® book from cover to cover or just pick out the information you want from our four useful boxes: e-questions, e-facts, e-alerts, e-ssentials. We give you everything you need to know on the subject, but throw in a lot of fun stuff along the way, too.

We now have more than 400 *Everything*® books in print, spanning such wide-ranging categories as weddings, pregnancy, cooking, music instruction, foreign language, crafts, pets, New Age, and so much more. When you're done reading them all, you can finally say you know *Everything*®!

QUESTIONS?
Answers to
common questions

FACTS
Important snippets
of information

ALERTS!
Urgent
warnings

ESSENTIALS
Quick
handy tips

DIRECTOR OF INNOVATION Paula Munier

EDITORIAL DIRECTOR Laura M. Daly

EXECUTIVE EDITOR, SERIES BOOKS Brielle K. Matson

ASSOCIATE COPY CHIEF Sheila Zwiebel

ACQUISITIONS EDITOR Lisa Laing

DEVELOPMENT EDITOR Katie McDonough

PRODUCTION EDITOR Casey Ebert

Visit the entire Everything® series at *www.everything.com*

THE
EVERYTHING®

IMPROVE YOUR WRITING BOOK

2nd Edition

Master the written word and communicate clearly

Pamela Rice Hahn

Aadamsmedia

In loving memory of my father, Homer H. Rice Jr. (1928-2003)

An Everything® Series Book.
Everything® and everything.com® are registered trademarks of F+W Publications, Inc.

Published by Adams Media, an F+W Publications Company
57 Littlefield Street, Avon, MA 02322 U.S.A.
www.adamsmedia.com

ISBN 10: 1-59869-510-X
ISBN 13: 978-1-59869-510-6

Printed in the United States of America.

J I H G F E D C B A

Library of Congress Cataloging-in-Publication Data
is available from the publisher.

This publication is designed to provide accurate and authoritative information with regard to the subject matter covered. It is sold with the understanding that the publisher is not engaged in rendering legal, accounting, or other professional advice. If legal advice or other expert assistance is required, the services of a competent professional person should be sought.

—From a *Declaration of Principles* jointly adopted by a Committee of the American Bar Association and a Committee of Publishers and Associations

Many of the designations used by manufacturers and sellers to distinguish their products are claimed as trademarks. Where those designations appear in this book and Adams Media was aware of a trademark claim, the designations have been printed with initial capital letters.

This book is available at quantity discounts for bulk purchases.
For information, please call 1-800-289-0963.

Contents

Essays in Particular / 133

Academic Writing: Research Papers, Master's Theses, and Dissertations / 145

Business Writing / 155

Job Search and Employment-Related Writing / 167

Grant Writing / 187

Technical Writing / 201

cknowledgments

For all their work on my behalf, I'd like to thank my agent Sheree Bykofsky and her associate, Janet Rosen. For all their input and help, I'd like to thank Lisa Laing, Katie McDonough, and everyone else at Adams Media, and David L. Hebert, Eric J. Ehlers, Jodi Cornelius, and Troy More. As always, additional thanks go to Lara and the grandkids (who make it all worthwhile), Ann Rice, Andy Rice, Tam Smith, and my mother, Pat Rice.

Top Ten Reasons
Why You Need to Write Well

1. Being a good, effective writer is one of the best ways to advance in your career, no matter what it might be.

2. Knowing all the proper writing etiquettes will help you maintain good friendships—from typing up proper e-mails to writing thoughtful personal letters.

3. Writing well will convey to others your knowledge and intelligence, garnering for you the respect that you deserve.

4. If you are taking classes, you need strong writing skills to get top grades.

5. Being able to write well enables you to put into words your thoughts, feelings, and ideas in a way that may move others.

6. You must be able to write well to teach others how to write, including helping your children with homework.

7. Writing is a wonderful way to relax and keep track of your life.

8. Being able to craft well-written and clear business letters may prove rewarding (especially if the letter is a complaint).

9. From invitations to essays to reminder notes to fax cover sheets—our daily lives are constantly filled with activities requiring the written word.

10. Someday you could write a bestseller!

Introduction

▶ OFTEN, THE SEEMINGLY overwhelming part of writing may stem from the secondary decisions about your communication format (formal versus informal, handwritten versus typed versus typeset, and so forth). Ironically, such flexibility can appear stifling. That doesn't have to happen. Once you learn a few simple rules about putting things down on paper, you'll recognize that these rules don't restrict your creativity and free flow of ideas. Providing yourself with a map—whether it be a rigid formal outline or an informal listing of known purposes for the communication—actually frees your mind to get to work on deciding how best to complete the task.

Learning a few simple steps about how to plan your writing will simplify the task of actually doing the necessary writing. As you will see, you'll follow basically the same steps regardless of what it is you need to write. It all boils down to determining the five Ws and the H:

- Who?
- What?
- When?
- Where?
- Why?
- How?

Determining answers to these questions helps get you ready to write. The answers help you see what needs to be said, from beginning to end. In other words, the answers help form the vision for your work.

Think of this stage in much the same way as you would plan a trip. Unless you have an unlimited expense and time budget, you'd never embark on a journey without some preliminary planning. Mastering a few essential steps leads to effective, efficient, and productive quality writing, which results in easy-to-understand communication. Being able to attach that many adjectives to what you write is indeed an attainable goal!

1

CHAPTER 1

The Basics

There are a few decisions you need to reach regarding what it is you intend to write. Some will be specific, such as the message you need to convey. That message can be anything from accepting an invitation, announcing your engagement, or complaining about the lack of supervision at a community youth program. Answering preliminary *who*, *what*, *when*, *where*, *why*, and *how* questions helps you draw the map for your writing trail.

Who?

Who will need to read what you've written? Will that reader be able to determine who wrote the stuff she is reading? Your audience, the who, affects the final how answer you'll need more than anything else on your list of preliminary, fact-finding questions.

ALERT!

Relax. That task of putting something in writing need not be as daunting as it first appears. After all, you've already defined your goal. Now all you need to do is establish the priorities necessary to reach the desired outcome: having something down on paper.

Determine Your Audience

Unless you're writing in your journal, where the only audience you please is yourself, the first fundamental question you'll need to answer is: Whom am I writing for? Once that is settled, you're ready to refine the scope even further by resolving these questions:

- Does my reader already know me?
- Is my reader somebody "in house" or will I be writing to somebody outside my center of influence?
- Will my reader know anything about this topic?
- Will my reader be receptive to what I'm writing, or will I need to include any special motivation for continuing?
- Will I need to anticipate and overcome any objections or any ambivalence?

Establish the Voice for Your Writing

Next, you need to ask yourself: Who should the reader perceive as the author of this particular writing?

- Should the author of the piece be invisible to the reader? If so, then first-person pronouns, such as I or we, should not be used.
- Should the reader feel as if the author is speaking directly to him or her? If so, then you'll want to use the second person pronoun you a lot.
- Should both the author and the reader be invisible? Then only third-person pronouns should be used, with no reference to I or you. This is the way most novels are written, with clear boundaries separating the reader from the piece, while also keeping the author invisible.

What?

Answering this question helps you better determine the subject about which you need to write. What kind of information do you plan to disseminate? Are you writing an information piece about a new procedure in your company? Are you writing a short story about the survivors of a plane crash?

What will your readers already know? You've heard the expression, "beating a dead horse"—by including too much information that people already know, you lessen the impact of the new points you're making. Only give enough information necessary to provide context.

FACT

Always keep your audience in mind. For example, if you're writing a piece about how to change spark plugs, you don't also need to go into the history of piston engines unless you're writing for a specific market where that kind of background information fits.

When?

Knowing when to set your piece is a very important aspect of writing. Are you setting the piece in the past? If so, be careful to maintain the illusion and not include things that weren't invented yet. Having Blargg the Caveman whip out a ballpoint pen is completely absurd, as would be having William Shakespeare use a computer. Sure, these are extreme examples, but even something as innocuous as a tea bag could be just as incongru-ous in the period of the story. Research the historical context of the period you're writing about to avoid jarring inconsistencies.

Where?

Where, in some ways, is inextricably tied to when, but don't underestimate the importance of setting.

- Where do the major events of your story take place?
- If the events haven't yet occurred, where are they expected to take place?
- How does the setting affect the characters and their interaction?

Why?

No matter what you're writing, you should always have a grasp on the rea-son you're doing it. This keeps you focused and on point.

Is your objective to provide a step-by-step, systematic guide to accomplishing some task? Then the only thing that's really important is outlining the steps, along with enough information to give it context. Too much explanation bogs down the reader and can bury the point you're trying to make, lessening its impact.

How?

Determining the how for what it is you're writing will help you determine how best you should tell that story. (Taken to the extreme, this is what polit-ical speechwriters use to put the spin on what it is politicians will say, based on how they want their constituents to perceive that message.)

- How do you plan to get your point across?
- Do you want to tell a linear story?
- Do you plan to use flashbacks to establish the history of your characters?

Keep all of these questions in mind when you're plotting and coming up with the things you'd like to write. As a preliminary step, you might want to make a checklist and check off each item as you address it.

Style Is Important, Too

Have you ever noticed that as you read something written by a particular author, you get familiar with the writing style? As you move from one book to the next, you notice similarities between them. Style is something that is peculiar to each individual writer. Stephen King, for example, writes in a very different style from Janet Evanovich, and not just because each author tends to write about different subjects. Style is an amorphous thing that is attributed to a writer; many writers don't even realize that they have a particular style. They just write.

Bending the Rules

Many beginning writers think that they can bend the rules or do whatever they like, and call it their "style." As you gain writing success and get more familiar with the rules, you're allowed certain liberties. As you become more adept at the rules, you also gain a better understanding of where you can bend them and still get away with it. So in your early days, be attentive to the way things are done, and worry about breaking the mold later.

If you're writing a quick note to a friend, you're bound to use much different language than you would if you were, say, writing a letter to a lawyer. Tone, diction, and style vary between formal and informal writing. Don't be too formal with your friends, and don't be too informal otherwise.

But style is much more than sticking to the basic rules. Style also encompasses how you put the words together into sentences, how you put your sentences together into paragraphs, and so on. As you develop your writing style, it will turn into your personal "voice." The way you transform your thoughts into words will become almost habitual and completely natural to you.

Informal Versus Formal Writing

The rules for informal writing are more relaxed. You can get away with slang. You can get away with saying things like, "You can get away with slang."

Formal writing is often used in academic situations where the audience has a professional background, although it also exists outside the purely academic field. Law and science are two particularly apt examples.

You must be careful not to sound too presumptuous when writing formally; just because a setting is formal does not mean that you should use only big words. You can use nice small words, and nice short sentences, too, but you should not use colloquialisms or other informal conventions. Stick to traditional punctuation styles and grammar usage.

CHAPTER 2

How to Write What You Mean

It's extremely important to be clear in your writing. Except in certain artistic forms, writing isn't about making things sound pretty. It isn't about choosing words that have a nice ring to them. Writing is communication. When it comes to writing, the most important thing is that you get your point across. Communication only takes place when the meaning of what you write is clear and concise.

The Elements of Effective Writing

When broken down into its simplest form, effective writing has three parts:

1. A beginning
2. A middle
3. An ending

Sure, it sounds trite, but everything has to start somewhere, right? Your writing will be much better if you consider each of these components. When you start writing, don't just jump in and start anywhere. Take a few moments to figure out where you want to start, what you're going to say, and how you're going to wrap things up.

Effective Openings

Despite the association with "once upon a time" as the beginning for make-believe stories, the consensus for most fiction today is that you "start with the action." If there are things the reader needs to know about the "beginning" (which is known in fiction as "backstory"), then there are devices such as flashbacks that can be used to supply that information, or it can be worked into the story as you go along. Today's world is a fast-paced one. People used to moving at a fast pace are not patient. Effective writing, regardless of whether it is fiction or nonfiction, reflects this trait.

Literature has evolved over the years to reflect the demands of the public. Consider the long, wordy passages in novels of past centuries: In Chapter 11 of Emily Brontë's Gothic *Wuthering Heights*, Mr. Lockwood muses, "I am now quite cured of seeking pleasure in society, be it country or town. A sensible man ought to find sufficient company in himself." A novelist writing for today's readers, who are used to getting their news in easily digestible sound bites, would probably simply have a character say, "I find pleasure in my own company."

Other beginnings are even less easy to define. As you'll see in later chapters, you don't get to the opening sentence of a letter until you write the "body." The beginning is the "opening," which consists of the recipient's address and greeting (and is not to be confused with the "heading," which consists of your information and the date).

Regardless of its name, an effective opening is one that engages the reader from the git-go. In formal writing, it's free of slang or colloquialisms (like *git-go*). An effective opening recognizes certain things about the reader (or audience), such as educational level. The writer takes those known factors into consideration when determining how best to appeal to that reader or audience.

If you're writing a romantic thriller, you want to introduce the hero and heroine, of course, but you want to do so with finesse. An opening scene might be the following.

Dick Meadows tilted his hat and boarded the aged train, pulling himself up with the handrails just as the train lurched slowly forward on its way to Nairobi. He heard a shout behind him, and turned to see a tall blonde woman running to catch up.

"Stop the train!"

He smiled. "Fat chance, lady," he thought to himself, before turning back to see the determined look on her face.

The train continued to move slowly as she ran alongside it. Bracing himself, Dick reached out his hand to help her up. She gave him a grateful smile as she climbed aboard.

That example starts with some action. It doesn't spend a lot of time developing the story, the setting, or anything else. It isn't necessary to establish how Dick or the lady got to the train station. Or why it's so important that the blonde catch the train. Or why she was late getting to the train. It simply jumps in where everything starts. This way, the reader joins the heroine as she hits the ground running, amidst the action, and hopefully will want to know more. The rest of that, of course, is continued in the middle.

Middle Matters

When it comes down to it, the "middle" is just a convenient way of separating your beginning and ending from everything else. The middle is where the substance occurs. The opening may set the tone, but the actual point of your piece will emerge through the unfolding of the middle. In a story, this is where the bulk of the story happens.

Your middle will actually be a series of events that slowly culminate in the big, final climactic scene. And after you reach that, it's time to end your story.

Wrapping Things Up

Just as you must be careful to start with the action in your opening, you must also remember to stop where the story ends. Many beginning writers continue writing long after the story is over, rehashing old material. In fiction, your writing is much stronger—and has a much greater emotional impact on the reader—if it leaves some things up to the imagination. As long as the major points of the story are wrapped up, you can leave some things unsaid.

FACT

An emotionally satisfying ending to a story with a few things left to the reader's speculation also leaves the author with the option of writing a sequel.

Consider the romantic thriller example. Suppose your story progressed to finding a giant ruby and smuggling it through various countries. Finally, Dick and the woman reach the coast.

Megan looked up into Dick's eyes. "So I guess this is it."
He nodded slowly. "Apparently."
Hoisting the satchel with the ruby inside, Megan slung it over her back. She smiled at Dick, trying not to cry, as she turned and began walking away from him, up the plank to board the ship.

Megan stopped at the top, hesitated, then turned to face him. Dick stood on the shore, with his hands on his hips, his hat slightly askew. Megan tried to push away the thought that this might be the last moment they would ever share. The last chance she'd have to look in his eyes.

"You sure?" she asked, biting her lip.

"Oh, what the hell," Dick muttered, and started to run up the plank.

Because the story ends that way, the reader doesn't know what happens to the ruby, or to Dick and Megan. Maybe they lived happily ever after, or maybe they had a fight on the cruise and decided to go their own separate ways. Those unanswered questions don't make it an ineffective ending. The point is that this is where this story ends. Anything more would merely be fluff and would most likely detract from the rest of the story. As long as you provide an effective emotional close to your piece, you don't have to have an answer there for everything.

Making a Good Impression

You may not realize it, but you are judged by what you write. Using correct grammar not only conveys a precise meaning, it also gives readers confidence that you know what you're talking about. This is very important when the reader is a prospective employer or editor.

Grammatical mistakes or spelling errors can make the reader doubt your abilities. To make the best impression, you should strive to use correct grammar and proper spelling.

Grammar is only one part of making a good impression. This chapter will help you understand the basic aspects of effective writing. When you use the techniques outlined in this chapter, your writing becomes stronger, which gives readers more confidence in you as a person, not only in your writing.

Active Voice

The voice of a sentence can be active or passive. When it is active, the subject of the sentence is performing the verb. With a passive sentence, however, the subject of the sentence is on the receiving end of the verb. Consider the following active example:

The cheerleaders danced to the half-time music.

The subject of the sentence—cheerleaders—is performing the action, namely dancing to the music. Now look at the following example of using passive voice:

The half-time music was accompanied by the dancing of the cheerleaders.

As you can see, the music isn't actually doing anything. The cheerleaders are still doing the dancing, but the action of the sentence has shifted. When you construct a sentence using the passive voice, the subject of the sentence receives the action of the verb instead of performing it.

There's a simple little trick to recognize when the passive voice is being used. If the word by is used in the sentence to indicate who is performing the action, it's probably a passive voice construction.

Omitting Unnecessary Adjectives

Adjectives modify nouns or pronouns. When used properly, they can add a great deal of depth to your writing. When used improperly, adjectives can make your writing seem unprofessional and stilted.

The elderly man picked up his ugly, rusty old razor and began to shave his craggy wrinkled face.

As you can see, too many adjectives in a sentence can make the reader stumble. It's a much better idea to break up your adjectives and intersperse them within a number of sentences; this puts them into bite-sized bits that are much easier for the reader to digest and swallow. Better yet, try to stretch out the description, so that you're not relying entirely on adjectives:

The old man picked up his razor. It was rusty, but it was all he had. He lathered up the soap and applied it to his face, covering up the wrinkles and stubble in preparation for his shave.

Compulsively Overusing Adverbs

An adverb is a word that modifies a verb. Adverbs can also modify adjectives, other adverbs, or even entire sentence clauses. They can convey degree, manner, number, place, or time. Adverbs can ask questions; they can also modify entire clauses in a sentence, like the word *however* does in the next paragraph.

Most adverbs end in *–ly*. *Quickly*, *angrily*, and *goodheartedly* are examples. *Who*, *what*, *when*, *where*, and *why* are all adverbs, too, and they're good ones to use. If adverbs appear too frequently in your writing, however, try to cut them out.

ALERT!

Overuse of adverbs can detract from your message, causing the reader to get hung up on the words instead of the point you're trying to make.

The following adverbs tend to appear too often in written English. Make sure that you use them sparingly. If you tend to use them a lot, cut them, and find other ways of getting your point across.

- Accordingly
- Also
- Anyhow
- Consequently

- Otherwise
- Still
- Then
- Therefore
- Yet

If you tend to overuse the words in the above list, don't fret; working around them is relatively easy to do. Simply restructure your sentence and try to do away with the adverb.

QUESTION?

Are there any things to look for in my writing that will help me find (and then get rid of) excessive adverbs?
Most often, excessive adverbs are used with compound sentences. Semicolons and commas tend to go hand in hand with adverbs, so use periods instead. This will help you break down those compound sentences into smaller portions. Nine times out of ten, you can just delete the adverb, change the comma or semicolon to a period, and end up with wonderful adverb-free sentences.

Before: I feel that I am the ideal candidate for this position. Accordingly, please accept the attached resume; also please accept the attached letter of reference. I am available weekdays; however, I am not available every second weekend. However, after Christmas, I will be able to work any weekend.

After: I feel that I am the ideal candidate for this position. Please accept the attached resume and letter of reference. I am available all weekdays. Until Christmas, I am unable to work every second weekend; after Christmas, I can work any weekend.

Good grammar never goes to waste. The rules of grammar are relatively easy to learn and will stay with you for your lifetime. You can get excellent grammar guides at your local library (Try *The Everything® Grammar and Style Book, 2nd Edition*) or conduct a Web search to find a grammar tutorial site.

Noun-Pronoun Agreement

Pronouns are words that take the place of nouns. They are nice to use because they are short and concise, and they avoid the needless repetition of nouns in a sentence. The following table shows common English pronouns grouped according to their function.

Common English Pronouns

Subject	Object	Possessive
I	me	my
you	you	your
he	him	his
she	her	her
it	it	its
we	us	our
they	them	their
who	whom	whose

Because a pronoun is used in place of a noun, it must have a noun to relate to. This is why some grammar teachers nail home the point that you should never start a sentence with *it*.

It ran the length of the track before it returned to the stable.

What exactly is it? How can you tell? You might be able to gain an inference from the sentence; after all, how many things will run a track and then return to the stable? However, this creates work for the reader, and any time you make a reader think, you run the risk of losing him or her along the way. A much better choice would be:

The horse ran the length of the track before it returned to the stable.

Not only must your pronoun relate to a noun, it must also relate to the noun in number, which is why you can never use *it* when you actually mean *them*, or vice versa. Be very careful with your pronouns and make sure that they agree in number.

In addition, you should be careful to make sure that the noun agrees in gender, too. Never use *her* for a male, and never use *him* for a female. By the same token, you should never use *they* to take the place of either *he* or *she* or *them* for *him* or *her*. For more information on this topic, refer to Chapter 4.

ALERT!

In conversation, many people use the pronouns they, them, and their even when referring to one person. This is not proper grammar. The correct choice is he or she when referring to a singular subject; him or her when referring to a singular object; and his or her when using a possessive adjective:

Wrong: Who left their shoes by the door? They did.
Correct: Who left his or her shoes by the door? She did.

Avoiding Ambiguous Pronoun Usage

You must be careful with pronouns, because using them improperly can result in an ambiguous sentence. If only two people of different genders are involved, the pronoun usage should be obvious. With two people of the same sex, or a group, confusion (or even the opportunity for it) can quickly result. Consider the following example:

"How is your shift going?" Matthew asked David, sitting down at his desk and running his fingers through his hair.

At whose desk did Matthew sit? Matthew's or David's? Moreover, whose hair did Matthew run his fingers through? Matthew's or David's? At first glance, it might seem obvious what's truly going on in the sentence, namely that Matthew sits at his own desk and runs his fingers through his own hair while he converses with David. The pronoun usage in the sentence, however, is far from specific and open to interpretation. If you were writing that sentence, the "alternative" interpretation is probably far from what you actually meant. So, it's a good idea to be careful. A much better sentence construction would be:

Matthew sat down at his desk and ran his fingers through his hair. "How is your shift going?" he asked David.

Remember that a pronoun must relate to another noun, and that that relationship should be obvious. If it is not, fiddle with your sentences until the pronoun usage makes sense. It's also a good idea to have someone else read over your work, not just to check for typos but also to check for problems with pronoun usage and other inconsistencies. If one of your friends is confused by a pronoun, there's a very good chance that someone else will be too. For other proofreading suggestions, see Chapter 4.

FACT

In fiction writing, each character's speech should appear in its own paragraph. If a new person speaks, then start a new paragraph. Depending on your own personal style, you may want to keep description and narrative in their own separate paragraphs, distinct from dialogue.

Sentence and Paragraph Structure

Sentence structure is usually a matter of style. As you gain more experience with your writing, you will develop your own personal style with the way you put words together into sentences, and the way you put sentences together into paragraphs. It helps if you keep these two things in mind:

1. **Keep your sentences as concise as possible.** Normally, this means "short," but don't oversimplify your sentences if you're trying to make a specific point. A sentence should be as long as it needs to be—and no longer.
2. **Try to keep your paragraph limited to one point or idea.** Rather than introduce multiple ideas in the course of one paragraph, break up the ideas and present them in their own paragraphs. This creates ease of understanding for the reader.

Beyond Using a Spellchecker

With the proliferation of computers and word-processing programs, many people have come to rely on technology to tell them whether words are spelled correctly. For most, running a spell check has become the final step in drafting a document; as long as error messages don't pop up along the way, people assume that the words have all been spelled correctly.

A spellchecker, however, is nothing more than a lexicon—a list of words. The computer will compare your word against its list of properly spelled words, giving an error message for anything that doesn't match up. This is why many names of people or places give errors. An error message from a spellchecker is simply a notification that the computer doesn't recognize the word after it compares the word to its internal lists. Sometimes, the computer will offer suggestions, but this is simply based on similarities between your word and the list of words it uses to compare. Remember, computers can't actually think.

Spellcheckers provide a false sense of security. It is possible that computers may become more sophisticated in the future, but for now, they can't tell the difference between different forms of homonyms.

Homonyms are words that sound the same but have different meanings. Examples are *their*, *there*, and *they're*; or *rain* and *reign*. Be careful with these kinds of words, because spellcheckers will only be able to tell you that they're spelled correctly, not used correctly. Consider the following:

Incorrect: It is our constitutional right to bare arms.

This example sentence is, of course, incorrect. The constitution doesn't say anything about naked arms; it does, however, have an amendment about weapons for personal defense. Therefore, the correct choice would be "bear," but at this point in time, a computer can't tell you that. You need to know for yourself how these words are used.

Correct: It is our constitutional right to bear arms.

The Value of a Good Dictionary

Get into the habit of reaching for your dictionary. A dictionary will tell you not only how to spell a word correctly, it will also tell you how that word is used. Chances are the few seconds it takes you to look up a word and read the definition will mean you'll never have a problem with that word again. That makes such dictionary usage time well spent.

If you use the Internet, there are a great number of dictionaries available online, such as Merriam-Webster Online at *www.m-w.com*. You merely have to type in the word, and the site will provide you with definitions from its database. However you do it, take the extra few seconds to make certain that you're using the proper word, and the proper spelling.

Don't Rely on a Thesaurus Alone

A thesaurus can be a great resource, too. It provides lists of synonyms, or words that have similar meanings. By consulting a thesaurus, you can come up with other words to help you say things a little differently. Many word-processing programs have a thesaurus included, and you can also find them on the Internet; in addition to the dictionary, there's also a thesaurus available at Merriam-Webster Online at *www.m-w.com*. A thesaurus can be a great resource to expand your vocabulary.

Never assume, however, that the words in a thesaurus are interchangeable. Among the suggestions, you will find similar words, but not words with identical meanings. Before you use a word you find in a thesaurus, look it up in the dictionary to determine its actual meaning. If you don't, you might end up using something that doesn't quite carry the meaning you intend.

Using Descriptive Nouns

A noun, as a basic definition, is a word that designates a person, place, or thing. Nouns can be simple and generic, like book, or they can be more descriptive, like romance, mystery, or thriller. The more descriptive your nouns, the more vivid your writing will be.

For example, consider the noun *dog*. *Dog* is a very nondescript noun that only conveys a very basic meaning. *Chihuahua, terrier*, and *dachshund* are more descriptive, and therefore effective, choices. Such words paint a recognizable picture in the reader's mind, making your writing seem more lively and specific. Try to choose nouns that are colorful and descriptive, rather than generic.

Choosing Action Verbs

Action verbs are verbs that describe action, as opposed to verbs that describe a state of being. To act, to sing, and to dance are all examples of verbs that describe action. To write is an action verb, too, because it describes something that you can actually do. At the opposite end of the spectrum is the verb to be, which is relatively flat and lifeless because it merely describes a state.

The verb *to be* is probably the most important verb in the language because it also serves as a conjunctive verb in complex constructions. For example:

Jessica is singing a song.
Martin is writing a play.

Even though both sentences contain the word *is*, which is a conjugated form of the verb *to be*, in those examples it is also used as a linking verb that serves to complete the conjugation of the other verbs *to sing* and *to write*.

John was singing a song.
John sang a song.
John had sung a song.

All of the above example sentences mean the same thing. The appropriate choice depends on the tense of the particular passage and how the activity of singing relates to what else is going on in the story.

It is very important to make sure that your verbs are used in the proper tense, but it's also important to try to make your verb usage as active as possible.

Remember, good writing should show, not tell, the reader what is happening. In crafting your story, try to choose verbs that show action. Sometimes, you will want to use weaker verbs like *to be* in order to establish your setting and mood. Use these sparingly. When describing action, be sure to use verbs that show the activity and serve to paint that vivid picture in the reader's mind about what is occurring in the story.

You should not make a habit of using action verbs to attribute dialogue when characters are speaking. Consider the following examples:

"Sarah and Tom tied the knot last week," Julie informed Sam.

"But I never thought they would actually marry," Sam intoned.

"None of us did. But they appear to have taken the leap," Julie added.

"How long do you think they'll be together?" Sam queried.

"Oh, be nice," Julie admonished. "You shouldn't be so negative," she advised.

As you can see, the action verbs used to attribute the dialogue actually slow down the flow of the conversation. In dialogue, what's important are the words being said. That's why when it comes to attributing dialogue, there is no better word than *said*. Not every line of dialogue needs to have a tag with it. When two characters are conversing in a selection of prose, it is usually pretty obvious which character is speaking. Attribution becomes necessary when there are long passages of dialogue, just to help the reader understand along the way.

Attribution tags are a storytelling technique, and it's a good idea to keep them as simple as possible. The beauty of the word *said* is that it becomes invisible to the reader. It is simply there as a pointer to keep the reader from getting confused. A reader naturally expects to see the word *said*; using other, fancy words can trip up the reader—something often referred to as "removing the reader from the story," which is something you don't want to do.

Analogy, Simile, and Metaphor as Descriptions

Metaphors, analogies, and similes are very similar in nature. Each is used to paint a picture with words. A simile is the most literal and straightforward; it uses the word like or as to make a comparison:

He's crazy like a fox.

He's as crazy as a fox.

The above examples are designed to make a comparison. The sentences do not make literal statements. Instead, they make figurative statements designed to add depth to the description.

A metaphor sits at the opposite end of the spectrum. It states that one thing is something else. A metaphor can create a very visual impact for your reader, so its use can be a very powerful tool. Its meaning is still figurative, but a metaphor causes you to read between the lines. Consider the following examples:

Don't pull my leg.
Don't pull the wool over my eyes.

Nobody's leg is actually being pulled in the first example. It simply means, "Be serious with me; don't joke around!" But the metaphor is, for whatever reason, that you're pulling on someone's leg by not telling the truth.

ALERT!

Be careful that the metaphor you use is not a cliché. Using a phrase, expression, or passage that has been overused (or has become a cliché) can have a negative effect on your writing, and as a result, cause it to lose its credibility. To have impact, your metaphor needs to be original or unique to the idea you're trying to convey.

The second example is a metaphor, too. It doesn't involve any wool, but it serves to paint the picture that somehow you're interfering with the view of the person involved. Pulling wool over that person's eyes is a figurative illustration that you're clouding the person's vision.

At the beginning of this discussion on metaphors, a metaphor was used. Did you notice it? "A metaphor sits at the opposite end of the spectrum." If you think about it, a metaphor can't actually sit anywhere—it's a thought, not something concrete. That sentence was a figurative metaphor, but it did its job conveying the meaning. That's how a good metaphor should be—invisible to the reader unless he or she is looking for it.

In between simile and metaphor is analogy. An analogy is usually a lot longer than either a simile or metaphor because you're using it to compare one situation to another. And that's the big difference—when you use an analogy, you are directly comparing two things. A simile is like a very short analogy; an analogy may use *like* or *as*, but your comparison is more likely to be much longer. It might even take up a paragraph. It will still have the aspects of simile and metaphor, but you provide more detail to convey the comparison. Analogy can be an effective tool because it allows you to point out the similarities between two situations where a simile or metaphor won't quite cut it.

To use analogy, just take a simile or metaphor and elaborate upon it. Stretch it out, and use the example to illustrate the point you're trying to make. Unlike a metaphor, it won't be a direct statement, and unlike a simile, it won't be a simple comparison. Use it when a simile or metaphor won't establish enough of the meaning you're trying to convey.

ESSENTIAL

A simile uses the word like or as to make a comparison. You can remember what a simile is by remembering that it states a similarity. A metaphor, on the other hand, goes the extra distance and actually says that something has certain characteristics. Both are important tools in the writer's toolbox.

Establishing Your Objective

All the fancy writing tricks in the world won't help if you don't have an established objective for your writing. To establish your objective, try to determine what the main point is that you're hoping to get across. If you're writing nonfiction, this should be relatively obvious. Even if you're writing fiction, you still need to have an objective. Even if that objective is merely to entertain, every word in your passage should contribute to that goal.

Many beginning writers get caught up in trying to "sound good." Try to avoid this pitfall. The following list contains many clichéd and hackneyed phrases that tend to get used by beginners:

Bad Choices	Good Choices
because of the fact that	since / because
for the period of	for
in many cases	often
in many instances	sometimes
in the nature of	like
the fact that he had not succeeded	his failure

CHAPTER 3

How to Keep 'Em Reading

A very important part of writing is learning how to make your readers want to continue reading. There are various ways to do this, from using pacing and hooks to involving the senses. Using the tips in this chapter can keep your readers entertained and turn your book (or whatever else you're writing) into a real "page-turner."

Impact

The impact of your writing merely describes how well you're getting your point across. Are you using the proper words? The proper diction? The proper voice? All of these things dictate the impact your story will have.

You increase the impact of your story when you make it interesting for the reader. When the reader wants to keep reading, your piece will have a greater impression on the reader's mind and imagination.

Pacing

Pacing is simply the time you take to convey your information. If you do it at a slow, leisurely pace, you will create a much different emotional impact than you will if you follow the action crisply and closely.

The pacing will also depend on the kind of manuscript you're writing. As you'll see in Chapter 21, there are a variety of fiction and nonfiction markets. Depending on what you're writing, each type of story or book (and each type of scene) will carry with it different requirements when it comes to pacing. If you're setting up scenes, a slow pace is probably effective. As previously mentioned, in a high-action scene, you want events to unfold quickly to keep the reader at a high emotional level of involvement.

Hooks

A "hook" is an interesting part of your story meant to grab the reader's attention. Much is said about the elusive hook, but with practice, you can quickly become adept at getting the reader's attention.

Using a hook merely means that you start your piece in a way that will engage the reader and make him or her want to read more. A hook can be a piece of dialogue or description. The key is to make sure it's interesting. Here are three different takes on starting off with an action hook:

Harold blinked as the old lady drew a gun out of her purse and pointed it at the convenience store clerk.

"Give me all your money," the little old lady said, waving a gun at the convenience store clerk.

The convenience store clerk looked on in disbelief as the little old lady drew a gun from her purse and leveled it at his chest.

The trick is to start with the action. How you actually start will depend on your objective and on your viewpoint. When you're starting a story, don't spend a lot of time establishing setting or character. You want the reader to want to read your story, and expounding information at the beginning of your piece is a sure way to lose the reader's interest. If you start with the action, you will pique the reader's curiosity; you can then work in setting and character after you've whetted the reader's appetite for more.

Likewise, whether in a piece of nonfiction or a letter, the temptation is to provide all sorts of details—or "backstory"—before getting to the point. Writing that states its objective (the action) up front is more effective.

Showing Versus Telling

Beginning writers are often admonished, "Show, don't tell!" Unless it's writing being done to narrate a slide-show presentation or other visual presentation, this instruction can create confusion for the writer if he or she is unclear how to go about actually doing that "showing" stuff.

QUESTION?

What's the difference between showing and telling a story?
Showing in a story merely means that you're allowing the reader to participate in the events rather than just rattling off what happened. When the reader participates, it creates involvement—he or she can see the events unfolding, and then is left wondering what is going to happen next.

If you tell the story instead of showing how the story unfolds, you risk boring the reader. And before you decide that you don't care about those readers who will get bored—after all, someone will surely find your writing spectacular, right?—remember that editors are readers, too. For that reason, the reader should always be first and foremost in your mind. To engage the reader, you need to show the story. Consider the following example of bad storytelling:

Greg went to the store. While there, he bought a gallon of milk. On his way out, he ran into his grade school teacher and spoke with her for a moment before proceeding on his way.

Not very interesting, is it? It's flat and lifeless and serves only as a grocery list (no pun intended) of what happened. Not only that, it robs you of the opportunity to involve your reader in the action and convey little bits of information about the characters in your story.

Now, see what it's like when you show the action:

Greg pulled open the door and stepped through. A slightly musty smell assaulted his nostrils as he walked into the old corner store and faced the high, cramped shelves. The scuffed floor creaked under his weight as he walked over to the ancient milk cooler. The clerk's eagle eyes never left him, giving the impression the clerk thought he might try to stuff a dusty can of peas into his coat pocket.

Greg opened the cooler and picked up a pint of milk, being careful to check the expiration date. Satisfied that it was relatively fresh, he took it up to the front counter.

As he was counting out change, the door opened. He glanced over and recognized Mrs. McGillicuddy, whom he hadn't seen since grade school, and who had barely changed a bit, despite the usual signs of aging. He smiled at her and called her by name.

She looked toward him, with a blank smile on her face. Suddenly, recognition lit her eyes. "Greg!" she exclaimed, smiling broadly.

Greg smiled back. "How on earth did you ever recognize me? It must be thirty years since I've seen you."

The elderly lady smiled mysteriously. "I always remember my star pupils."

Did the second version make you feel more involved? Did you find yourself transported into the small corner store? Did you find it more interesting?

While this example may not exactly be a literary masterpiece, it does serve to show you what it felt like to be in the store at that particular moment, which is something that the first example did not do. Not only that, it also raised some questions about each of the characters and probably made you want to learn more.

The power of showing serves to involve your reader and makes him or her want to participate in the story. Telling the reader what happened is about as interesting as reading a shopping list.

Involving the Senses

In the preceding section, the sense of smell was conveyed with the words musty and dusty. As you were reading, did you perhaps even smell a hint of it yourself? If not, you can probably think of other times when you've become involved in what you're reading and have actually felt the sensory cues being described in the story. For example: Have you ever been reading a story about a blizzard and felt a chill, despite being seated on your patio during the middle of summer? Or reading about the beach when you were interrupted by the doorbell, and then was momentarily surprised to see snow on the ground when you answered the door? That's the power of the mind.

To a lesser extent, the sense of hearing was also used with the creaking floor, and the sense of sight was used, too. The combination of all of these senses makes the reader feel as if he or she is standing alongside the characters, seeing what happens as the events transpire, which gives a feeling of involvement. Get into the habit of involving the senses in your writing:

- **Touch:** What kind of texture do objects have? Is the chair hard, or soft and plush? Show how the surroundings feel to the characters' physical touch.
- **Smell:** What scents can the characters smell in his or her surroundings? Fresh? Smoky? Sweet? Acrid?

- **Sight:** What kinds of things do the characters see? When describing the surroundings, use visual words that convey the color, shape, and other physical attributes of objects to show the reader what is being seen instead of just telling the reader that something is within sight.
- **Hearing:** What kinds of sounds are being made in the surroundings? If your characters are at the waterfront, can they hear waves lapping against the wharf? Can they hear seagulls calling?
- **Taste:** In books like *Babette's Feast* or *A Year in Provence*, information about how a meal tastes directly relates to the story. Unless it is something that directly relates to the story, you may not want to describe exactly how a meal tastes to the character. Small clues about things that involve the character's taste buds can help draw the reader into the action, however, so use your judgment about whether or not your story needs those details.

ALERT!

Remember, the setting of your scene should be secondary to what's actually transpiring in the story. You use senses to complement your scene, not construct it.

It might be a good idea to make up a small list and tape it to your computer monitor to serve as a reminder to involve the senses in your writing. As you're writing a scene, try to use at least two of the senses to make your reader feel like he or she is participating in the story. The more you can use, the better, but try to avoid forcing it.

Voice

The voice of your piece is determined by how you plan to tell the story. In fiction, especially in novels, the voice most often used is third person. The author is invisible and unknown, and the reader is not spoken to in the prose. In many nonfiction books, as in the one you're now reading, the author and the reader are both acknowledged as active participants.

Both types of writing reflect a different voice, because each type of work has a different objective. In a novel or short story, you are trying to paint a picture using words, giving the reader something to enjoy. In non-fiction, frequently you are conveying information or expertise, so the use of first-person pronouns can be completely acceptable. For much the same reason, second-person pronouns are acceptable too, because you're often speaking directly to the reader.

FACT

First-person voice won't work in stories in which you want to have scenes that take place away from the main character. Keep that in mind before you choose a particular voice.

First-person novels, however, are a different story. In them, the voice is usually that of the protagonist. There are some exceptions, however; many people would agree that Sherlock Holmes was the protagonist of Sir Arthur Conan Doyle's stories, but the first-person narrator was Dr. Watson.

First-person writing gives a direct involvement with the reader because the reader is allowed to climb directly inside the head of the narrator. Because you're limited to one person, novels written in the first-person voice tend to be easier to write as far as one aspect is concerned. Much of the preliminary work is already done for you as the author because there's no need to decide which character's viewpoint would best describe each scene, since you're only dealing with one person.

Rhythm

The concept of rhythm can apply to many parts of your writing. On a sentence level, the way the words fit together and how they sound can create a certain poetic cadence. But rhythm goes much deeper.

Short sentences convey urgency. Look! The shorter the sentence, the more urgent the feeling. The incomplete nature of sentence fragments, like the one you just read, creates a quickening of the pace as well. If you are writing a dramatic scene, short sentences hurry the reader along. Longer sentences create a more laid-back feeling, taking away some of the urgency. Consider the following example:

Jessica gasped as she watched the man walking toward the house. She ducked low behind the hedge, being careful not to be seen, and tried to remain quiet so as not to attract the man's attention. She thought that she could see the hint of a knife in his hand, but she wasn't entirely sure.

Now, look at this:

Jessica gasped. She shifted her position, covertly cowering behind the hedge. She watched the unshaven man approach. She was close enough to catch his scent. It wasn't pleasant. She could see a glint of shiny metal. Was he holding a knife? She couldn't tell.

Which example made you feel more tense? The rhythm of the scene is dictated by the objective you're trying to accomplish. If you want the reader to feel nervous and scared, then short sentences with lots of action are the way to go. As you write, consider the rhythm of the scene and make sure that you're not making things less interesting for the reader along the way.

Transitions

Whenever you move along from one scene to the next, you need to use a transition. After all, you can't expect your reader to spend every moment with the character from the time she wakes up to the time she goes to bed. You need to select the scenes you wish to include, and then you must make the gaps seem logical. To do this, you use transitions.

There are a number of different types of transitions you can use to move from one scene to the next. At its essence, a transition is simply a way to notify the reader that a passage of time has occurred. The trick is to do it in such a fashion that it is obvious to the reader that it's happened so the reader won't feel lost as he or she continues reading.

Jessica dropped the letter in the mailbox. The next afternoon, she realized that she'd forgotten to put a stamp on it.

Kind of rough, isn't it? When making such a time transition, you need to make it obvious to the reader that a time shift is coming up. Consider the following:

Jessica dropped the letter in the mailbox. It wasn't until the next afternoon as she rearranged things on her desk that she realized she'd forgotten to put a stamp on it.

Your job as a writer is to make it easy on the reader, allowing the story to unfold in the reader's mind. The use of transitions serves to telegraph to the reader that a time shift is coming up, which makes the time shift easier to accept in the reader's mind. Without effective transitions, you risk confusing the reader, who may have to spend some extra time trying to figure out what just happened.

Here are some common transition forms you can use to shift time in your story. For maximum effect, learn how to use all of them; never rely on one or two. The more you mix and match, the more varied and interesting your writing will be.

Hiatus

A hiatus is a series of blank lines separating paragraphs. The initial paragraph after the hiatus will begin in the new time period, and the reader will automatically know that the shift in time is occurring because of the "break" in the page. If your hiatus falls at the end of a page, you need to indicate the break with a series of three asterisks centered in the middle of the break. Be careful not to overuse this device; the hiatus should only be used when there is a clear break between scenes.

One-Liners

If a series of actions occur that aren't integral to the story line, you can quickly gloss over them in one sentence, just to fill the reader in on what has taken place. If no important action occurs during the activities, you can sum everything up and continue.

Bill managed to accomplish all of the errands on his to-do list before he got home.

This way, you don't need to show that Bill went to the dry cleaners, stopped at the grocery store, visited the gym, or any of the other mundane yet necessary things he accomplished.

Time Phrases

You can also use stock phrases like "the next day," "that afternoon," "the next morning," or broader passages of time, such as "the next month" to convey time. Use these sparingly, as too many will make it seem like you're telling the reader instead of showing.

Scenic Transitions

You can even create an entire, but short, scene to convey that time has passed. Using this type of transition lets you elaborate upon your setting and deliver more information about your character. Consider the following:

Phil looked up the walk but didn't enter the yard. The house looked empty at the moment. Continuing down the street, he watched the sun slowly begin to set. Shouldn't take too much longer, he figured. He circled the next block leisurely, watching as blue-collar workers pulled into their suburban driveways after a long hard day of work. Kids happily ran from houses, greeting their fathers, leaving Phil with a small tinge of longing for the family he never had. Eventually, he circled back, coming again to the house. The lights were now on, and he proceeded up the walk toward the door.

Reading this short passage, the reader wonders why Phil is at that particular house and what he expects to find there. The reader is also introduced to the surroundings, understanding that the house is situated in a blue-collar, working-class neighborhood where a number of families live. The reader is also left wondering about Phil's past and is given the opportunity to empathize with Phil's feelings about the family he never had. Rather than glossing over the waiting period, you can use this type of scenic transition to allow reader identification to occur.

Using Dialogue

When your characters speak about doing something, it's not much of a logical jump for the reader to expect that they actually start doing it.

"Let's get some lunch," Dick said.
"Sounds great!" Linda said as she grabbed her purse.
The restaurant was packed, but they managed to find a table toward the back.

Now, the reader is carried along with Dick and Linda without having to get in the car with them, drive the distance, park, and go through all of the other steps that really aren't integral to the story. Such transitions are economical because the reader is quickly carried along with the flow of the story without even realizing that a transition has occurred.

Using Habits

Habitual actions can also be used to signify the passing of time. The nice thing about this is that they tend to be economical, conveying the time passage in very few words:

Bill went through four cigarettes before the door to the waiting room opened.

Of course, smoking isn't the only habit you can use. Cups of coffee, sticks of gum, or even the number of magazines read can signify time passage just as effectively.

When Literal Isn't Best (Literal Versus Literary)

Sometimes you will want to use literary techniques that aren't true statements of fact.

- **Allusion:** When you create an allusion, you are pointing out the similarities between two concepts. You are pointing out their similarities on a basic level, without going into too much depth.
- **Analogy:** In an analogy, you compare one type of situation to another. By framing the analogy, you're pointing out the similarities and the differences between the two situations. You're not saying that these things are exactly the same, merely that they're similar.
- **Hyperbole:** Hyperbole is when you exaggerate for emphasis. The statement "There has to be a six-foot mountain of snow out there!" might not be very factual, but it delivers a mental image of the amount of snow and the character's reaction to it.
- **Metaphor:** When you use a metaphor, you are saying that something is another thing; as a result, you're indirectly stating that the two share similarities. A metaphor is always figurative.
- **Personification:** In personification, you give an inanimate object the qualities of a human. You can also do the same with insects and animals.
- **Simile:** A simile uses the words "like" or "as" to compare something.
- **Understatement:** Understatement is kind of like the opposite of hyperbole. When using it, you are underplaying the fact you are presenting, making it seem less important than it actually is.

These devices will come up most often in fiction writing, but they can also be used in nonfiction writing to emphasize a point.

CHAPTER 4

Editing and Proofreading Techniques

Someone once said that the only constant in life is change. That's especially true when it comes to writing. You need to learn to develop a thick skin, because there's a very good chance that what you wrote will have to change. In an employment situation, senior managers may insist that reports be worded differently than what you had in mind or that the focus of them should change.

4

Sentence Structure

Once you get your first draft onto the page, it's time to clean up the words and make sure that you're conveying the proper meaning. The following points are things you should consider while you're editing.

Many beginning writers fall into the trap of believing that their words are sacred. If you want to become an effective writer, then get used to the idea that everything is subject to change.

Subject and Verb Agreement

The verbs you use must always agree with the subject to which they correspond. For example:

He goes to the store every Tuesday.
They go to the store every Tuesday.

Note how the form of the verb changes to match the pronoun.
Of course, not all of your subjects will be pronouns. Often, you will start sentences using regular or proper nouns:

Sam goes to the store every Tuesday.
Sam and Bill go to the store every Tuesday.

Two singular subjects, when acting together, will take a plural verb. Make sure that your sentence construction uses the proper agreements.

Verb Tense Agreement

There are three basic tenses in the English language: the past, the present, and the future. In most writing, you will use the past tense, especially when you are describing events that have already occurred.

The past tense has further divisions, too. You can talk about events that occurred in the past, and you can also talk about events that occurred before those events. You have to be careful to make sure that you are using these tenses properly, or mass confusion could result. Even if confusion doesn't arise, improperly constructed sentences can still look silly; this also makes the reader wonder if the author knows what he or she is talking about, so if you're not careful, you could risk losing credibility in your writing.

Verb tense agreement can be hard to get used to at first, but it's really not that difficult. Consider the following example:

Mandy walked into the bathroom, picked up the towel, and began to dry her hair. When she was done, she put the towel back where it was.

Wasn't the towel just in her hair? Where, exactly, would Mandy be putting the towel, then? In the first sentence, all of the verbs are in the immediate past tense. In the second sentence, the verbs are still in the immediate past. When it comes to where the towel was, however, the verb is referring to where the towel was before the other events took place. Therefore, a slightly different tense is needed:

Mandy walked into the bathroom, picked up the towel, and began to dry her hair. When she was done, she put the towel back where it had been.

Now the verbs clearly show that Mandy put the towel back in the place it had been before she picked it up. When compared to the other example, it is much clearer (not to mention grammatically correct). Pay careful attention to your verb tenses to make sure that your writing refers to the correct time period.

Run-On Sentences

Some people just fall into the habit of making their sentences run on too long, so that you end up with really long sentences, and with other clauses tacked onto the end without any bit of a break, making up one of the longest sentences you could ever hope to find, no matter how hard you look, and you end up going on forever before you ever come across a period, and even then it seems almost like an afterthought.

See, then, how bad a run-on sentence can be? As a general rule of thumb, a sentence should only have one point. Sometimes you can add on another point as a sub-clause, but if it gets any more complicated than that you should consider breaking it up into much smaller bits.

Sentence Length

You should always try to vary the length of your sentences. Intersperse them. Don't use a lot of short sentences unless you're trying to establish a scenic objective, such as suspense. Or immediacy. You're much better off staggering the sentences so that you have longer ones broken up by shorter ones. This creates variety and keeps things interesting for the reader.

Readership Level

No matter what you write, you should always keep your readership level in mind. If you're writing for a group of children, you'll want to use simple concepts and simple language to convey your meaning. Historical references must often be explained for them to have meaning and establish the context you intend. If you're writing for a group of academics, your language will be aimed differently. But unless you have an idea of who your readership will be, you should err on the side of caution and assume a readership level of about seventh to tenth grade.

FACT

Some dictionaries contain listings that show "spelling" words for each grade level. However, academic standards change. Check with your local school office for suggestions on where you can obtain such grade-level lists and use them to compare the words used in your writing against those suggested for your intended audience. If you're already working with a children's book publisher, check with your editor or consult the publisher's writing guidelines for suggestions.

A good rule of thumb is just to keep all of your writing as simple as possible. That way, it can be understood by a reader of almost any level. You may not want to write for a grade-school level, but aiming for a high-school crowd is completely acceptable in most circles. Of course, sometimes a higher level of diction is called for, such as with an academic crowd. The trick is to figure out who your audience is and then aim appropriately.

One of the magic things about the English language is that there are so many ways to say things. You can convey information in a very formal manner, or in a number of degrees of informal ones.

Punctuation

Punctuation is a very important part of writing. Punctuation marks tell us when sentences end and when new ones begin. They break up the grammar of the sentence so that we can quickly understand the meaning. They give a context to the words we use.

The following punctuation marks are important to writing. Make sure that you understand how to use them properly and effectively.

An English professor wrote the words, "Woman without her man is nothing," on the blackboard and told his students to add punctuation to the sentence.

The men wrote: "Woman, without her man, is nothing."
The women wrote: "Woman! Without her, man is nothing."

—Author Unknown

Serial Comma

Unless you're writing to magazine, newspaper, or Web page guidelines that suggest otherwise, whenever you have three or more nouns listed in a sentence, use a serial comma to avoid ambiguity. A serial comma simply means that the comma is repeated in between the nouns:

Tom, Dick, and Harry are my friends.
I bought a shirt, a tie, and a pair of socks.

Historically, the serial comma was used to separate all the nouns. A modern convention, though, is to omit the last comma from the series, leaving the conjunction to tie them together:

Tom, Dick and Harry are my friends.
I bought a shirt, a tie and a pair of socks.

In the United States, omitting the final comma was for a time considered the modern, preferred convention, but because the lack of that final comma can often inadvertently distort the meaning of a sentence, the preference is once again to use the serial comma. Outside the United States, some places prefer the old-fashioned way of including the final comma in the series. Depending on which market you're writing for, structure your serial commas accordingly. If you're writing an article for a magazine published in the United Kingdom, you can save your editors a headache by writing in their preferred style.

Serial commas can work with other conjunctions, too, so don't think that it's only sentences with *and* that you have to worry about. Consider the following:

I want to go to the store with either Tom, Dick, or Harry. (with serial comma)
I want to go to the store with either Tom, Dick or Harry. (without serial comma)

So far, you have seen examples that use three nouns to create the serial comma. If there were only two, no serial comma would be needed, because a simple conjunction like *and* would suffice. But a serial comma can be used with more than three, too:

There are a number of things you will need to bake bread. The necessary ingredients include yeast, eggs, flour, and water.

If you are using long compound phrases instead of simple nouns, or compound phrases in which an internal comma is present, then consider using a semicolon instead.

I only have four things left to do. I must go to the store and pick up some candy; stop at the dry cleaner's; go for an oil change; and buy roses for my wife.

Is a comma the only punctuation mark used in a series?
No. Sometimes, you may also come across serial semicolons. Semico-lons are sometimes used to break up bits that are too complex to sustain using commas:

Exclamation Points

An exclamation point is a very powerful form of punctuation. It delivers a real impact! The overuse of exclamation points, however, clouds writing and makes it look amateurish. Use exclamation points very sparingly. If you constantly use exclamation points in dialogue, the results look absurd:

Bob picked up the newspaper. His picture was on the cover! He picked up the phone and quickly dialed his girlfriend. "Bess! You'll never believe it!"

"I know, I know! I saw it!" she said excitedly over the phone. "You must be so thrilled! Congratulations!"

There's a reason you never see this kind of exchange in books. You may come across it in comic books or on the Web or in e-mail—where you'll often even see multiple exclamation points strung together, but in most of the publishing world, this is considered overkill and amateurish. You don't want your writing to look like the transcript from an online chat room. Sometimes it's appropriate to use them, but you should never do it all the time. Here's a much cleaner version:

Bob picked up the newspaper and found that his picture was on the cover. He quickly picked up the phone and dialed his girlfriend. "Bess! You'll never believe it."

"I know, I know! I saw it," she said excitedly over the phone. "You must be so thrilled. Congratulations!"

Now, the emotion of the situation is still conveyed, and the characters sound far less maniacal, too.

E ALERT!

As a rule of thumb, use exclamation points sparingly in dialogue. And never, ever use it in prose or narrative unless you're very sure it's necessary.

Chances are, however, that with some thought and careful editing, you could improve on that passage even further and eliminate most of the exclamation points (and the adverb "excitedly") by letting the action conveyed by your verb choice serve as the intended emphasis.

En and Em Dashes

Dashes are also an effective punctuation tool. The names may sound funny, but there's a logical explanation for them. An en dash is shorter than an em dash. This harkens back to the days of printing presses; an en dash was simply a dash as long as the letter *n*, and an em dash was one as long as an *m*—or roughly double the length of an *n*.

You can use an em dash to break up parts of your sentence—like when you're including something aside from your main point—but don't do it very often. If used too often, like the exclamation point, it loses its emphasis and becomes distracting.

Many word-processing programs fill in the proper dash if you just use a hyphen, normally located right beside the zero on your keyboard. You can also use alt codes to insert the dashes. Simply hold down the alt button on your keyboard, and using the numeric keypad, key in the appropriate four-digit number. You then let go of the alt button, and voilà! Your dash appears.

En dash (–): alt + 0150
Em dash (—): alt + 0151

The plus symbol is merely there to show you that you key in the numbers while you're holding down the alt key—you don't actually type that symbol in. And remember that you must do it using the numeric keypad—this trick won't work using the regular top row numbers on your keyboard.

Possessive Pronouns Versus Contractions

One of the biggest mistakes in written English is the improper use of apostrophes. Consider the following examples:

Wrong: The dog wagged it's tail.
Correct: The dog wagged its tail.
Wrong: The book is her's.
Correct: The book is hers.

In the wrong versions of these example sentences, an apostrophe is used to indicate possession. When you're using pronouns, you don't use an apostrophe because in the English language we have what are known as possessive pronouns.

Many people become confused about these constructions. You should also be on the lookout for the tendency to make words plural by using an apostrophe with an *s* at the end. An apostrophe *s* is only used to indicate possession or contraction, not to make a noun plural.

Whose dog is that?
That's Sara's dog.

The apostrophe *s* following *that* indicates a contraction. If the sentence were spelled out in full, it would read "That is Sara's dog." The apostrophe *s* takes the place of the *is*. The apostrophe *s* following *Sara*, however, is a possessive adjective. It could be stated differently too:

Whose dog is that?
That's the dog of Sara.

Yes, the sentence sounds terrible that way, but it serves to illustrate another way you can indicate possession. (A better way would be: That dog belongs to Sara.) When you're using apostrophes, then, verify that you're using them in the right circumstances by seeing if you could construct the sentence any other way. If the word with the apostrophe is a contraction, it can be stretched out to its full version. If it's a possessive apostrophe, you should be able to reconstruct the sentence using the word *of* to indicate possession. If you can't do either of those, then it's probably used with a plural noun that should not take an apostrophe in the first place.

It also sometimes helps to wiggle the words in your sentence the other way: If you're confused about whether to use *its* or *it's*, remember that *it's* is the contraction of *it is*; *its* therefore is the possessive pronoun. Likewise, *whose* and *who's* also often cause confusion. *Who's* is the contraction of *who is* (as in "Who's coming to dinner?") and whose is the possessive pronoun (as in "At whose house will we be meeting for lunch?").

Bias-Free Language

Simply put, bias-free language means that you don't exclude members of the population. This means that you never use only masculine pronouns or adjectives (he, him, or his) to refer to persons when gender is unspecified, because you're excluding approximately half of the population. On the flip side, using only the feminine pronouns (she, hers, or her) will exclude the other half.

Using bias-free language and avoiding sexist terms doesn't mean you need to re-create the language to accommodate the prevailing "political correctness" of the day. *Herstory* may have its place in humorous, informal writing, but it's out of place in formal writing, regardless of the sex of the person making that history. Shortcuts like *s/he* may be fine in your personal notes or even in some informal writing, but these kinds of shortcuts have no place in formal usage.

One of the common mistakes beginning writers make is to use what is perceived as "gender-neutral" language. So, they use words like *they, them,* or *their* to create an inoffensive catchall that can count for everybody. This works great in theory, but grammatically, it's wrong.

Some publishers choose to overcome this challenge by alternating forms. In one passage, the word *him* will be used, and in the next passage, the word *her*; alternating, then, is simply for the sake of illustration. Often, a note will appear somewhere toward the front of the book stating that this is the publisher's objective to obtain a gender-neutral, all-inclusive message. This is merely one way of doing it.

There is another way, and it has been done for many, many years. If you want to be gender inclusive, just use both:

Once we select the correct candidate, we will have him or her fill out the proper tax forms before beginning employment. If he or she wishes, the forms can be completed on the first day of employment, rather than beforehand.

The use of *he or she* tends to be relatively invisible. If you overuse it, it may look a little clunky, but you can become quickly adept at restructuring sentences so that you're using the words appropriately. Never use *they* when you mean *he or she*, and never use *them* when you mean *him or her*. Not only is it grammatically incorrect, but it can also add ambiguity to your sentence, because people may have to start trying to figure out who you're talking about.

Cultural Differences in Language

In the 1970s, the Nova was a popular vehicle. Wanting to expand the market, the company that made the Nova decided to market it worldwide. The company executives were red-faced when they learned that the words no va mean "it doesn't go" in Spanish. Here they were trying to market a vehicle, and a considerable portion of the world found it hilarious.

It's a great idea to have someone else read over your work. Other people will be more likely to notice these kinds of mistakes, and the more diverse your support group, the better. While terrible gaffes may not happen often, they still sometimes slip through. Doing all that you can to avoid such gaffes is a true sign of professionalism on your part.

If you're working cross-culturally, that is, if there are a wide variety of cultures in your market, you have to be careful how you write and what words you choose. This is a subset to your consideration of readership, but it's still important to keep in mind. Certain words may take on a unique meaning in a particular geographic area. The "slang" meaning may be quite different from the actual meaning, and you can run into embarrassment by using the wrong words. The word *fag* is slang for cigarette in the United Kingdom, and once was in other English-speaking countries, too, but it's now a derisive term in North America, for example. That's why it's essential that you're careful when you use slang or other colloquialisms, even in fiction. Avoid them altogether in formal writing.

Proofreading Techniques

Although the edits to your manuscript are completed, you're not quite done. You still need to ensure that you have a clean manuscript without spelling mistakes or grammatical mistakes. Just as with getting input for cultural sensitivity, getting other people to read your work can help in other areas, too.

If you don't have a writers' group you can rely on to proofread for you, you can gain this objectivity yourself by putting the manuscript away for a few days, ignoring it completely, and coming back to it when you've gained enough distance. You'll be more likely to notice mistakes when you're fresh.

Another technique that works well is to slowly read what you've written out loud. (The "out loud" part is essential because you'll find that you'll "hear" when you "trip" over the words; your ear will pick it up when a sentence contains awkward word choices or groupings, or grammatical errors.)

CHAPTER 5

Letter-Writing Basics and Specifics

In this age of e-mails and text messages, you may think letter writing is a thing of the past. While these and other technology-forward forms of communication are becoming more prevalent every day, a standard letter is still sometimes the best way to go. Moreover, letter-writing doesn't need to be the intimidating process many people fear. In this chapter and the two that follow, you'll learn how to tackle the most common types of letters that you'll likely need to write.

Why Write a Letter

Perhaps you're one of those many individuals who dreads putting your thoughts on paper, feeling a phone call would be a quicker way to handle things. In fact, you'll find that there are a number of reasons why a phone call isn't usually the best course of action.

1. **Avoid playing phone tag roulette.** With a letter, you know your message will reach its intended audience at a time when it's convenient for that person to sit down and absorb the information, rather than just listen.
2. **Take the opportunity to be more considerate.** Receiving information in a letter saves the recipient from the chore of recording information given to him or her over the phone. This is especially important when it comes to address and phone information or other pertinent numerical data someone might not want to forget.
3. **A letter is less emotional.** A letter allows both parties some "space" to absorb the message. A letter can help you soften any anger you may feel and put it in proper perspective before you complete the final draft you'll send; likewise, it allows the recipient to overcome any defensiveness he or she may feel about your message.
4. **A letter is less embarrassing.** The recipient of a thank-you or compliment isn't put in the position of immediately replying or showing appreciation, saving that person from any awkwardness that he or she might feel.
5. **A letter provides documentation.** This is an especially important consideration when it comes to complaint letters or other communications for which you may later need proof as to what's transpired.

Planning Your Letter

Writing a letter is like any other form of writing. There are steps you can take to help you organize (or outline) your work. Doing this streamlines the editing process, thereby saving you time overall.

For those times when you already have a good idea of what you need to say in a letter, writing it out in a stream-of-consciousness flow of words may be quicker than actually preparing an outline. Once that's done, your only remaining task is to edit your letter before you print it out.

Other times you may need to do a bit of brainstorming to help you focus on what needs to be included. One way to go about this type of brainstorming session is to compare what you're preparing to a grocery list.

Chances are that when you're about to embark on a major shopping trip at the local grocery store, you begin by making out your list. In that case, your menu plans and any special considerations, such as items needed for a party or holiday feast, determine what goes on your list. When it comes to preparing a "list" for your letter, you'll write out those things you believe you should include. Don't be overly judgmental at this point. List anything that comes to mind.

Next, you probably arrange your grocery list according to where you'll encounter what you need within the store, saving yourself time and steps once you're ready to do your shopping. You'll save yourself steps when you write your letter if you put the items on your brainstorming list in an order of importance.

Before you actually leave for the market, you probably take one last look at your list and compare it to the grocer's ad for that week. This helps you determine which items will best fit within your budget. One practice is to put some sort of indication beside those products that are on sale so that they stand out on your list. In the case of your brainstorming list for a letter, you'd likewise highlight any essential sentiments. Once that's done, you'll know what is and what isn't important to include in the letter.

As you learned in Chapter 1, unless you're writing a work of fiction like the screenplays for films such as *Pulp Fiction* or *Memento* (which each contain many flashbacks altering the expected chronological narrative progression), what you write should follow a linear progression and have a recognizable beginning, middle, and ending. In the case of a formal letter, different sources label those parts in different ways. Essentially, the parts of a formal letter include the following:

1. **Salutation and introductory comments.** "Dear <name>" is known as the salutation. The first introductory line or lines of your letter should then set the tone. The introductory comments convey what the letter will be about.
2. **Body.** This is the part of your letter that contains your message.

3. **Ending sentiment and complimentary close.** The ending sentiment consists of the final sentence or sentences in your letter, the intent of which is to leave a positive impression with the recipient. The complimentary closing is your parting phrase, such as Sincerely.

In most cases, an informal letter or note will still contain the same parts. An informal letter is just less rigid about the tone, meaning that you can use more familiar or casual language, such as a complimentary closing like *With Love* or *Hugs*.

Stationery

Use letter-size. Make people's job easier. Standard 8½" x 11" paper is easier to file. The personalized stationery you got for Christmas may be lovely, but it isn't appropriate for formal or business-related correspondence. You wouldn't wear your absolutely lovely bunny slippers to a formal dinner party. Your letter should likewise be appropriately dressed for the occasion.

When using stationery that shows an executive's name and title, omit that information when typing out the letter closing. Simply type out the name of the person sending the letter.

Formal, Typed Letters

Whether you use plain paper or personal or business stationery, formal letters should be typed or printed. See Appendix B for letter format examples.

With all of the different fonts that are available on the computer, the temptation is to use them all and go artistic when printing out a letter. While it's okay to use one or two alternative fonts in your letterhead (whether you use one done for you by a printer or create one yourself on the computer), limit the letter itself to one of the following fonts.

Font	Type
Courier New	12 point
Garamond	12 point
Times New Roman	12 point

Handwritten Notes

Unless a disability (or lousy handwriting) prohibits doing so, most personal communications should be handwritten. You'll see suggestions on how to handle different types of letters throughout this and the next two chapters.

Informal, handwritten letters can be done using:

- Informal stationery,
- Note cards or fold-over-style cards,
- Personal or business stationery, or
- A greeting card.

Complaint Letters

Whether you call it a claim letter or a consumer-action letter, an effective complaint letter gets results because it provides the recipient with something that demands (literally and figuratively) attention. Don't misunderstand: When making "demands," your letter shouldn't be one full of ultimatums. Quite the contrary. A complaint letter with tactful, logically arranged details effectively presents your grievance—and provides you with a record of your message, too. Complaint letters may be called for in situations such as billing disputes, neighborhood problems, order delays, incorrect or incomplete shipment receipts, and policy disputes.

Personal Complaint Letter

(Date)

Dear Mrs. Jones,

I'm writing to you about concerns my wife and I have about your dog. Your dachshund's barking has us concerned that should your dog ever escape from your own fenced-in backyard, it would pose an attack threat to our children when they play in our yard. I believe we should set up a meeting within the next week to discuss this situation.

Sincerely,

Paul Smith

Keep in mind that your complaint letter has a better chance of getting the results you desire (a resolution to your complaint) if written in polite, logical terms.

FACT

A complaint letter should state the problem and ask for what you feel is a fair resolution to that problem. To be effective, it should be no longer than one page. If you feel that you must provide extraneous details that would extend that length to beyond a page, you should strive to put such information in an enclosed supporting document instead.

Consider any letter that you write while angry as a form of therapy—a way to vent your frustration and brainstorm the first draft of your complaint letter at the same time. Then, once you've had a chance to distance yourself from your anger and be objective, edit the letter so that its wording states the problem in terms that will help you reach your objective.

Dispute Letters

For service disputes or complaints about merchandise, you should provide supporting documents with your letter, including either photocopies of or a written record of your:

- Dated receipt
- Place of purchase
- Product description, including model and serial numbers

Whenever possible, direct your letter to a specific person. Finding out the name of the person to whom you should send your letter is usually as easy as placing a phone call to the company and asking the receptionist or party who answers to whom you should direct your letter. It isn't necessary to give the receptionist any details about your specific complaint. A question as general as "I'm having a problem receiving a shipment and I need to know the name of the person I should contact; to whom do you suggest I write to direct my concerns?" or a statement like "I need the name of your shipping department's supervisor" should suffice.

Your complaint has a better chance of being handled if it is, by virtue of how it's addressed, a named person's responsibility to take action. A letter sent to a "department" can be shuffled from desk to desk before somebody researches your complaint and writes your reply, or worse, ignores your letter altogether.

There will be times, however, when it isn't possible to obtain a name. In such an instance, be as specific as possible when you address the letter. Supplying a department name within the address and your letter salutation helps ensure that your letter lands on the proper desk.

Formal Complaint Letter

(Date)

Dear Presto Software Company Customer Service Supervisor:

I returned a software package to your company almost a month ago and I have yet to receive the promised replacement for those damaged goods.

Supporting documents you'll find attached with this letter are:

A copy of the letter from the local post office, stating the software was not shipped in sufficient protective packaging to ensure the CD wasn't damaged during shipment

A copy of my letter sent when I returned the software package as proof that it was received in a manner in which I was unable to install the software, which would have voided the return policy conditions (The CD was bent in half!)

A copy of the receipt showing the package return postage cost

A copy of the dated and signed receipt indicating that the package was received by your company

Please see that my replacement software is shipped immediately. If I do not receive it within ten business days from this date, I will expect a full refund for my purchase, plus the return shipping costs.

Sincerely,
Adam Dotcom
Enc.

Complaint and Dispute Letter Replies

If a matter justifies a complaint or dispute letter, that letter deserves a reply. You can find examples of such replies in Appendix B.

In some cases, a letter regarding a complaint that needs (or warrants) immediate attention can be sent by fax. For an example, see Appendix B.

CHAPTER 6

Social Writing

There are countless social occasions that require some sort of written communication out of courtesy toward a business acquaintance, friend, or relative. Some require a predetermined course of action. Others are more flexible about how you can respond. Should you write a note? Send a letter? Is it okay if you type it? Because of that flexibility, there often isn't one right or wrong way to go about structuring your response.

Congratulatory Notes and Letters of Congratulations

One of the nicest "gifts" you can give someone is an acknowledgment for a job well done or other achievement. Letters offering congratulations can be sent for:

- Adoptions or births,
- Anniversaries (marriage, business, or other special event),
- Awards,
- Birthdays,
- Engagements,
- Graduations,
- New homes,
- New jobs,
- Retirements, and
- Special achievements (honor roll, college acceptance, publication of a book, and so forth).

A letter of congratulations should be short and sweet. It should include the word "congratulations" and an acknowledgment of the accomplishment. (Never include extra news of your own. Save that information for a letter.)

Congratulatory Letter

(Date)

Dear Taylor,

I just read in the paper that you made the honor roll. Congratulations!

Sincerely,

Laura

Condolences and Sympathy Letters

Some sources say that a condolence letter is one only sent in sympathy for a death, while a letter of sympathy or a sympathy letter can be sent for a death or other loss. According to Merriam-Webster Online, *www.m-w.com*, condolence is defined as sympathy with another in sorrow or an expression of sympathy. For that reason, this book treats all three as interchangeable terms for any letter expressing empathy for any hardship.

Often referred to as a sympathy letter or letter of sympathy, a condolence letter is not an easy thing to write. (That's why so many people take the "easy way out" and send a sympathy card.) You should write a condolence letter when an event occurs that affects somebody important in the life of a business associate or employee, friend, neighbor, or relative, such as:

- An accident or injury
- A death
- A devastating natural disaster or other financial loss, such as a job loss or bankruptcy
- A divorce
- A miscarriage or stillbirth
- A serious illness or injury
- A terminal illness
- A violent crime

Often those unfortunate occurrences in somebody's life—the types of things you've been told that you "don't talk about," such as mental illness or addiction rehabilitation—are times when a sympathetic, understanding letter can offer needed encouragement in otherwise seemingly hopeless circumstances.

Following the examples given in Appendix B will help you deal with planning the letter—deciding what to write. Some appropriate things to include are the following:

- An explanation of how you learned of the news
- A brief, appropriate expression of your feelings of loss or grief
- An offer of thoughts or prayers in keeping with your faith, stated in a way that doesn't offend the beliefs of the letter recipient
- A sentiment offering affection, comfort, concern, or hope for the future
- A specific suggestion about how you'd like to offer any help or assistance
- The victim's name

The purpose of your letter isn't necessarily to make the recipient feel better. That may come later. However, at the time the letter is received, the recipient is grieving. You're under no obligation, nor is it appropriate, to try to cheer up the person. A condolence or sympathy letter acknowledges the grief. It's a written reflection of the compassion you feel for and share with those grieving.

There are some things you should leave out of a condolence letter, such as overly dramatic adjectives to describe the loss. Phrases like "he's in a better place" or "God's will" can be insulting rather than comforting. Lastly, while it's appropriate to express your feelings about the loss, don't belabor the point. The intent of your letter is to offer condolence, not to elicit sympathy from the letter recipient for yourself.

Whenever possible, a short letter or note written in sympathy for a friend or family member should be handwritten on plain, personal stationery. A card is also appropriate if you include a handwritten sentiment as well. Longer messages, or those sent to a business acquaintance, client, colleague, customer, or employee with whom you did not work closely, may be typed. Examples of such typed letters are shown in Appendix B.

QUESTION?

I have some fond memories of happy times spent with the deceased. Is it out of line to relate those in my condolence letter?
It's not only appropriate; in most cases, it will be appreciated. Also include things such as an explanation of those traits the deceased possessed that you admired or an acknowledgment of any special award or service he or she received or performed. Including such specifics helps make the letter more sincere.

Death

(Date)

Dear Becky,

I was sorry to hear about the death of your brother. While growing up, I remember how onvious I was of your having an older brother. Matthew was always so considerate whenever I visited your house. I never once remember hearing him complain when he had to help us fix one of our bikes or later, when we were older, drop us off somewhere if he was going to be using the car. It's a sad fact of life that living so far away has meant that I've lost touch with some of those peripherally close to my life. I'm glad that we've remained friends, even at such a long distance—and I want to let you know that even though I'm not physically there to help, I am here for you in your time of loss.

With love,

Sue

Natural Disaster

(Date)

Dear Cheryl,

I just learned about the fire. Thank goodness everybody in the family is safe! Still, our hearts go out to you in what has to be a difficult time. I know how much pride you take in your home, and grieve knowing you've not only lost possessions, but treasured and sentimental keepsakes as well.

Larry and I are planning a trip to visit his parents next weekend, so I'll give you a call later this week to inquire about what you need—and about how we can help.

You remain in our hearts and prayers. Hang in there!
Warmly,

Sarah

Victim of Crime

(Date)

Dear Chris and Jeremy,

Powell and I just heard about the vandalism done to your place. Any invasion of your home is not only frustrating—it invades your sense of safety, too. Your home should be your haven and if there's anything we can do to help restore some semblance of order to the chaos created by this crime, you only need to ask. In fact, I'll make it easy for you to ask by giving you a call before the weekend to see when and how you can use our help.

Sincerely,

Baxter

Death of a Pet

(Date)

Dear Mildred,

Please accept my condolences on the death of your beloved Shadow. I know she was more than a cat; she was a part of your family. There's seldom a day that goes by that we don't talk, but sometimes such familiarity can lead to the assumption that things are understood. I didn't want to take that chance. This note is to let you know that I care.

Warmest wishes,

Gertrude

Keep in mind that the purpose of a condolence letter is to express sympathy, not pity. If you have any doubts about the message you've written, have someone whose opinion you trust read it. Even better: Read the card aloud to that person so you both can "hear" whether or not your sentiment conveys its intended purpose.

Loss of a Baby

(Date)

Dear Gloria,

John and I were saddened to hear that you lost the baby. We know how much you and Benjamin were looking forward to having another child. If there is anything we can do to help you during your grieving process, please know that we're here to help.

With love,

Judy

Serious Illness or Injury

(Date)

Dear Gloria and Mark,

David and I were devastated to learn about Jeremy's illness. As parents, we do all within our power to protect our children. For those times when life throws something in our paths that we're powerless to help a child avoid, all we can do is pull together—and find the strength to endure. Please know that all of you are in our thoughts and prayers.

Warm regards,

Janet

Terminal Illness

(Date)

Dear Joshua,

I hope you don't mind, but Jason told me about your illness. Please know that you are in my heart and prayers. I'll give you a call soon. I'm hoping you'll feel up to having me drop by for a visit.

Also know that if, at any time when I call, you don't feel up to talking or a visit, I hope you'll tell me so. I won't be offended. I'll understand. I only want what's best for you.

I'm looking forward to seeing you as soon as you're up to it.

Fondly,

Janet

A terminal illness doesn't mean that the victim's death is imminent. Treatments for cancer and AIDS now offer patients extended hope for the future. Despite relapses and crisis moments, chances are the patient will continue to enjoy life for years to come. Keep that in mind when you write your message.

Get-Well Notes and Letters

Whether you're sending a get-well card or writing your sentiment on stationery, your get-well message should be an optimistic, cheerful one. If appropriate, such as for a friend or relative coping with a lengthy recovery time following major surgery, you'll want to offer any assistance you can provide to help out.

Acknowledge the reason for your message without being overly dramatic about it. "Your fall on the ice" is more sincere than "that unfortunate accident."

Get-Well Note

(Date)

Dear Bert,

I was sorry to learn that you sprained your back when you fell on the ice. I'm writing this note to let you know that you're in my thoughts while you recover, and to let you know that you don't need to fret about keeping your walks and driveway cleared. Until you feel up to doing the work yourself again, I'll gladly bring my snow blower next door. I'll see that my son Dennis follows along behind me with the snow shovel. (Miraculously, I've managed to convince him that when he shovels snow, he's building those biceps that so impress the girls.) I'll give you a call in a few days to see if there's any other way I can help out. After all, what are neighbors for?

Rest up and you'll feel better before you know it!

Sincerely,

Andrew

Invitations

Wedding and graduation invitations are traditionally formal, engraved announcements. Other special occasions that warrant invitations can include the following:

- **Business Events:** Trade shows, open houses, exhibitions, new product introductions, premieres, new business openings
- **Business Parties:** Birthdays, employee relocations, maternity leaves, promotions, retirements
- **Civic and Cultural Events:** Art shows, commemorative occasions (such as the renaming of a bridge or street in honor of a local citizen), concerts, fundraisers, historical society exhibitions, stage productions
- **Educational Events and Programs:** Conferences, open houses, seminars, speechs, workshops

- **Family Celebrations:** Anniversaries, baby showers, baptisms, bar or bat mitzvahs, First Communions, graduation, holiday celebrations, reunions, weddings, wedding receptions, wedding showers

Creating an Invitation

Invitations are as varied as the events for which they can cover. While a personalized invitation is always the best option, sometimes it isn't a practical one. The nature of the event will set the tone for the appropriate type of invitation.

Once you've chosen a format for your invitation, you need to decide on the content. It's essential that an invitation contain all of the *who, what, where, when,* and *why* information. In addition, the *how* information is often *how much*. (If there is a fee for attending the event, somehow you need to state so up front.) Place this information in a logical order.

Information about attire should go on the lower right-hand corner of a formal invitation. Attire descriptions include black tie, casual, costume, evening attire, formal, informal, semi-formal, and white tie.

Invitation

The Mercer County Art League

Invites you to attend

The Twenty-Fifth Annual

Local Artist Recognition Open House

to be held at

The Grand Lake Lighthouse Pavilion Banquet Room

on Sunday, the twenty-seventh of April

Two thousand and eight

One o'clock to five o'clock

Refreshments   Informal Dress

Open Bar

When typing an informal invitation, it's acceptable to list things. Lists make the items stand out, so they're more easily noticed and remembered.

Informal Invitation

(Date)

Dear Alex and Amanda and family,

Summer's almost over so it's time to make plans for our Annual Neighborhood Labor Day Weekend Cookout. (Where has the time gone?)

We'll be holding the cookout on Sunday, September 7. As usual, we plan on eating at about 3 p.m.—and throughout the rest of the evening, as long as the food holds out.

As in the past, we're hoping you'll bring a side dish and a dessert to share.

Dennis will be up at the crack of dawn, smoking ribs and getting all of his other specialties ready for the grill. We'll provide the:

Buns
Paper plates/Napkins
Silverware
Meat
Beverages

However, feel free to bring along any extra soft drinks, heartier beverages, or other things you wish to share as well. (Your homemade bread and butter pickles were a hit at last year's event!)

Hope to see you there!

Sincerely,

Dennis and Ann

Invitation Acceptance

Formal, engraved invitations often include an engraved reply card and self-addressed envelope for your R.S.V.P. For informal invitations to which you R.S.V.P. with a phone call, it's also a courtesy to send a short, handwritten note confirming your invitation acceptance. In the note, you can volunteer any additional information, such as an offer of assistance on the day of the event.

Letter of Confirmation

(Date)

Dear Ann,

As we discussed recently on the phone, Homer and I are looking forward to attending your annual cookout. We'll be there early, with the kids, our side dish and dessert, and our appetites!

I know how hectic things can be while you're doing those last-minute preparations, so I'll give you a call before we leave to see if there's anything you need us to pick up.

Fondly,

Pat

Declining an Invitation

When declining an invitation, it isn't mandatory that you give a reason why you can't attend. In the case of an informal reply to a well-known acquaintance, however, it is a courtesy to do so.

Letter to Decline an Invitation

(Date)

Dear Dennis and Ann,

Unfortunately, we won't be able to attend this year's event. Alex's parents will be spending that weekend with us. They're stopping by on their way to Florida, leaving earlier than usual so that we can attend an out-of-town family reunion on Saturday. We'll be spending the weekend with relatives, and not returning home until Monday.

I'll drop off a jar of my bread and butter pickles sometime before we leave. Let us know if there's anything else you need, too.

Know that we'll be with you in spirit, even though we can't be there in person.

Regretfully,

Alex and Amanda

Announcements

An announcement is a formal or informal notification of news of an event, stated in the fewest possible words. Such brevity only refers to the announcement itself, which needs to include the important who, what, when, where, and why details. The reasons why you may need to send an announcement are lengthy:

- Adoption
- Address change
- Birth
- Death
- Divorce
- Engagement

- Graduation
- Name change
- Promotion
- Job Change
- Meeting
- Retirement
- Wedding

FACT

Business announcements can range from news of an acquisition to a collection notice or product recall. See Chapter 14 for more information.

Impersonal (sent to business associates)

Following the divorce, the former Rebecca (Becky) Millford adopted her maiden name and is now known as Rebecca Brown. She continues to reside at 2345 Homestead Lane, Smalltown, OH 45822, (419) 555-5555.

Personal Announcement
(used in handwritten notes to friends and relatives)

Because of my divorce, I've decided to go back to my maiden name. So, from now on, I'll be known again as Rebecca (Becky) Brown. I still reside at 2345 Homestead Lane, Smalltown, OH 45822, (419) 555-5555.

CHAPTER 7

Thank-You Notes and Letters

Although a verbal thank-you for a gift may seem simpler to do, it just isn't as effective as sending a sincere thank-you note or letter. This is even truer today, when letter writing is almost a lost art. As a general rule, thank-you notes are flexible when it comes to the beginning, middle, and ending format. Regardless of the style you adapt for such letters, you should strive to acknowledge the gift or event (giving detail or providing sufficient explanation) and end with a sentiment that leaves a lasting impression.

Accompanying a Thank-You Gift

When sending a thank-you gift, a short letter adds a nice touch.

Letter Attached with a Thank-You Gift

(Date)

Dear Mr. Jones:

On behalf of the Wheat Fields Public School PTA and myself, please accept this framed photograph of you presenting your generous check to our organization as our sincere way of saying thank you for all that you've done to help support our school.

Because of your financial assistance, we were able to meet our goal. This summer's Reading is FUNdamental Program will be possible because of your help. Throughout the summer, we'll keep you posted about how the program is progressing. In fact, should you be able to find time in your busy schedule, we're hoping that you might like to attend one of the sessions. I'll send you a copy of the dates and times for those sessions as soon as it is available.

Thank you again for your thoughtful gift.

Sincerely,

Anthony Rice
Secretary

FACT

When sending a thank-you note along with flowers or a gift to a group of people who provided a service, such as the nurses on duty during a hospital stay, it's okay to omit the heading and "address" the accompanying card with a sentiment like, "Sent with special thanks and appreciation to all the fifth floor nurses at St. Rita's Hospital."

Gifts

There's no specific rule about how to go about thanking someone for a cash gift or a check. It's up to you as to whether or not you name the amount. If you feel more comfortable writing "your gift of $100" and then name the specific use you found for the money, then by all means, do so. Otherwise, "your generous gift of cash" or "your check" will suffice.

Gift Thank-You Note

(Date)

Dear Uncle Norman and Aunt Beth,

I just received your generous gift of a Palm Pilot. Your gift will help me keep track of all my commitments at college. I'm already entering items in the address book, so I'm well on my way to getting organized. Your gift matched my needs perfectly.

Your nephew,
Archie

Check Thank-You Note

(Date)

Dear Granddad Jones,

Thank you so much for your generous check. I deposited most of it in my college tuition fund; however, I did keep out enough to buy a backpack. (I wanted to get something to remind me of you every time I go to class.)

With love,
Amber

E ALERT!

Address the recipient of a heartfelt, informal thank-you note as you would do so in person, such as "Gramma Pam," "Nana," or "Auntie Boo."

A handwritten note is usually your best choice when sending a short thank-you card. However, if your handwriting skills leave something to be desired—or if a condition like carpal tunnel syndrome makes writing difficult—consider using a handwriting font.

Wedding Check Thank-You Note

(Date)

Dear Dennis and Ann,

Thank you for your generous check. We used the money to buy a set of prints that now hangs in our dining room. We'll give you a call next week so we can set up a time for you to visit—and take a look at the prints.

With love,

Nolan and Kristy

Wedding Gift Thank-You Note

(Date)

Dear Aunt Anna,

Thank you for the beautiful hand-embroidered pillowcases. We're using them in the guest bedroom. They look lovely! Knowing how much time and love went into making them makes them even more special.

Love,

Randy and Lara

Condolence

In some cases, it is appropriate to use the note cards provided by the funeral home. You can acknowledge those who lent support following a death in the family by sending such notes to anyone who:

- Provided food or hosted dinners
- Provided overnight accommodations for out-of-town relatives
- Sent condolence messages
- Sent flowers or a donation
- Offered other types of support, like taking a family member shopping for appropriate clothing

Even though a cash donation made in the deceased's memory will be acknowledged by the recipient, you should still send a personalized thank-you to the donor.

Personalized Thank-You Note

(Date)

Dear Jon,

Thank you for your contribution to the Red Cross in memory of my late husband Stan.

I truly appreciate your generosity and thoughtfulness.

Sincerely,

Bethany Schlueter

Personalized Thank-You Note

(Date)

Dear Pastor Dunn,

On behalf of the entire Emans family, I want to thank you for delivering the homily at Dad's funeral. We found comfort in your kind words.

Dad spoke highly of you and the work you do at the church. We now have a better understanding of why he respected you so much.

Please continue to keep us in your prayers.

Sincerely,

Patricia Emans Wright

QUESTION?

When is it appropriate to send a thank-you note?
Never overlook an opportunity to thank someone. Any time you feel gratitude, you should express that gratitude in a note. Just remember that the formality of the circumstance, occasion, or event for which you are offering your thanks will dictate your choice of whether your note should be on your personal or company stationery—or if it should be hand-written or typed.

Dinner Thank-You Note

Even an invitation to dinner can merit a personalized thank-you. When a dinner party is hosted by more than one individual, be sure to send a personalized thank-you to all hosts. For an event hosted by an organization, a thank-you letter should be sent to the chairperson and the board of directors. (This way you include the secretary/treasurer, vice president, and other officials of the organization.)

Dinner Thank-You Note

(Date)

Dear Lara, Randy, and family,

Thank you for a truly delightful evening. I have to admit, when Lara first said that she was going to let the kids "build" their own pizzas, I thought she was asking for trouble—or at the very least, a very messy kitchen by the end of the evening. Instead, everything worked out well, the pizza was delicious, and the kids are still talking about how much fun they had. (Your kitchen seemed to survive, too!)

I was especially impressed by how well everything was organized. Having all of the toppings set out on the table where they were within reach of even the youngest child was evidence of that. Thanks to your well-thought-out plan, there wasn't a fussy eater in the bunch.

Thank you so much for inviting us to take part.

Fondly,

Laura, Mark, and family

A thank-you note is one place where extra adjectives are acceptable. Just keep in mind that your language needs to sound sincere, not overly dramatized. The amount of flowery language you use is determined by how familiar you are with the person to whom you're addressing your letter.

Thank-You Note for Hospitality

Even if you've already thanked someone in person or during a phone conversation, a special favor deserves a special written thank-you note.

(Date)

Dear Dennis and Ann,

Thank you for the invitation to spend the weekend with you at your vacation condo. Rick and I had a wonderful time.

Sincerely,

Tam

Thank-You Note for Personal Favor or Service

Time is a precious commodity. Nobody has enough of it, which is why when someone does you a personal favor or provides a personal service of some sort, that person deserves a note thanking him or her for that favor or service.

Thank-You Note for Service

(Date)

Dear Pat and Homer,

Thank you so much for volunteering to let the kids spend the night. Your thoughtfulness meant that I was able to get to the hospital early enough for mom's surgery without needing to roust the kids out of bed and take them to the sitter's. They always have such a good time at your house, so they were thankful for the chance to have an extended visit, too.

Warmly,

Connie

Personal Thank-You Note

(Date)

Dear Janet,

Thank you so much for listening. Because of your insight, I believe I am now able to reach a good decision, based on logic, not anger. You helped me put things in perspective, and for that, I am grateful.

Fondly,

Debbie

CHAPTER 8

Layman's Journalism

Whether or not you're actually writing a story for the newspaper (as a freelance writer or in the form of a press release submitted by your club or organization), you'll use the same techniques the professional journalists do. Regardless of how you structure the beginning, the middle, and the end of your story, it needs to include that ever-essential who, what, when, where, why, and how information.

The Inverted Pyramid

The simplest and most common story structure is one called the "inverted pyramid."

It is also the most practical, because news stories need to be a particular length to fill up a predetermined amount of space in the newspaper. Editing to make such stories "fit" is done under severe deadline pressure. A story written in inverted pyramid format can be edited by trimming it one paragraph at a time, going from the bottom up, until the story is the right length. The editor doing the edits can do so confidently, because even though information is being cut from the story, it is being cut in ascending order of importance.

Think of the "inverted pyramid" as an upside-down triangle, with the narrow tip of less information pointing downward and the broad base of news-worthier details across the top. Stories written in inverted pyramid format therefore have the most newsworthy information at the beginning of the story and the less important news at the end.

Story Leads

The first paragraph of a news story is known as the lead. Most often, the lead is one long sentence that summarizes the facts of the news story in order of most newsworthy to least newsworthy. This helps the reader know at a glance what the story will be about. The lead also sets the structure for the rest of the story.

Typical Story Lead

Because of concerns over the growing menace of the West Nile virus and the need to educate physicians on newly developed diagnosis techniques, doctors from the Centers for Disease Control (CDC) met today with representatives from the American Family Physicians Society.

Other Types of Leads

The other most frequently used leads include the following:

The News Lead:
The news lead usually describes specific actions.

In one of the most gruesome incidents in years, a Palestinian suicide bomber grabbed an Israeli child from his mother's arms before killing himself, the child, and ten others when he detonated the bomb he had strapped to his waist.

The Quote Lead:
The quote lead is especially effective when the quote makes the reader automatically want to know more—if it motivates the reader to ask questions.

"I felt the crunch before the tingle."

The Description Lead:
The description lead is often used at the beginning of feature articles, and is used to provide a descriptive image of the subject of the feature.

Looking out of place wearing a tie, as evidenced by the rash around his collar that seemingly grew brighter with each word he spoke, farmer Jacob Miller sat straight-backed in his chair as he addressed the members of the congressional committee.

Eight Tips for Conducting Interviews

Whether you're talking to somebody in person, or interviewing him or her over the phone, there are a number of things you should do to prepare for the interview and during the interview itself.

1. **Do your homework.** Learn as much as possible about the subject of your interview in advance. Visit the company (if interviewing a businessperson) or other appropriate Web site (such as the Web pages for a college department if interviewing an expert). Make notes about what you find there, especially about that which you hope to learn during the interview.

2. **Have open-ended questions ready in advance.** Prepare more than you'll have time to ask—in anticipation of the interview going well and the subject of your interview asking you to stay (or talk) longer. Such advance preparation also demonstrates that you have done your homework, and that you respect the interviewee's time.

3. **Be courteous.** Such courtesy includes being on time. If the interview is to take place in person, dress appropriately, introduce yourself, and have a business card or paper with contact information ready to give to the subject of your interview.

4. **Allow a brief period of time to get to know one another before you start asking questions.** Ask the subject of the interview if he or she has any questions to ask about you or the interview protocol before you begin.

5. **Ask for permission to tape the interview.** Have your taping equipment—with an adequate fresh battery supply and appropriately sized tapes—ready in advance. Regardless of whether or not you receive permission to tape your discussion, also have a notepad and pen or pencil ready so you can take notes. (If the interview is in person, also take notes about the atmosphere and any body language.) Never rely on your memory alone.

6. **Confirm and clarify, and then confirm again.** Ask for proper spellings for any names or terms about which you're unsure. Confirm that you have the correct spelling of the name of the subject of your interview. Get clarification on any new terms brought up during your discussion.

7. **End the interview on friendly terms.** Thank the subject of your interview for his or her time. Ask for a convenient time to contact that person again, should you have additional questions or need additional clarification.

8. **Transcribe your notes from the interview as soon as possible.** Don't let too much time pass before you type up and organize your notes; you want to do so while your overall impressions and the facts are fresh in your mind.

When to Use Direct Quotes

A direct quote repeats what the subject of your interview said exactly, and is enclosed in quotation marks. Otherwise, when you paraphrase what was said, quotation marks aren't used—although they are sometimes used around a quoted portion of a paraphrased segment to add emphasis.

The preacher looked out over the crowd, took a deep breath, and commented about how glad he was to see so many "faithful followers" in attendance.

Direct quotes are used:

- To answer how, what, who, or why questions
- To include exact or official information, especially when it's important that it come from an obviously authoritative voice
- When the interviewee's language is particularly descriptive

Press Releases

Much of what you see or read in the news doesn't just appear there because the news agencies have battalions of reporters off doing investigative journalism, tracking down information while they're on break from doing that covert work they hope will uncover political shenanigans. Reporters usually show up to cover an event because they first learned about it from a press release.

Unless it's a part of a complete press packet, any photo that accompanies a press release should be clearly identified (such as by labeling it with a soft marker on the back of the photo) and attached to the press release with a paper clip.

A press release is a written announcement of some sort of event, ranging from a fundraising dinner to a new product release to a job promotion.

A press release that doesn't require immediate attention can be delivered in person or by mail; otherwise, for late-breaking news, it's permissible to use electronic distribution, either by fax or e-mail.

Unless it's via e-mail, a press release should be typed on letterhead (or other professionally designed paper). The proper format also includes the following:

- Contact information, including the name and daytime phone number of the person
- Release date (traditionally "For Immediate Release"—although some now consider that line superfluous, or "For Release On (or After) <Date>")
- Headline (centered and in bold type)
- Dateline (the city name in all capital letters, followed by date of release)

Here are a few more tips:

- The body, or the actual news release itself, should contain the essential how, who, what, where, when, and why information and be double-spaced on one side of 8½" x 11" paper.
- If the body of the release extends beyond one page, center and type "(CONTINUED)" or "(MORE)" at the bottom of the page.
- Number consecutive pages by placing the release title or a keyword from the release title and the page number flush left at the margin at the top of the page.
- Center one of the following to indicate the end of the release: ###, – 30 – , (END).

FACT

For a short, one-page news advisory-style press release announcing an upcoming event, substitute the words "News Advisory" for the release date, and center all of the essential information in bold type directly below the headline to make it easy for a reporter or the calendar editor to scan it quickly.

Press Release

FOR IMMEDIATE RELEASE   Contact: Tony Rice
Creative Visions Club
555 That Boulevard
Celina, OH 45822
Phone: (555) 555-5555
Fax: (555) 555-5556
E-mail: tony@domain.com

THE CREATIVE VISIONS CLUB TO HOST
SECOND ANNUAL ANIMATIONFEST

CELINA, April 1—Over the weekend of April 6–8, local animators will once again gather at the Florence Convention Center in downtown Celina for the Second Annual Animationfest.

Joining local artists and scriptwriters will be nationally known figures such as keynote speaker Jemma Smith, creator of RubbaDubbaHubba, and seminar instructor Taylor Sutton, the force behind Wild Animal Extravaganza. [List other important event data]

"We're proud to once again be having so many distinguished artisans teaming up with local talent," said Tony Rice, president of the local Creative Visions Club. "We already have more than a thousand people registered to attend the classes and seminars," he continued, adding, "but there's still time for anyone who's interested to participate," indicating there are still a few registration slots open for the event.

This year's Animationfest will conclude on Sunday, April 8, with an open house and reception, open to the public—although registration at the door will be limited to the first thousand people who attend. Animationfest participants will be available to autograph merchandise—like special video packages, prints, and animation cells.

All profits from the event go to support the Creative Visions Club mentoring program.

CHAPTER 9

Research

Choosing a topic to write about is a start. But it's only the start. Odds are, before you can write in-depth about a given topic, you'll need to do some research. Research is more than just locating information, however. You must first spend some time analyzing your topic. This helps you get a head start on finding the relevant information that will help you organize your piece.

9

Determining the Scope of the Research Needed

Before you can begin your research, you need to know what to look for. Only then can you figure out where you need to look.

That probably seems overly simplistic, but think about it: The task ahead of you will seem overwhelming until you know the scope of that task. Only then can you break your work down into manageable steps.

Think back to the first time you assembled a model. You attached part A to part B and continued through the process until you had something ready to display proudly on the shelf in your room. But attaching those parts wasn't the first step you took to getting the job done. First, you had to decide what you wanted to build. In that case, you probably viewed the boxes sitting on the shelves at the hobby store in much the same way you'd think about all the books facing you on the shelves at the library.

As you looked at the rows in front of you, the boxes may not have been as well organized as those books filed under the Dewey Decimal System at the library, but they were in categories all the same. Even if you walked into the store knowing that you wanted to build a car, that wasn't enough. It was still overwhelming until you decided what type of car you wanted to build. And at what scale. And in what color. You didn't actually determine your objective until you selected the specific model you were going to build. Even then, your job was far from over.

Once you got the model home, you spent some time looking at the picture on the box. That picture became your "focus" because it represented what your final "product" should look like.

Next, you emptied the contents of the box onto the table in front of you. At that point, while you had everything you needed in front of you, you were far from having the job done. You still had to look over the instructions, arrange all of those pieces and parts in some sort of logical order, and figure out what other tools (glue, paint, brushes) you still needed. Eventually, you treated those instructions in much the same manner as you would research—digesting it until you had a thorough understanding of your intended product. Those parts assembled in logical order became your outline. Your tools were your aids to getting your vision into tangible form. Throughout the entire process, that picture on the box never lost its importance either. It allowed you to maintain (or refresh) your focus. It helped you "see" the goal in front of you.

Why is that focus so important? Focus is what lets you narrow a broad topic down to something manageable. Focus allows you to glean your specific "thesis statement" from general subject matter.

There's a reason that one of the most popular search engines based its name on "googol"—the mathematical term for "1 followed by 100 zeroes." Google (*www.google.com*) is now able to search billions of Web pages. There is a vast amount of information available online, which is a mixed blessing: Chances are if you know how, you'll be able to find the information you need, but unless you know how to "refine" your search, finding the information can be a daunting task. For example, in 2003, a search on the word "herb" on *www.google.com* garnered 2,290,000 hits; in 2008, it came up with 56,700,000 hits. The astounding amount of information available is why in much the same way that you hone the focus of your subject matter, you also must customize the nature of any of your quests for information—whether it's while looking through resources at the library, posing questions to experts, or conducting searches online.

You can read more about how to determine the focus of what you're writing in Chapter 11.

When to Use the Library

Any research that you do will consist of using two types of sources:

- **Primary:** Published and unpublished materials that can include (but aren't limited to) public records (birth certificates, deeds), research notes, first-hand anecdotal observations (oral history or personal diaries), and so forth.

- **Secondary:** Published works such as almanacs, books, directories, encyclopedias, and so forth.

Secondary sources are the easiest to track down, and therefore less costly—both in money and in time. Because of their ready availability, these materials are most helpful during your preliminary project-planning stage, when you need to read more generalized information to gain a better overall grasp of the subject. Such general information helps you isolate the options as to which specialized direction your project can take. It shows you what is already known about your topic, what aspects have been covered by others and in what ways, as well as other details you'll need to ascertain before you can truly establish your focus. (Remember: It's your focus that lets you find your voice for your writing project and prevents you from simply rehashing something that's already been done.)

ESSENTIAL

One method of obtaining primary source material is to go directly to the source and interview someone. Whether you need anecdotal information or verification of facts from an expert, many aspects of conducting such an interview are the same. See Chapter 8 for more information.

Libraries are the best means for locating secondary sources. As you'll soon learn, starting your research at a library doesn't necessarily mean you have to physically make a trip there. Many libraries now have their catalogs online, so you can see which books are available on the shelves and through interlibrary loan. More and more of the information that was once only available in those reference books not available to be checked out of the library is now making its way into online archives. Often the best information of this type is only available through expensive subscription databases, but even that doesn't mean you must pay those high subscriptions fees yourself. Many libraries let you access those services through their Web sites.

The types of resources available to you on-site will depend on the type of library you use: an academic library at a large university, a public library in a large (or small) community, a high school library, or a specialized library.

Printed materials available at the library include the following:

- Directories
- Nonfiction books (including textbooks and reference books)
- Newspapers
- Periodicals (popular, trade, and scholarly magazines and journals)

There are also magazine and other subscription databases that you can access on your home computer, such as:

- **Biographies Illustrated:** H. W. Wilson's collection of more than 100,000 biographies from over fifty reference titles, thousands of biographical magazine articles, with over 32,000 printable images. Searches can be done by name, profession, ethnic background, place of birth, and more. Literary criticism articles are also accessible from the author's biography.
- **Discoverer:** Interactive general reference database that consists of full-text articles constructed from more than 1,200 magazines, newspapers, and U.S. government documents. This online resource is geared for the younger (K–8 reading level) researcher.
- **EBSCOhost Databases:** Provides access to academic journals, magazines, newspapers, and books and monographs, that include the Academic Search Premier, Alt Health Watch, Business Source Premier, Computer Source, Eric (the Educational Resource Information Center), Health Source: Nursing & Academic, MAS Ultra–School Edition, MEDLINE, Middle Search Plus, Newspaper Source, Primary Search, Professional Development Collection, Psychology & Behavioral Science Collection, Regional Business News, Religion and Philosophy Collection, Sociological Collection, and Vocational and Career Collection databases, plus these databases:
- **MasterFILE Premier:** Updated daily, this multidisciplinary database provides full text for more than 1,730 general reference publications with full text information dating as far back as 1975, 500 full-text reference books, 84,774 biographies, 100,554 primary source

documents, and an image collection of 235,186 photos, maps, and flags.

- **Newspaper Source:** Selected full text for twenty-five national (U.S.) and international newspapers and full-text television and radio news transcripts, and selected full text for more than 260 regional (U.S.) newspapers.
- **Primary Search:** Another database primarily geared for children, this one includes *Encyclopedia of Animals*; *World Almanac for Kids*; Funk and Wagnall's *New Encyclopedia*; a compilation of essential documents in American history; and collections of pictures, maps, and flags. Includes the full text for nearly seventy popular magazines for elementary school research, each of which are assigned a reading level indicator (Lexiles). Full-text information dates as far back as 1990.
- **Middle Search Plus:** A daily updated database for older elementary students that includes Primary Search and adds full-text articles from over 140 K–12 magazines, full text of fifty-two reference books, and over 5,000 book reviews, with full-text backfiles dating to 1990. Middle Search Plus also contains 84,774 biographies; 100,554 primary source documents; and an image collection of 235,186 photos, maps, and flags.
- **Funk & Wagnalls *New World Encyclopedia*:** This database provides over 25,000 encyclopedic entries covering a variety of subject areas.
- **TOPICsearch from EBSCO:** Current events database of social, political, and economic issues, scientific discoveries, and other popular topics. TOPICsearch contains full text for over 139,800 articles from more than 4,800 diverse sources.

Whether you limit your searches to the subscription services available from your library or search databases on the World Wide Web, you'll encounter selections that are stored as:

- Full or complete text
- Index and abstract
- Representation or summary

FACT

Once you're ready to find more information, pick up the book you've found most informative about your topic thus far and check out the bibliography. Those are the books the author found most helpful; chances are some of them will aid in your research, too.

One advantage of being at the library in person is that you can walk up to an actual reference librarian and ask for help; however, because most libraries also now post the e-mail addresses for reference librarians on their Web sites, you can ask questions even if you're accessing the library from your home computer. You simply write out your question and submit it by e-mail. The answer won't be an immediate one, but what you lose in speed you gain in the convenience with which the reply can be copied and pasted directly into your notes.

On-Your-Own, Computer-Aided Research

One disadvantage of conducting your research directly on the World Wide Web is all the pesky pop-up ads and other distractions you can encounter. Another is the fact that you can't always trust the information you find: As *www.snopes.com* and other urban legends sites will attest, tall tales abound on the Web. Despite those problems, as long as you keep your online searches focused (something not always easy to do when each site links to other equally fascinating sites, which may not always be directly related to the task you've set for yourself), the World Wide Web offers advantages, too. You can:

- **Do a keyword search at online bookseller sites** (*www.amazon.com, www.bamm.com, www.bn.com*, and others) to see what books are in print or about to be published in your topic area.
- **Do a Web search.** The potential sources of information via this route are endless. You can check the Web sites for organizations or associations, many of which include an FAQ (Frequently Asked Questions) or "about" page that can provide you with an overview about

a topic. You can find anecdotal information on personal Web sites, newsgroups, and mailing lists.

- **Read recent news articles.** You can find current editions of newspapers—both large (*www.nytimes.com, www.washingtonpost.com*) and small (*www.dailystandard.com*)—online. (Many newspaper sites do charge for any but the most recent articles in their archives; however, you can often access older articles through a library subscription database.) In addition to the services offered through your library's subscription database, for medical news you can search Web sites like WebMD (*www.webmd.com*). You can also find the latest headlines at sites like Yahoo! News (*http://news.yahoo.com*) or Google News (*http://news.google.com*).

ESSENTIAL

The University of Louisville Information Technology department moderates CARR-L, the Computer-Aided Reporting and Research List. You can find more information about this useful research service at *www .louisville.edu/it/listserv/archives/carr-l.html*.

Search Engine Search Syntax

You'll save yourself a lot of time (and hours of frustration wading through nonessential information) if you learn a few simple rules about how to conduct an effective search. Those "rules" involve learning how to speak the language, or "search syntax."

Search syntax is the set of rules that lets you refine a Web search so that you retrieve only that information that is most relevant to your needs. It allows for searches based on combinations of terms, exclusion of nonessential terms, and multiple forms of words, synonyms, and phrases. The most used forms of search syntax are wildcards and truncation, discussed in the next section.

Wildcards and Truncation

This syntax allows a symbol in the middle of a word (wildcard) or at the end of the word (truncation). This feature makes it easier to search for related word groups, like "man" and "men" by using a wildcard such as "m*n." Truncation can be useful to search for a group of similar words like "invest, investor, investors, investing, investment, investments" by submitting "invest*" rather than typing in all those terms separated by ORs. This search would also yield pages that include "investigate, investigated, investigator, investigation, investigating." To solve this problem, combine your wildcard search with related terms and the appropriate Boolean logic operators:

invest* AND stock* OR bond* OR financ* OR money

Boolean Logic
Use AND, OR, and NOT to search for items containing both terms, either term, or a term only if not accompanied by another term. Be sure to check the instructions for the search engine you're using. In most cases, "and" is assumed, so it isn't necessary to type in the word "and"; separating your search words by spacing is sufficient. Also, some search engines now offer advanced search pages. The logic on those pages is the same, but rather than use the Boolean operators, you place your search words in the appropriate spaces on the search form.

Capitalization
Use capitalization when searching for proper names. For example, a search on "Herb" would exclude most instances of garden or culinary herb, yet give you those pages with the name Herb. It can also be used if you want to look for a particular pattern of capitalization, like WebMD.

Field Searching
Database records are separated into fields, which can help if you recall the domain on which you found what you needed but only remember certain keywords from a title. For example, the results from searching for these keywords "silk shirt blueroses.com" include the Web page for the short story *My First Silk Shirt* on that domain.

Phrase Searching
This search is useful when you are looking for something where you know specific words always appear next to one another, such as in a quote.

On most search engines, the phrase itself should be enclosed in quotation marks: "a rose by any other name."

Proximity

Also known as a NEAR search, some search engines (like *www.altavista.com*) let you search for terms that appear near one another, within so many words or paragraphs, or adjacent to each other.

Be careful that when using NOT to exclude a word that you don't limit your search too much, especially if used in combination with a wildcard. For example, your intent may be to use "herb NOT stor*" to exclude (online) store or stores, but you'd also be excluding another topic that might prove helpful, like storage.

Evaluating Your Sources

Finding reference materials to use isn't the only important part of any research. You also need to determine the reliability of that material.

You can find a number of checklists to use on the Evaluating Web Resources page at *www3.widener.edu/Academics/Libraries/Wolfgram_ Memorial_Library/Evaluate_Web_Pages/ 659/.*

One of the most basic things to do is to check the copyright date of a book you intend to use. While this information won't be as critical in a book about the Civil War, it can make a difference if you need to write about something more current. A book about breast cancer treatments published in 1990 may still include what will be a great deal of useful information, but you can't rely on it for details on treatments in use today.

Citing Sources

While the order in which such information is presented may vary, the primary citation elements of a bibliographic reference are the same for most styles of documentation. Primary citation elements usually include the name of the author, the title of the work, the place of publication (city and state in publisher's address), the publisher's name, the date of publication, and a description of the location (or the page number) of the reference. Many styles also include a category for the publication class or type.

Electronic sources do not always contain all of those elements, and often contain other elements that relate to this new era of publishing. Such differences can include the following:

- Login name, nick (online nickname), or alias instead of an author's name
- File name instead of a title
- Protocol and address (such as a URL) instead of the place of publication and the name of the publisher

FACT

When citing an online work, the date the researcher accessed the site may be the only way to designate the edition of that work; not all sites show a date of publication.

Another difference when it comes to citing a reference found on the Web is that a work may consist of only that one page, regardless of its length. Pagination—as well as the need for an index—used in print publication becomes redundant when any word or phrase within the text can be found via a "Find" on a given work. Therefore, while published works usually show navigational references such as page, section, or paragraph numbers at the conclusion of the citation (separated by commas), most online works citations omit those entirely.

Regardless of the differences in how you cite a work, you still must cite it somehow. According to the *Columbia Guide to Online Style* (*www.columbia.edu/cu/cup/cgos2006/basic.html*) "When in doubt, it is better to give too much information than too little."

Citing Sources Within the Text

Sources mentioned within the text of a document are cited within parentheses. Such parenthetical, or in-text, citations of print publications usually include the author's last name and the page number of the reference (humanities style) or the author's last name, the date of publication, and the page number of the reference (scientific style). For online sources, the parenthetical citation done in humanities style usually just includes the author's last name or, when no author name is available, the file name; for scientific style, the online citation includes the date of publication, or the date of access if no publication date is available.

For scientific style citations for Web pages that do not indicate a publication date or date of last revision or modification, the citation should show the date of access instead, in day-month-year format: (30 Aug. 2002).

ALERT!

While in a print source citation it's acceptable to omit the author's name in subsequent references to the same work (giving only the different page number or location, if applicable), when citing an online source, repeating the author's name may be the only way to acknowledge where the information originated.

Bibliographic Citations

Any bibliographic citations should follow the format for whatever style you are using: generally MLA or Chicago for humanities style or APA or CBE for scientific style. Here are some examples of how you can modify those basic formats when citing online:

Humanities Style

Author's Last Name, First Name. "Title of Document." *Title of Complete Work* [if applicable]. Version or File Number [if applicable]. Document date or date of last revision [if different from access date]. Protocol and address, access path or directories (date of access).

Ehlers, Eric. "An Online History of the Literature of Comics." *Comics History.* 2002. *http://www.thelemur.net/comics.html* (28 Aug. 2002).

Scientific Style

Author's Last Name, Initial(s). (Date of document [if different from date accessed].) Title of document. Title of complete work [if applicable]. Version or File number [if applicable]. (Edition or revision [if applicable]). Protocol and address, access path, or directories (date of access).

Ehlers, Eric. (2002). *An online history of the literature of comics. Comics history. http://www.thelemur.net/comics.html* (28 Aug. 2002).

Unless the style guidelines you're using for a work state otherwise, it's generally acceptable to use the "hot link" feature of your word-processing program to underline a URL and display it in a different color (usually blue).

Research Organization Techniques

Whether you keep them on your computer, a series of note cards, or in a notebook, the fact remains that: You'll need to take notes.

Don't rely on your memory. Keeping track of what you found—and where you found it!—is an essential part of effective research. Carefully recording your sources in the bibliographic format at the start will save you the hassle of having to backtrack to find that information later.

It also helps if early on you establish some logical groups in which to organize your materials. Doing so will help make inadvertent gaps in your research stand out. During your next trip to the library or your next online search, you'll know for which specific areas you still need to find resources.

By keeping your research organized, you'll easily be able to determine when you've reached the end of your research and are ready to begin doing the writing itself. Here are just a few of the Web sites that can help you find materials that will aid in your research:

AltaVista (www.altavista.com)

The advantage of this search engine and directory is that it also includes the Boolean logic operator NEAR, which finds documents that include the designated words when they appear within ten words of one another.

bizjournals.com (www.bizjournals.com)

A site for city business journals. Another business-related site that might prove helpful is Fast Company (*www.fastcompany.com*). Free market data can be found at the U.S. Department of Commerce Market Access and Compliance Web site (*www.mac.doc.gov*) and market statistics at the U.S. International Trade Administration site (*http://trade.gov/index.asp*). Public company filing information is available for download at the U.S. Securities and Exchange Commission Web site (*www.sec.gov*).

Library of Congress (www.loc.gov)

This is the largest library in the world, with 29 million books and other printed materials, 2.7 million recordings, 12 million photographs, 4.8 million maps, and 58 million manuscripts. You won't find everything online, but you'll be amazed at what you can locate there.

Open Directory Project (www.dmoz.org)

While this site may not be as pretty as some of the commercial sites, it's one of the most helpful because the directories are maintained by humans. It's the largest directory edited by humans on the Web with nearly 5 million sites in more than 590,000 categories.

Six Steps to Productive Research

The following six steps will help ensure that your research efforts are efficient and accurate:

1. **Cross-check all information.** Don't assume anything. Despite even the most meticulous publishing standards, mistakes can still occur. When,

in doing so, you encounter contradictory data between two of your reliable sources, go back to their original sources to see if the information there can help you resolve the inconsistency.

2. **Whenever possible, consult the original source.** In many cases, this will involve questioning an expert. (See Chapter 8 for more information.)

3. **Use the telephone.** Don't forget that the phone can be one of the most useful weapons in your arsenal. Use it to talk to a reference librarian when you need suggestions (like when you encounter a roadblock or a dead end in your research) or an answer to a specific question. If that librarian isn't able to help you, call another library. If you encounter a business name for which you're unable to locate a phone number, call the Chamber of Commerce in the city in the last known address; chances are the person there will be able to tell you if the business has changed names or moved out of town.

4. **Consult bibliographies.** Remember, there's a wealth of information in bibliographies. Experts write books and articles. Likewise, don't overlook the names of people quoted in your research material.

5. **Ask for referrals.** When you finish interviewing one expert, ask if he or she can suggest anyone else you should speak with about the subject.

6. **Keep things fresh.** Check the publication dates on the materials you use. Remember that a book released this month was probably written at least a year ago or longer. If you have any doubt about whether or not there may be new findings since that time, contact the author and ask.

Your reputation can hinge on the reliability and accuracy of the information you present. It may seem unfair that even one error in a multithousand-word document can undermine your credibility, but that's the reality of how perceptions are formed. Even one error can cause a reader, or your audience, to doubt the accuracy of all of your other information. Conducting thorough, effective research helps ensure this doesn't happen.

CHAPTER 10

Copyright Matters

A copyright is the law that covers only the form or manner in which ideas or information have been manifested, often referred to as the "form of material expression." Copyright is not designed or intended to cover the actual idea, concept, fact, style, or technique which is exemplified in or represented by the work; it covers how that idea, concept, fact, style, or technique is expressed by the owner of the copyright. Copyright protection extends further than the written word. Songs can carry a copyright, as can artwork, movies, and television shows. In this chapter, however, you will read about copyright law as it pertains to your writing and that of others.

Copyright Law

Copyright law is a balance between two competing interests. On the one hand, it encourages authors and artists to create work; it ensures that they will be able to receive adequate compensation for their efforts. On the other hand, in a free and democratic society, the communication of ideas should be encouraged. Copyright law, therefore, tries to strike a balance between the two interests. The doctrine of fair use serves to balance out the potential monopoly created by copyright law by allowing people to use certain aspects of literary and other works without infringing on the copyright. Fair use will be discussed in detail later in this chapter.

As a basic introduction, copyright gives the owner the right to reproduce the work in any form, to make derivative works based on the original work, and to distribute copies of the work. Usually, the owner of the work is the person who creates the work. As mentioned above, a work can be defined as including many forms of expression. The definition of literary work may include a short story, a novel, a poem, a nonfiction article, a play, a screenplay, or virtually any other form of written communication.

Another qualification of copyright is that the work must be original. Original simply means that the creator expended some effort in creating it. Originality does not require that the work be innovative, just that the creator actually went through the steps of producing it.

FACT

There are some things that cannot be copyrighted. Titles, for example, cannot be the object of copyright, but other legal protection may exist for the infringement of titles, such as trademark law. In addition, there is some question as to whether e-mail and newsgroup postings can be the subject of copyright.

The most important aspect of copyright is that it protects only the actual expression of an idea, not the idea itself. Ideas are for the benefit of society, and therefore must be free. For example, Einstein would never have been able to copyright his famous formula. He could have claimed copyright in the words he used to express the idea, but he could never copyright the idea of $E = mc^2$. The only thing that can be protected by copyright is the actual form of expression.

This is inextricably tied to one of the basic qualifications of copyright law: In order to claim copyright in a literary work, it must be fixed. This simply means that the work must be written down. Since the only thing protected is the expression, a thing must actually be expressed in some way before it can be protected.

It used to be that a literary work had to be registered with the copyright office to assert a claim; this is no longer the case, and copyright begins at the moment of fixation. So, as soon as you write something down, or type it into a word-processing document and save it to your hard drive, you are the copyright owner. Copyright law has had to catch up to technology, so it now includes works that aren't actually set out on paper. Computer hard drives are fine, as is a document stored in a personal digital assistant: As long as the work is stored and can be retrieved, it is protected by copyright.

Work-for-Hire Agreements

Sometimes, a work is specifically commissioned by a publisher. In such circumstances, the agreement between the author and the publisher may be a work-for-hire agreement in which the owner of the copyright is the publisher, not the author.

ALERT!

Similar to a work-for-hire agreement, an employee who creates a work while under the employment of another person may find that the work is owned by the employer, depending on the scope of the work and the nature of the employment. If you work for someone and routinely create written works in the scope of your job, check your employment agreement.

Duration of Copyright

The current term of copyright protection extends from the date of the creation of the work until seventy years after the death of the author. After this point, the work enters the public domain and can be copied freely without regard to copyright infringement. This provides authors with long-term protection of their works.

Unless the terms of the contract specify otherwise, in the case of works commissioned under work-for-hire agreements, the copyright will last for ninety-five years after the date of publication. If the work is unpublished, the copyright of commissioned works under a work-for-hire agreement lasts 120 years.

Works created earlier than 1998 will enter the public domain earlier, depending on the original date of publication. This is still of historical interest when trying to determine when a particular work from the past is to enter the public domain, but any works created after 1999 will follow the rules outlined above.

Collective Works

Sometimes, articles or short stories are collected and published together in an anthology. In such a situation, many of the individual components of the collective work will still carry their own individual copyright, which is owned by the author; however, copyright also exists for the anthology. Basically, this means that no one else can compile the same works together and publish them. In most cases, unless the contract agreement specifies otherwise, the rights to the individual stories or articles are still retained by the original authors.

If you look at the beginning pages of an anthology of short stories, you will often see a page listing the individual copyright notices of each short story in the collection. This is done to maintain the copyright interest of the story's original copyright holder (usually the author of the story).

Joint Authors

It is possible for two authors to own an interest in the copyright of a work if both authors contribute to the creation of the work. The contribution, however, must be relatively substantial; merely suggesting ideas or titles does not give rise to a claim for joint authorship. There must be a contribution of actual work.

If you collaborate with someone, it is essential to have a collaboration agreement to govern the work. In such an agreement, you can specify which authors receive what percentage; if it comes down to determining the interests in a court case, the split may be fifty-fifty. If you don't want this to happen, it's a very good idea to enter into a collaboration agreement right from the start. This will clearly specify each author's respective copyright interests, while also protecting your individual legal interests with things such as payment, expected contributions, and so forth. There are a slew of sample collaboration agreements available on the Internet. You can use any form you like, as long as it addresses the following five points:

1. The parties to the agreement, with full contact information clearly spelled out
2. The expected contribution of each of the parties
3. The agreed ownership split
4. Provisions for the division of advances and royalties
5. A clause that stipulates the name of the literary agent to be used, if applicable

Selling or Licensing Your Copyright

Copyright is a form of intellectual property. Intellectual property also encompasses trademarks and patents; all of these are relatively intangible things that usually wouldn't be considered as "property" if not for the laws passed to protect them. Copyright, then, becomes a form of property that can be transferred, licensed, or sold.

A license, however, merely grants permission to another to use the copyright. In many cases, it also allows the licensee (or the person who buys the license from you) to enter into legal action against third parties who infringe upon the work. Publication is, in a sense, a licensing situation, where, for agreed-upon terms, you allow the publisher to print and promote your work. After your agreement with the publisher has expired, you are again free to license the work.

FACT

If you transfer or sell your interest in the copyright, you give up all subsequent claim to it. This is different from a work-for-hire agreement, where you never held copyright in the first place; in a work-for-hire agreement, it is usually expressly stipulated that the publisher (or other commissioning party) will be the first copyright owner. Selling your interest subsequent to creation is a little different, but the result is basically the same.

Many authors talk about "selling" their reprint rights, which is a bit of a misnomer; sure, you get paid for reprints, but the copyright is still usually owned by you. If you truly sell your copyright, you will have no subsequent interest in it. If someone offers to "buy" your work, read your agreement carefully so that you are aware of the nature of the transaction. Make sure that you aren't actually permanently selling your copyright interest if that isn't your intention. If in doubt, enlist the services of an attorney.

Fair Use

The doctrine of fair use was not originally a part of copyright law, but developed slowly through a number of court decisions. It is now an official part of the copyright law as enacted by legislation. Basically, it sets the parameters as to what use other people can make of a copyrighted work before they must secure permission (or risk infringing the copyright).

Unfortunately, the lines drawn by the doctrine of fair use are not always that clear. There is no set number of words, or percentage, or any other clearly delineated factor. Rather, it has to be a subjective analysis based on the use to which the copyrighted work is put.

The following bulleted list is culled from the 1961 *Report of the Register of Copyrights on the General Revision of the U.S. Copyright Law*. The wording is verbatim; the only change is that the individual examples have been broken down for easier reading. It will give you an idea of the government's approach to the doctrine of fair use. Fair use allows:

- Quotation of excerpts in a review or criticism for purposes of illustration or comment.
- Quotation of short passages in a scholarly or technical work, for illustration or clarification of the author's observations.
- Use in a parody of some of the content of the work parodied.
- Summary of an address or article, with brief quotations, in a news report.
- Reproduction by a library of a portion of a work to replace part of a damaged copy.
- Reproduction by a teacher or student of a small part of a work to illustrate a lesson.
- Reproduction of a work in legislative or judicial proceedings or reports; incidental and fortuitous reproduction, in a newsreel or broadcast, of a work located in the scene of an event being reported.

The doctrine of fair use, then, tries to strike a balance between the copyright owner's interests and the interests of society at large to benefit by additional information being produced. To determine the scope of the doctrine of fair use, section 107 of the Copyright Act sets out four criteria to consider:

1. **The purpose and nature of the use of the copyrighted material.** Is the reproduction being used for a commercial use? Is it for nonprofit or educational uses? Is it being used for scientific research? Is it being used for the purposes of criticism or commentary? All of these questions shed light on the analysis of the first point. The more commercial the use is, the less likely the use will be considered to be "fair" for the purposes of the doctrine of fair use. Uses such as teaching and research are given more breadth. The nature of criticism and commentary usually requires that a portion of the work being considered be

quoted to some extent; as long as the reproduction isn't too substantial in the context of the criticism, the use should be considered fair, too.

2. **The nature of the copyrighted work.** Is the work being reproduced merely factual in nature? Or is it something that came from the imagination of the author? Is it something that was written for the betterment of society, or is it purely entertaining in form? Is it something that was written specifically for commercial exploitation? The nature of the work that is being produced is as important as the use to which it will be put.

3. **The amount of the work reproduced, relative to the copyrighted work as a whole.** Reproducing one or two lines of a poem or a song may be acceptable, while reproducing the whole thing will probably be seen as an infringement. What is important is how much of the work is being reproduced. If the answer is "most," then you're probably on your way to infringement, and you should either find another way of doing things or start seeking permission from the copyright owner. In the professional world, obtaining permission is sometimes referred to as "clearance." Either way, it's always a good idea to get permission if you're using a poem or a song, since even one line can be a very substantial portion of such a work. With other types of work, a paragraph or two is probably okay. What is important, again, is the relationship between the work you are reproducing and the original work as a whole. Condensing the original work into a précis (a condensed, summarized form of the original work) will probably be an infringement, because you are reproducing a substantial part.

4. **The potential market impact and how it may affect the copyrighted work.** If a work is out of print and not commercially available, reproduction of a part of it (even a relatively substantial part, depending on the circumstances) will probably be considered fair. If the owner of the copyright is in a position to charge a fee for the use of the material, this tips the balance out of the realm of fair use, but this also must be considered alongside the other factors. If a work is commercially available, your use may replace the need for a consumer to purchase the original work, and therefore any reproduction you attempt will probably not be considered fair.

Of course, the doctrine of fair use merely allows you to use the material without first seeking permission. If, after considering the factors outlined above, you decide that your proposed use would not fall within the fair use doctrine, you can always contact the copyright owner to obtain permission. In some cases, the payment of fees is required; however, a great number of authors are happy to see that their works are being cited and readily grant permission.

If you are concerned about a particular use and whether or not it will be considered fair, it may be best to consult an attorney for a legal opinion determined with regard to the particular facts.

When to Use Citations

Copyright and plagiarism are related concepts, but they come from completely different backgrounds. Copyright exists primarily to benefit the copyright owner economically. Plagiarism, on the other hand, is not a legal concept; it is entirely a moral concept, outside the purview of the law. However, it can still have serious repercussions. Many academic institutions, such as colleges and universities, treat plagiarism with the utmost severity, even permanently expelling students for violations. Don't risk it—use citations where appropriate.

Quoting or Referring to Experts

Because copyright protection does not extend to the ideas expressed in the work, you can safely state the ideas and conclusions of others without regard to existing copyright. Copyright cannot be used as a monopoly for an idea, so these types of quotes can be used as long as the usage does not infringe upon the copyright of another. It's still good form, however, to quote your source.

If you are not writing an academic paper, merely acknowledging the source should be sufficient, as in the following example:

According to Professor Bloggs of the University of Arkansonia's literary studies department, 37 percent of male teenagers like to read spy novels, while only 12 percent of the adult male population likes to read them.

Derivative Works

One of the rights reserved for the copyright owner is the ability to make derivative works. This is most obvious in the form of fiction, where fictional characters are cast in events to create a story. As long as a fictional character is sufficiently sketched out, it is a proper object of copyright.

For instance, you couldn't use the Harry Potter characters in your own work without permission. This is one of the rights reserved to the copyright owner. The right to create derivative works also encompasses the creation of other forms of work based on the original, such as movies or TV shows or even merchandise bearing the likeness of the characters. For years after the death of Sir Arthur Conan Doyle, anyone who wanted to use the Sherlock Holmes character had to have permission from the estate. As an author, you too are afforded the protection of your fictional characters. By the same token, you must take care not to violate the copyright of others.

Protecting Your Interests

Protecting yourself from infringement is only one half of copyright; you'll also want to protect your work, too. The following section provides information on protecting your own work from infringement.

Copyright Notices

Earlier in history, in order for a claim for copyright to be supported, the work must have carried a copyright notice. Now, a notice of copyright is not required—a work is still protected by copyright even if it doesn't have a copyright notice appearing on it, but it is still a good idea to include it. Some writers argue that because copyright exists once a work is saved to a reproducible medium, such copyright is always implied. However, one of the defenses to an accusation of copyright infringement is lack of knowledge that copyright existed in the work, and that defense is not applicable if the work bears a copyright notice. Therefore, including such a notice provides the copyright owner with his or her best copyright protection.

ALERT!

The copyright symbol © has a special legal meaning. People sometimes use a small c surrounded by parenthesis, as in (c), but this does not have the same legal meaning. The only acceptable alternative to the © symbol is spelling the word "copyright" out in full. Just remember this handy little copyright notice phrase: If in doubt, spell it out.

Although the word and symbol are often used together, for a proper copyright notice, it is really only necessary to include either the word "copyright" or its symbol, a small "c" with a circle around it (e.g., ©). It should also bear the date of creation. And, unless the author or owner of the work is clear elsewhere in the context of the manuscript, the copyright notice should also bear the name of the author or owner of the copyright. For example, if your work is titled "The Autobiography of Pamela Rice Hahn," and you are Pamela Rice Hahn (which would mean there are two of me out there), the copyright symbol followed by the year should suffice. Otherwise, it's a good idea to include your name in the copyright notice.

Therefore, it's a good idea to include a copyright notice on all of your works, and place it prominently either at the beginning or the end of your work. Positioning your notice close to the title is always a good bet. As a quick summary, any of the following are acceptable:

- Copyright © 2008 Pamela Rice Hahn
- Copyright 2008 Pamela Rice Hahn
- © 2008 Pamela Rice Hahn

Proof of Ownership

You may have heard that you can secure a copyright by mailing a copy of the work to yourself. This is sound in theory, but it isn't necessary, nor is it definitive proof of ownership.

The idea behind mailing yourself a copy is that you then possess proof of the date of creation, based on the federal postmark on the canceled stamp and envelope. If a copyright issue arises based on the work, you can present the sealed envelope to a judge at trial, who would then open it and find your original work inside, with the date stamp on the outside of the envelope giving an indication of when the work was created. However, the other party could challenge this evidence, saying perhaps that you mailed the envelope to yourself unsealed and then inserted the work at a later date. While it might seem like a far-fetched defense, it is possible that it could succeed at trial, depending on the particular situation that surrounds the events leading up to the copyright infringement.

You can certainly still mail yourself a copy of your works as prima facie evidence, but it's not a good idea to rely on it as sole proof of ownership and creation. It's also a good idea to hang onto your notes and research, especially if you get into the habit of dating them. The more evidence you can provide, the better.

Much of this talk, however, is probably a little extreme. The chances of someone stealing your material are very, very slim. It does happen, but not to the extreme that beginning writers suspect. If you are careful about keeping your records, you shouldn't have any problem. You should also keep records of where and when you submit your material, and any response you receive.

If you have a really good story, and you really want to make certain that your work is copyrighted, you may wish to register it with the copyright office. In order to do this, you will have to send in an application form, the required fee, and a copy of the work. The Library of Congress retains a copy of all registered copyrighted material, whether published or not. Depending on your particular circumstances, you may have to submit two or more copies instead of one. You can get all the details you need by contacting the federal government's copyright office at: Library of Congress, Copyright Office, 101 Independence Avenue, S.E., Washington, D.C. 20559-6000, Phone: (202) 707-3000, *www.copyright.gov.*

CHAPTER 11

Essays in General

In one form or another, the essay is the basic structure of almost every form of nonfiction writing, such
as editorials and opinion pieces, legal opinions, magazine articles, newspaper features, speeches, and
report summaries. The principles of essay writing
can also be applied to descriptive passages in fiction
or entire works of nonfiction, such as this book. This
chapter will show you how to write effective essays.

Strategic Essay Preparation

Regardless of which strategy you use to plan your essay, it's important that you have one. Stream-of-consciousness writing might work for writing entries in your journal (or as one of your essay-planning exercises), but that practice seldom produces a polished final draft.

Without an organized set of notes from which you can outline the salient points you plan to make, your writing will be a disorganized chore. A contractor doesn't begin building a house before he gets the plans for doing so from the architect. Likewise, you need to be the architect drawing up the plans for your essay before you become the contractor doing the actual writing itself.

When given the option of choosing your own topic for an essay, pick one about which you feel passionate. Such a topic will hold your interest throughout the entire process; your writing will reflect that passion and will be better as a result.

Work in the way that's most comfortable for you. Some people like to do their planning on scraps of paper or note cards that can be physically rearranged. Others prefer to do all work directly on the computer, figuring that copying and pasting the points in order is more efficient for their work habits.

How you plan your essay will depend in part on the type you need to write.

If it's for a *How I Spent My Summer Vacation*–type assignment, your job is easier. You already have your topic. You analyze the question, and determine what will be your central issue and other key points.

If you need to come up with your own idea, you need to determine your subject area and isolate the topic or subtopic about which you want to write. A subject is an overall category; topics and subtopics then fall within each subject. Think of them in the following way:

Subject
    Topic
        Subtopic
        Subtopic
        Subtopic
    Topic
        Subtopic
        Subtopic
        Subtopic
    Topic
        Subtopic
        Subtopic
        Subtopic

QUESTION?

How can I simplify finding a topic for my essay?
One option would be to access The Library of Congress's online catalog (*www.loc.gov*), which now has more than 14 million records in its database. Names and subjects searches are available through their separate service, Library of Congress Authorities at *authorities.loc.gov*. The Library of Congress is only one resource and it offers endless options for choosing a subject from which to pick a topic.

Brainstorming Potential Topics

Write down anything that comes to mind, without being judgmental about anything at this point. Don't worry about how much research a topic will require, whether or not you'll need to talk with experts, or even putting your topic ideas into "fancy" phrases. The purpose of this exercise is to see what you can come up with; from there, you can choose the subject about which you'd prefer to write.

The time I broke my leg
The importance of rhyming poetry (and why it doesn't deserve the scorn it gets)

Developing Pro-Con Issues

Should Internet Sales Be Subject to Sales Taxes?
Pro: Equalize competition between online stores and storefronts.
Con: Logistics nightmare: Would sales taxes be charged for the location where the sale originates, for the buyer's location, or for where the purchase is to be shipped?
Pro: Raises money for states.
Con: Adversely affects an already troubled dot-com economy.

Topic Focus

Choose a keyword for a broad topic that interests you, then brainstorm related terms from which you can choose the focus for your essay.

Topic Keyword:
    Herb
Related Topics:
    Culinary Herbs
    Medicinal Herbs
    Herb Gardens
    Organically Grown Herbs
    Preserving Herbs

Once you've settled on a topic idea, write down any related ideas or observations that come to mind. From this brainstorming will emerge what will become the central issue or theme on which you'll concentrate your essay—or, in other words, your focus. You'll discard some of the things you write down. Keep those that seem like logical extensions of that central theme; arrange them in what now seems like their logical order. (That may change once you get into your research, but this will give you the beginnings on which to base your outline.)

All this work will lead you to the point where you'll have the three main things you need for a well-written essay:

1. **Your introduction.** The essay beginning, in which you essentially give the "mission statement" for your essay, or explain what it will be about.

2. **Your arguments.** This is where you'll transition into the major supporting points directly related to the focus of your essay, usually devoting a paragraph to each.

3. **Your conclusion.** This is just what it sounds like: At this point, you'll be ready to summarize your suppositions and wrap things up, ending your essay.

Set Realistic Expectations

As you choose the topic for your essay, it's important to take into consideration how much time you have to complete the project. Most writing projects can end up taking longer than you expect, so it's better to err on the side of caution when you make your calculations. You'll need to budget your time for the following:

- **Initial brainstorming:** The process during which you choose your topic, determine the focus of your essay, and write your thesis statement.

- **Research:** The time you allot for this should include both the amount of time you anticipate it will take you to track down the research (online searches, trips to the library, etc.) and the time you'll need to fully read that research and compile your notes.

- **Writing the first draft:** As a rule of thumb, figure at least two hours to write each 250-word page. Therefore, if your essay assignment is for ten double-spaced pages, you'll need twenty hours to do the writing.

- **Follow-up research:** Budget a few hours for additional trips to the library or for other research needs that surface while you write your first draft, such as the need to make another phone call to one of your experts to verify some information.

- **Editing and rewriting:** Again erring on the side of caution, it's a good idea to allow half the time it took to write your first draft for editing (which includes inserting earlier missing information) and rewriting your essay. In other words, plan on budgeting an hour per page.

Choosing Your Focus

It's in your best interest to establish the focus of your essay as early as possible. This will prevent you from spending unnecessary hours tracking down and reading research that isn't on-topic for what you need to write.

One way to do this is to track down a recent general audience periodical or newspaper article about the topic. From that article, you should be able to ascertain whether or not the topic is one that excites you: After reading the article, do you find you want to know more? The questions you write down (about those things you want to know more about) will help shape the direction of your research.

Keep your focus in mind while you read. Is that focus broad enough to support the entire essay, while being direct enough to fit the size and scope of your assignment or project?

It's okay to remain somewhat flexible at this point. You still have time to adjust the scope of your research once you've honed your focus.

Identify Your Topic Question

Once you've arrived at what you believe should be the focus of your essay, see if you can now phrase that focus in the form of a question.

Broad Topic: Transportation in lower Manhattan

Topic Question: How have the transportation needs in lower Manhattan been affected by the events of September 11, 2001?

Such a topic question would suffice for a short paper. For a longer essay, you might want to consider broadening the topic to first give some past history of the transportation needs (and shortages) in that area, then describe how those needs were affected by 9/11, and conclude with information about how those needs are being met and projections about what plans are underway to meet those needs in the future.

A topic question is important because it helps you:

- Direct your research
- Identify the method of analysis you'll use in your essay
- Determine your thesis statement

FACT

Be sure to keep your topic question open-ended. A question that can be answered with a simple yes or no won't supply the direction you need to develop your thesis statement.

Relating Personal Experience and Learning to Your Essay

While it isn't necessary to write about only that which you know (read *Writing to Learn* by William Zinsser for fascinating information about this theory), in anything that you write you bring along your personal biases based on your life experiences. Those biases are the filters through which you strain what you encounter. Even when you approach a subject with an unbiased objective of looking at "both sides of the equation," you'll still be influenced by your built-in prejudices.

Prior knowledge is also a plus, however. It means it'll take you less time to become informed about recent developments about the topic. When appropriate, it'll mean you can write about how your personal experience relates to the topic.

Brainstorm, Brainstorm, and Then Brainstorm Some More

Keep a notepad with you so you can jot down ideas as they occur to you. (This is good advice for any writer, although some carry a micro-cassette, PDA, or notebook computer with them for this purpose.) Also, bounce ideas off of others. Another person can often provide a fresh perspective, or suggest something that hadn't yet occurred to you.

In an essay, as in any form of writing, it's essential that you determine the audience for which you'll be writing. See Chapter 1 for more details.

Write the Thesis Statement

In essence, your thesis statement is a brief statement of the opinion you'll be developing in your essay. The thesis statement becomes the main point about which you compose your essay introduction and therefore sets the tone for the entire essay. You'll keep this thesis statement in mind as you do your research—gathering specific information, refining your focus, and intentionally looking for the critical points to help substantiate your assertions. In other words, as you research, you become an investigator. Research is the time you spend finding evidence to support your opinions and conclusions.

A thesis statement is expressed in a single sentence that both provides a summary of the position you will be arguing and sets up the pattern of organization you will use in your essay to present the proof necessary to support your argument.

Your thesis statement will do the following three things:

1. Proclaim the position you will take in your essay.
2. Establish the way you will organize your discussion.
3. Point to the conclusion you will derive based on the evidence you present.

ALERT!

In your thesis statement, don't include any subsidiary information that you intend to back up in your essay.

Essay Notes Worksheet

One way to make planning, then writing, your essay easier is to establish a fill-in-the-blanks-style worksheet:

Essay Notes Worksheet

I. Topic Question and Thesis Statement to Be Used In Essay Introduction

_____

_____

_____

II. Essay Arguments

A. Paragraph 1:

1. Supporting Point 1

_____

_____

_____

2. Evidence (that supports the thesis statement) for Supporting Point 1:

_____

_____

_____

B. Paragraph 2:

1. Supporting Point 2

_____

_____

_____

2. Evidence (that supports the thesis statement) for Supporting Point 2

_____

_____

_____

C. Paragraph 3:

1. Supporting Point 3

_____

_____

_____

2. Evidence (that supports the thesis statement) for Supporting Point 3

_____

_____

_____

III. Conclusion

_____

_____

_____

Developing an Essay Outline

Using the Essay Notes Worksheet, you're now ready to plan your essay. The following example shows one way in which your essay might develop. NOTE: This example assumes the essay writer has already completed some additional preliminary research, and is keeping the notes from that research on his or her computer.

Essay Notes Worksheet

I. Topic Question and Thesis Statement to Be Used in Essay Introduction

Topic Question:
What's the big deal about chronic fatigue syndrome when a lot of people are sleep-deprived and tired in today's busy society?

Thesis Statement:
When an illness affects more than a million people in this country, it becomes important to improve public awareness so they realize that "fatigue" means more than just being tired.

II. Essay Arguments

A. Paragraph 1:

1. Supporting Point 1

Definition of the syndrome (and the names by which it is known)
Write definition so that it includes the reasons why CFS is a significant illness, including details about the devastating lifestyle changes that accompany a diagnosis

2. Evidence (that supports the thesis statement) for Supporting Point 1:

Notes from *www.cfids.org* (word/essays/cfs/research/cfids_org.doc)

B. Paragraph 2:

Essay Notes Worksheet (continued)

1. Supporting Point 2

How fatigue is more than just being tired:
> How the chronic fatigue in CFS differs from the symptom of chronic fatigue in other illnesses, such as chronic depression
> Muscle weakness (How when someone with CFS walks a block, it's comparable to how an untrained, healthy person would feel after running a marathon. Brief explanation of lactic acid release in muscles.)
> Fatigue comparable to how somebody feels on chemo
> Cognitive skills impairment
> Headache, flu-like, and other ongoing symptoms
> Related and associated illnesses (CFS patients often also cope with fibromyalgia, multiple chemical sensitivities, heightened allergic symptoms, migraines, irritable bowel syndrome, etc.)

2. Evidence (that supports the thesis statement) for Supporting Point 2

Doctor interviews (word/essays/cfs/research/med_prof_interviews.doc)
Centers for Disease Control info (word/essays/cfs/research/cdc.doc)
Anecdotal patient info (word/essays/cfs/research/cfs_patient_online.doc, word/essays/cfs/research/cfs_patient_interviews.doc)
Notes from *www.cfids.org* (word/essays/cfs/research/cfids_org.doc)
Symptoms (word/essays/cfs/research/cfs_symptoms.doc)
Related illnesses (word/essays/cfs/research/cfs_other_illnesses.doc)

C. Paragraph 3:

1. Supporting Point 3

Importance of patient, caregiver, and medical provider education
"You don't look sick"

2. Evidence (that supports the thesis statement) for Supporting Point 3

Notes from *www.cfids.org* (word/essays/cfs/research/cfids_org.doc)
Controversial or uninformed media quotes and rebuttals to those quotes
(word/essays/cfs/research/cfs_controversy.doc)

III. Conclusion
As simple as it may seem, it's important for someone coping with a devastating illness to know that he or she has a support group that does not trivialize the symptoms of that illness. Such respect is necessary for the patient to maintain the self-esteem necessary . . .

Be sure the research you include in your essay is that which supports your thesis. "In a January 2002 press release Surgeon General Dr. David Satcher put the number of people diagnosed with CFS at 1 million"—an interesting fact, but a statistic of that nature should only be in your essay if it is necessary to support one of your arguments.

At this point, the outline is only a working outline. The example above includes more things under each point than could obviously be covered in one paragraph. What's important at the time you complete your outline is to get what you know thus far down on paper. (This also helps your subconscious go to work on essay development problems you may be encountering.) You may need to add or delete points later, depending on the overall length of the essay and the space necessary to develop each argument.

Be sure to allow enough space in the outline so that you can insert the transition sentences you'll use to move from one point to the next. Also keep in mind that you'll need to be able to reiterate your main points. The more that you can "see" taking place on your outline, the easier it will be to transform that outline into the first draft of your essay. This outline "map" is necessary for you to conscientiously impose structure around your ideas and avoid an essay that's rambling and ineffective. Eventually, your outline should stand on its own, with the ideas in a logical order. Then, as you add content around your main points, choose each word so that it supports and reinforces the logic of your outline. Ideally, your outline (and eventually your essay) should build to where it ends with an insightful thought in the conclusion; the evidence presented in your essay supports that insight.

As you revise your outline, arrange the evidence in chronological order or in order of importance. Writing your transition sentences will help you figure out how best to organize that evidence. It's important that it's clear in your essay why one point follows another. Chapter 12 provides further information on developing your outline and effective outline formats.

Using Evidence

Remember that the evidence for your essay includes the anecdotes, clarifying examples, facts, and illustrations you've gathered from your research. Each piece of evidence you include should support your thesis statement. In most cases, you'll want to start by giving general statements and build your arguments from there, ending with specific facts. Your evidence should be:

- Accurate
- Arranged in a logical manner
- Authoritative
- Relevant
- Straightforward, and not manipulated
- Sufficient to support your thesis (prove your point)

Using Reasoning

When your essay relies on reasoning, you'll want to arrange your evidence in its most logical order. Some examples of how this can be done include the following:

- Complex to simple
- General to specific
- Highest-priority item first
- Least climactic to most climactic
- Lowest-priority item first

- Most climactic to least climactic
- Simple to complex
- Specific to general

Reasoning is the way you find it most logical to present the evidence you've chosen to support your thesis.

Tips to Help Streamline the Essay-Writing Process

The ability to organize your thoughts quickly and write them down in essay format is a useful skill. Even beyond writing an essay, you'll use basically the same skills whether you need to summarize a report or complete an essay exam. Like any skill, it improves with practice.

Remember that an essay is a logical presentation of facts that begins with a preparation period (during which you brainstorm potential ideas and gather your evidence), followed by the actual writing of the essay.

Here are some helpful tips:

- **Underline keywords.** This works to emphasize key thoughts within your brainstorming notes and your research.
- **Think of yourself as a reporter.** As you peruse your research, write down probing questions that come to mind as you discover gaps in what you read. (This will help you know what additional research materials you need to gather and can also provide you with questions to ask experts when you interview them.)
- **Keep things colorful.** Use different colored highlighters to mark up your notes, distinguishing different types of facts (e.g., yellow for quotes, blue for expert names, etc.) and to mark off material once you've used it.
- **Ask yourself a question.** If you find yourself stuck at some point in the essay-writing process, ask yourself: What is the most important thing I have learned/discovered while doing research for this project?

- **Summarize your main points.** Write your opening and closing paragraphs in advance and then complete the writing about those points necessary to support your summary.
- **Simplify your transitions.** If you're having difficulty knowing how to make the transition from one point to the next, start out using "the first point I'd like to make" and "the next point I'd like to make" and so on; you can then revise those when you edit your draft.

Keeping these tips in mind throughout your essay project will ease whatever burden you may feel about the task at hand. Because they help keep you on track by focusing on the essential elements of your essay, the tips can help ease any initial intimidation you may feel.

CHAPTER 12

Essays in Particular

Knowing how to write a thesis statement and a con-clusion for your essay isn't enough. You also need to decide how to structure the information that will go in the middle (the body) of your essay. In this chap-ter, you'll learn how to structure your essay argu-ment, format your essay, develop a thesis, and create an outline, as well as how to treat specific types of essays such as academic essays and admissions essays.

Structuring Your Essay Argument

In an essay, your argument is how you choose to present the evidence. You can do this in a number of ways:

- **A discussion:** Giving both sides to a debate.
- **An explanation:** Describing your evidence in detail.
- **An exposition:** Arguing a point of view.

How you choose to present your evidence will depend on how you analyze and organize your research information, and sometimes vice versa. (It's kind of like the chicken and the egg: In some cases, you'll be hard-pressed to know which came first. Other times, you'll know the point of view you intend to take when you begin.)

When you analyze the evidence you've gathered, you break it down into its logical parts. From that exercise, you'll be able to discern how those parts relate to each other. How you demonstrate that relationship within your essay depends on the point of view you adopt. You may choose to present information from different sources that examine unique aspects about your topic, deconstruct that information to illustrate the relationships between the different sources, and then merge them into a whole concept.

In some shape or form, the simplest way to describe the process is that you assemble your evidence so that piece by piece they eventually merge to present the "big picture." This can be accomplished using different organization patterns:

- **Advantages and disadvantages:** This format takes a pro-and-con approach, describing both sides of the equation, and then drawing conclusions from that evidence.
- **Cause and effect:** This is the format most often used to describe a life-changing experience or to write about someone who or something that has greatly influenced your life. You describe how you understand and appreciate the effect that other incident or person had on your development and maturity.

- **Chronological:** This journal-style format progresses point by point, with details about each point given in the order in which it occurred.
- **Comparison and contrast:** This method compares one aspect of an object or situation with another, such as describing what it's like to live at the poverty level in the United States versus the poverty lifestyle in a third-world country.
- **Description:** Similar to the chronological structure except that instead of systematically proceeding through increments of time, it is a point-by-point explanation of a place, person, or thing.
- **Example:** This is the structure of the traditional academic essay, which begins with a main argument or thesis statement, continues with at least three pieces of evidence that support the thesis statement argument, and concludes by stating what the essay has shown.
- **Narrative:** This method involves writing your essay in story format, and is often used in what are referred to as personal essays—those that describe a personal event in the writer's life and the writer's reaction to that event. By design, it will incorporate another method as well, such as when the story is described in a chronological order of events.

FACT

It's a common misconception that formal academic writing must be done in the third person. The voice you choose for your essay will depend on your topic. First person can also be effective, and, unless instructed otherwise by your professor, should be used when writing personal experience or opinion essays.

The Academic Essay

The academic essay differs from fictional or personal writing in that it has a formal structure. The entire message for the writing is not limited to individual sentences or paragraphs, but rather relies on the overall structure and organization of the essay, the content of which is individual and reflects the writer's argument and research.

In almost all instances, the academic essay must contain an argument or claim. The essay must address an issue or raise a question, presented through appropriate data or information (evidence) that exemplifies, analyzes, and comments on that evidence in a logical manner. The essay will make reference to sources, often also pointing out any illogical data found, such as inconsistencies or omissions in a source argument. In addition to being graded on their writing ability, students are assessed on their ability to select the appropriate and relevant evidence to justify their arguments or claims.

FACT

The amount of evidence gathered for an essay isn't as important as the quality of the information cited. A lengthy bibliography and reference notes aren't enough. The evidence used must be relevant to the thesis.

Essay arguments may vary in how they are written and how the argument is expressed, but a good essay should show the development of a thesis, supported by evidence. It should also be written in a way that effectively anticipates and overcomes objections or counterarguments.

The Parts of an Academic Essay

The clichéd explanation of how to write an academic essay is to "tell me what you're going to tell me, tell it, then tell me what you told me."

In almost all instances, American academic essays are "thesis-driven," which means that the writer explains the main point of the essay—the thesis statement—in the beginning of the essay. As covered in Chapter 11, a thesis statement is a sentence or two that provides a summary of the position you will be arguing. It also sets up the pattern of organization you will use in your essay to present the proof necessary to support your argument.

In an academic essay, the beginning, middle, and end of the essay are known as the introduction, body, and conclusion:

- **Introduction:** The opening sentences where the topic statement (the what, who, and when) must be introduced. It is also here where the central issue (the why and how) is addressed. Additional comments about the aim and outline structure of the essay are also sometimes included.
- **Body:** It is here that you will cover the analysis or explanation, namely your examination of the evidence you've chosen to support your thesis. The body will also include your evaluation of that evidence. (The essay argument style you've chosen will dictate the manner and order in which this analysis and evaluation are presented.)
- **Conclusion:** The end of the essay refers back to the introduction and explains how you met the goals of the essay. The limitations of the present work and recommendations for future action, study, or more research are also often part of the conclusion.

ESSENTIAL

Present perfect tense is often used in the conclusion of an academic essay, to state what the writer has done and learned from the experience. Phrases such as "I have been doing research that leads to the conclusion that . . ." or "experts have said . . ." are in the present perfect tense.

Formatting Your Essay

Your academic essay will not only be judged on your writing and how well you present your evidence (and the quality of that evidence regarding how it supports your thesis), the printed format for your essay is also important. In addition to showing that you know how to follow instructions, a properly formatted essay is also easier for the instructor to read and grade. (You want as many things in your favor as possible.)

The information in this section is given as a common example of what is expected in such formatting. It's important that you follow the guidelines set forth by your professor because papers that fail to meet the expected standards are usually penalized, and in extreme cases, are sometimes rejected outright and not graded.

Common formatting instructions include the following:

- Print (or type) your essay on regular white, 8½" x 11" paper.
- Staple the pages together (unless instructed otherwise).
- Use at least 12-point type size throughout, in a regular serif font, such as Times New Roman or Courier.
- Double-space the text.
- Set up margins of at least one inch on all four sides.
- Include a title page.

Admissions Essays

Free information on college admissions essays and how they relate to the college selection process is available from the National Association for College Admission Counseling (NACAC), 1631 Prince Street, Alexandria, VA 22314 or on its Web site (*www.nacacnet.org*).

Some Web sites that offer suggestions:

- **CollegeBoard.com (*www.collegeboard.com*):** Information on "Three Steps to a Great College Essay" in the "Essay Skills" portion of the student "apply to a college" section.
- **PersonalEssay.com (*www.personalessay.com*):** This is a Web site for a "for-a-fee" essay-editing service; however, the site also has some free essay-writing tips.
- **Petersons.com (*www.petersons.com*):** The "College Planner: Student Edition" section provides admissions essays tips and suggestions.

ESSENTIAL

Remember that once you write an essay for one college, most often you can save time by adapting that essay for the applications you submit to other schools. Be creative and you'll probably find that you can lift entire paragraphs, and apply them to different questions. Just make sure that in doing so you have answered the question asked. Pay attention to the introductions and conclusions because this is where answers can stand out if they're not properly adapted.

Developing a Thesis

The most common failure in academic writing is the failure to establish a clear thesis. The thesis is the reason for being for any academic paper. It gives direction to your writing and lets the reader (who is very frequently the one evaluating your work—remember how nice it is to please this person) know what the heck it is you're going to talk about.

Many professors demand a specific thesis sentence. An advanced writer can often give a good idea about what his or her thesis is without relying on a single sentence to define it; however, even when such a sentence doesn't physically appear in the final paper, chances are that the writer wrote one before beginning the work in order to be cognizant of the paper's main theme.

While it's true that the thesis is a tool for the reader, you should also be aware that the thesis is a tool for you as you write. By constantly referring to your thesis, you can more easily keep your paper on-topic and make a cleaner, more intelligent-sounding presentation.

Often in the sciences (and frequently in any research paper), the thesis will come from a hypothesis formed before you do your research. A hypothesis is the idea you believe will be proven (or disproven) by the experiment or research you do. Once you've done the research, your thesis may discuss if your hypothesis was proven correct or incorrect. It should also probably explain any implications of your research.

A thesis on a literary topic may be what you feel is a message of the work, or the significance of a theme or motif in the work. It should be a subject that is meaningful to you and relevant to the topics you've uncovered in your research. Most importantly, it needs to be a subject you are interested in. If you enjoy the subject, you'll have a much easier time writing about it.

Developing exactly what you want to say about an assigned subject can be a difficult task, but finding and using a solid thesis can make or break a paper, so it's worth it to put a lot of work into writing your thesis. If your paper assignment comes in the form of a question, you can often rephrase the question as a statement for your thesis. If this doesn't work, and you feel you are stuck, you may want to try writing down all your thoughts on the subject. Once you've seen what all your ideas are, you can choose a statement that will allow you to include the greatest portion, or even better, the highest quality of the ideas you wrote down. Using this method, you may have half your paper written already. All you need to do is organize it and smooth out the transitions. Once you have chosen a thesis, you are ready to get approval from your professor. Many papers, such as a master's or doctoral thesis, require that you get formal approval from your advisor. Even if your paper doesn't require it, however, very few professors will object if you explain to them what your thesis is and how you plan to approach the discussion in order to get the professor's input on the subject.

If you are required to write a formal proposal, you will probably also be given a set of guidelines for the proposal. Such proposals should include your thesis statement, the approach you will take toward your research, the sources you think you will use, and frequently the organization your paper will use. Many of these items are variables, so don't worry if your paper evolves such that the end result is different than your initial proposal. Professors normally accept that a proposal is a fluid document, not something chiseled in stone.

The Outline

The outline is a method of approaching the writing of a paper that often chafes people. Part of the reason the outline is bothersome is that some people find it restrictive. To avoid feeling this way, you need to remember that, like the thesis statement, the outline is a tool for you, not a taskmaster.

The thesis statement will keep you straight on what direction to take in your paper. The outline is the path you plan to take to keep you pointed in that direction. It is important to remember that your outline should be fluid. As you have new ideas, you should make changes to accommodate them, dropping or adding items as necessary.

If you take the time to have your ideas placed in relation to each other, you don't have to worry about repeating yourself as you write. You will also be able to manipulate the order in which your thoughts appear, which in turn will allow you to see the entire paper conceptually.

When you start writing ten- or twenty-page papers, having an abbreviated list of what ideas should be presented provides you with a handy visual tool, letting you know where to insert new ideas or how to arrange aspects of the paper effectively.

There are two primary reasons for making an outline before you begin your writing: first, to organize your ideas; and second, to keep those ideas within view.

Academic writing is very demanding in the organization department, so it's good to have all of your ideas proceeding in a logical and related sequence. Outlines can be very helpful, enabling you to see how your ideas progress.

Outlines also help make sure you don't forget any of your ideas. If you have all your ideas written down and in the order you wish to present them, you don't need to worry about whether you've inadvertently omitted anything. You can simply move from idea to idea, checking them off as you proceed with your writing.

Effective Outline Formats

There are two effective ways to make an outline. The first is the traditional format. Main subjects are marked with Roman numerals (I, II, III, IV, etc.). In short essays, you can use these to mark paragraphs. In longer papers, they work better as section markers. Topics within those subjects are indented one level and defined by capital letters. As you get more specific (say you feel the topic marked "C" needed more notes to help you remember where you wanted to take your discussion), you indent again and use Arabic numerals (1, 2, 3, 4, etc.). You can get as detailed as you want, using lowercase letters, lowercase Roman numerals, etc. Again, this is your tool. If you want to use a different alphanumeric sequence, just make sure you can remember it. No one else needs to. You just need to remember how it is broken up.

Outline for "Comics: Giving Them the Respect They Deserve"

I. Establishing Comics as Literature
    A. Function of comics
        1. communication
        2. storytelling
            a. genres
        3. aesthetic response
    B. How to read comics
II. Characterization
    A. Hero and Heroine
    B. Villain
    C. Everyman
III. Story Progression

Another option that seems less confining to most people is to use stacks of 3" x 5" cards. One method is to color code them with a marker or a sticker to separate main topics, then put them in the sequence in which you want to discuss them. You may want to play around with the marking system until you find one that works for you (after all, the outline is a tool for you, not the other way around). A major advantage of this method of outlining is that you can easily reorder the topic cards without spending time editing a document you made. It is just as easy to add or remove topics and subjects as any other outlining method.

If, while doing your research, you write your notes from your sources onto your index cards or within your outline document, you'll have your quotes and citations already prepared for your report.

Note cards are also useful in that you can either stack them to save space on your desk (or at the library) or lay them out on a flat surface in order to see everything at once. Do what helps you work best.

For Longer Essays Only

One final note on outlines: They may take more time than they're worth for very short essays. In high school you may have learned the "five paragraph" format for essays. In this method, you introduce what you want to say in one paragraph, specifying three things you will use to prove your thesis. The next three paragraphs each discuss one of those three topics. The final paragraph restates your thesis and what you did to prove it. This sort of essay is very effective and is solid writing, but a full outline for this sort of essay is tantamount to writing it twice! In this case, simply write a thesis statement and jot down the three things you will discuss to elaborate your thesis. This should be sufficient. (It is also a good habit to have for when you need to complete the essay portion of the SAT test.)

Remember: An outline is intended to be a tool to help streamline your work; it isn't something that should become a tedious chore or create more work.

CHAPTER 13

Academic Writing: Research Papers, Master's Theses, and Dissertations

Frequently, people are under the misconception that only poetry and fiction constitute "creative" writing. Don't be one of those people. Every piece of work, including academic writing, requires you to use your creativity, and most of the rules about writing for any subject will apply to academic writing.

Getting It Down

All professionals in academic circles, from physicists to literary historians, have to write about their research, theories, and discoveries. It's not only a part of being a student; it's also a part of being an academic professional.

Academic writing sometimes seems like a tricky task because most disciplines want you to use certain conventions. As with any other writing project, you should read papers and books in the relevant discipline before writing your own papers. This will help you get a feel for some of the conventions and practices specific to your field. This chapter will of course cover some of those conventions, but it would be impossible to cover every usage in every field. Being familiar with writing in your discipline will be an invaluable skill for all academic writing.

If you are a student, remember that your most important aid for writing is your professor. No book can help explain the questions and topics proposed by your professor. Most professors are happy to be able to discuss with you the documentation, subject, or problems specific to your paper.

The "voice" of your paper is also important to consider. The hard sciences tend to be much less personal in their writing, achieving a feeling of greater objectivity. In the humanities, writings tend to be more informal, often using first-person and second-person pronouns (e.g.; I, we; you).

Some professors are adamant about the voice you use in your paper. If you are unfamiliar with the publication or professor's preferences, it is a good idea to ask directly.

MLA Documentation Style

There are many types of style for quoting sources used in academic writing. One of the most important functions of a style guide is to instruct you as to the proper form for such documentation. Many academic organizations each have different systems for documenting sources: footnotes, endnotes, internal citation, and so forth.

This chapter will give an overview of one of the most common documentation styles, the one developed by the Modern Language Association, or MLA.

The MLA documentation style uses internal or parenthetical citation, which means when you cite a quote or an idea from someone else, you immediately begin a set of parentheses, inside of which you place the author's name and the number of the page from where you pulled the information:

There are those who claim that comic books were destroyed by the advent of censorship from the Comics Code Authority, but others claim the Comics Code Authority actually was a long-term benefactor to the comic book industry (Nyberg, x–xi).

At the end of a paper written in MLA format, you must place a list of all the works you cited within the paper. List cited works by the name of the author, the title of the article (if there is an article title), followed by the name of the publication, all separated by periods. Lastly come the details of publication, including the page numbers of the article, the city where it was published, the publishing company, and the year of publication. Here's an example using the book referred to in the previous example:

Nyberg, Amy Kiste. Seal of Approval: The History of the Comics Code. Jackson: University Press of Mississippi, 1998.

FACT

Some professors don't care which documentation style you use, as long as it's done properly. However, it is important that you check with your professor or target publication when there is any question as to whether or not there is a preferred style.

Magazine or serial articles may also require that you include the issue and volume number of the publication. The punctuation in both the internal citation and the works cited list is important for proper use of the documentation and should be observed closely. In addition, the second and following lines of the works cited entries are indented while the first line of such entries are not. These are important for clarity of the information.

Obviously, not all of the works you cite in an academic paper will be from a book or even from a printed source. With the advent of the Internet, CD-ROMs, and even broadcast media (like TV or radio), there are many possible sources of information. A listing for how to cite all of these possible sources would take many pages. However, the *MLA Handbook for Writers of Research Papers* by Joseph Gibaldi has a very comprehensive listing with plenty of examples, covering nearly any media or information source you may use.

For more details, you can look at the style guide published by the MLA, which is currently in its second edition and widely available for purchase at university bookstores. (Refer to Appendix A for further information on these suggested titles.)

Other Documentation Styles

There are other styles of documentation. If you prefer to use one of these (or your professor prefers that you do), be sure to be familiar with the style. A good source of information on these styles is *A Manual for Writers of Term Papers, Theses, and Dissertations* (Chicago Guides to Writing, Editing, and Publishing) by Kate L. Turabian.

A Manual for Writers of Term Papers, Theses, and Dissertations, often referred to as "Turabian," presents a different method of documentation. Turabian uses footnotes to cite works, sometimes placing the complete bibliographical information inside the footnote as well as occasional annotations (both of these are discussed below). These footnotes may provide the citation information for sequential references at once.

Turabian also occasionally prescribes a "notes" page at the end of the main text for endnotes containing tangential but relevant information.

QUESTION?

What does "tangential" mean?
"Tangential" means "of little relevance," so such sources would fall within the purview of trivia or secondary information more so than pertinent information.

Finally, Turabian's method of listing the bibliographical information differs from the MLA style. Papers written in Turabian style may have several works on the bibliography page that were not directly cited, and the format for the same information is different. The book cited above would look like the following in Turabian.

Nyberg, Amy Kiste. 1998. *Seal of Approval: The History of the Comics Code*. Jackson: University Press of Mississippi.

Most fields, including biology, chemistry, geology, linguistics, mathematics, medicine, physics, and psychology, have preferred documentation methods. To have a full understanding of their requirements, you should refer to a handbook published by organizations in the appropriate field. You don't want to get your documentation wrong!

Refer to Appendix A for information on additional commonly used style guides.

Bibliography, Footnotes, and Endnotes

As mentioned earlier, you will need a works cited list (often called a bibliography) at the end of your paper. This will list all the books, articles, Web sites, interviews, and other sources you referenced or quoted throughout your paper. You should start making this list before you even complete an outline; sometimes, you may even want to start making the list before you come up with a thesis. As soon as you find a work you think you'll use, write down all the bibliographical information. This should be done in the documentation style format you'll be using for your paper, such as the MLA style. You can always remove a source from your list if you find that it isn't needed, but going back to gather the information is a nuisance.

There will be times when you will not want to remove those unused items, however. Frequently, papers will be required to have a bibliography that lists books on the subject for further research. These lists will never be complete for normal student research papers or dissertations. An exhaustive bibliography of all works on almost any subject takes many, many pages. In fact, books that are nothing but bibliographies have been published.

Bibliographies published as books or articles without any associated paper are generally annotated, and often students are asked to annotate their own works cited lists. To annotate, you simply add a sentence or two after the publication information for the work's entry. These sentences will discuss the thoughts presented in the work and perhaps mention how useful the work is as a whole.

Footnotes and endnotes are a touchy subject. Some professors don't like them. Some documentation styles require that you use footnotes or endnotes to refer to the cited work. Using footnote citation is popular with some people who claim that the internal citation method used by the MLA is distracting. They want the information available if they want to investigate the idea further, but they don't want their reading pace interrupted by a parenthetical reference to an author and page number.

In general, there are two reasons to use a footnote or endnote:

1. **To cite a work.** This should always be used if the documentation style requires it, and never used if your documentation style asks for internal citation.

2. **To provide information interesting or relevant to your paper's discussion, but still tangential.** These should be kept to a minimum, and as mentioned earlier, some evaluators may not like them, in which case they should be eliminated entirely.

There aren't many instances where the information you would put into a footnote can't be worked into the regular text of your argument.

With modern word-processing software, endnotes and footnotes are very easy to create. Generally, it's a matter of opening a menu and choosing whether you want a footnote or an endnote. Most software will keep track of the numbering of your notes and will automatically adjust them if you delete or add a note.

Writing Your Paper

After you've chosen a thesis and have an outline, you're ready to get to the meat of writing a paper: the writing!

Now you're in really good shape to begin. All you need to do is shape the ideas into coherent sentences, flesh out those ideas that need more elaboration, and make sure you have good sentences that transition between thoughts and your proper paragraph format.

Without a thesis and outline, you will probably spend time at this stage rambling and faltering as you try to find your voice, cutting and then adding entire sentences or paragraphs as you realize they either don't make sense or wander off topic. This isn't necessarily bad, but in most cases it takes more overall time to write the paper, causes unnecessary stress, and results in less confidence in what you've written.

An Interesting Introduction

There are a few things to pay attention to at this stage, however. The first is the introduction. In short essays, this may only be a paragraph. In longer papers, you may use an entire page. The introduction should have some sort of hook. It need not be as gripping as the last novel you read, but it should at least bring up the general topic you want to discuss. Longer introductions should have information that explains the controversy prompting your paper, or they may mention the lack of knowledge that led to your research or experimentation. Another idea is to detail briefly the counter to the thesis you are about to present. The introduction should always either contain your thesis statement or at least summarize the thesis enough to make it clear to any reader what the rest of your paper will discuss.

The Body

The next portion of your paper should discuss all those ideas you wrote down in the outline. Whether you want to break your paper into artificial sections or simply transition between paragraphs is a personal decision (but one that may be tempered by the preferences of your professor or publisher).

When it comes to the style in which you write your paper, remember that some fields prefer formal writing while some like a more personal voice. This is why you should have read your textbook and the sources from which you got all of your quotes; they help you know what the expectations are in the field for which you're writing.

A Strong Conclusion

Make sure you have a strong conclusion to your paper. The conclusion should mention the thesis and may reiterate the primary arguments or idea of your paper, but this alone will be insufficient. You will also need to mention the implications of your discussion. If you made a new scientific discovery, extrapolate potential applications. If you made a new observation about the meaning of a philosopher's main thoughts, be sure to mention the potential ramifications for philosophers who came later and how the idea may change philosophical thought going forward. The best papers are ones that point out where further discovery or observations may come in the future. Make sure you bring closure to your discussion, but also remind the reader that other discussions are still waiting on the same subject.

Getting Your Paper into Final Form

If you've followed the steps above, you probably have a good paper so far, but as in all writing endeavors, the first draft is never, ever enough. This rule is almost as important as the plagiarism rule (which, as you remember, is to properly cite all of your sources at all costs). You will always have proofreading to do, and in most cases, you will need to rewrite sections.

Finish your first draft with enough time to take a break before coming back to look at it again. Look over your draft closely. Ask yourself these questions as you check the phrasing of every sentence:

- Did you choose the best words to prove your point?
- Did you state everything clearly, in an interesting and grammatically correct manner?

You also need to proofread. Word-processing software is a great tool, because it helps you move text quickly. It reduces the amount of paper wasted and lets you correct mistakes efficiently. As discussed in Chapter 2, software spellcheckers can't catch all mistakes. Nor can a program's grammar checker do an even halfway decent job of catching grammar errors. English grammar and phrasing rules are not consistent in every application. Grammar checkers may prompt you to make a change to something that is more wrong than what you wrote!

If you can't rely on your software to catch your mistakes, then what can you do? You have several solutions:

1. **Read your paper out loud.** Many errors in phrasing will become evident because you'll be more apt to trip over them as you're reading aloud than if you're simply skimming the paper.

2. **Have someone read your paper out loud to you.** You will be even more apt to pick up errors because phrasing or word problems will sound harsh to your ear. (It can help to devise a plan so that you can signal your friend so that he or she knows when to mark whatever passages you wish to go back and review; despite any found errors, such a signal will allow your friend to continue reading without interrupting the flow of your paper.)

3. **Have a friend proofread your paper.** Make sure your friend knows to indicate any sentence he or she had to read twice to understand.

4. **Take advantage of your college's writing center.** Most universities offer this service for free. Just be sure to check in advance so you allow enough time for one of the workers or volunteers to look over your paper.

A paper free of language errors will make a great impression and make it easier for the reader to focus on what you have to say.

Adapting Your Work for Publication

If you plan to progress within your academic field—that is, you want to become a professor or a research worker in the field, you'll eventually need to publish your academic writing. The best place to publish academic writing is in scholarly journals specific to your field. It may be nice to have an article in a magazine or your local newspaper, but such publication credits don't carry as much significance with academic-related employers and universities who are looking at your application.

You should recognize that these journals may have different criteria for evaluating documentation, writing style, or format than the professor who first graded your paper. Be sure to find out the format in which journals want to see manuscripts. Comply with these guidelines to the letter.

Most academic publications have more stringent requirements than professors do for student writing submitted in their courses. They will require your ideas and research to be even more significant and original than student papers, and the demand for familiarity with any relevant writing in the field will be much greater. Refine your work to its peak of perfection before submitting. Frequently, this will mean rewriting the paper several more times.

You may also need to alter the content of your article. Determine whether there is an innovative approach to your paper that will be more significant. Perhaps changing the thesis slightly will make it fit better within a specific journal's area of concern.

Academic writing can be a daunting challenge, especially if you are inexperienced with writing and your area of study is mostly unrelated to language usage. However, the key to academic writing is organization. You don't need to be a brilliant wordsmith to write a good paper, even one deserving of publication. You just need to document correctly, establish and maintain your direction, and organize your thoughts.

CHAPTER 14

Business Writing

Your life may not depend on your ability to accomplish the writing you need to do for business, but that ability—or lack thereof—can certainly affect your financial life. Success in business relies on effective communication, which can take many forms. Understanding the particular formats needed for specific business writing tasks is the first step in achieving that necessary ability to communicate effectively. This chapter will help you work your way through the basics.

Request for Proposal (RFP)

Whether it is unsolicited or requested, a proposal is a written presentation that addresses a specific need. As a full description of a proposed plan for action, the entity (person, business, or organization) submitting a proposal should make certain it contains information about the following:

- Benefits of working with the entity
- Cost breakdowns
- Delivery (date of completion) details
- Performance standards details
- Qualifications and ability to perform the actions
- Schedule of events to be addressed
- Time requirements

The proposal should then conclude with a summary that includes the proposal writer's recommendations.

Businesses and organizations usually deal with three types of proposals:

1. Internal, for change or proposed budget adjustments within the entity.
2. External, for change or budget recommendations outside of the entity.
3. Product, for sales or technology product or service recommendations.

While entities often submit unsolicited proposals within the organization (in the form of a suggestion for a procedural change, for example) or to another entity (in the hope of establishing a need in order to solicit business), when a proposal is specifically solicited, it is known as a Request for Proposal (RFP), also sometimes informally known as a "request for a bid."

The following example is written specifically for a meeting and catering RFP and assumes it is being used as a "form letter"; however, if such requests are made frequently, the form should be maintained by electronic means (as a word-processing or other program file) so that it's easy to customize. The essential elements would be the same for other RFP requests, too.

Meetings & Catering Function Request for Proposal

To: Director of Sales
[Business name, address, phone, and other pertinent identifying information]

From:
(Contact's) First Name:
Last Name:
Title:
Company or Organization:
Mailing Address:
City:
State/Province:
Country:
ZIP/Postal Code:
Phone:
Alternative Phone Number (cell phone or pager):
Fax:
E-mail:

Event Information:

Name of meeting or event:
Type of event (check all that apply):

❑   Business   ❑ Other:
❑   Meeting   ❑ Social
❑   Conference   ❑ Meeting
                     ❑ Wedding
                     ❑ Bar/Bat Mitzvah
                     ❑ Reunion

Is catering required?
❑ Sit Down   ❑ Buffet   ❑ Reception

Preferred date:

Preferred time:
Alternative dates:
Alternative times:

Number of people:

Need for guest rooms or suites? Yes / No
How many?

Special considerations:
A/V setup:
Other:

Additional information:

Press Packets

Also known as a press kit, the press packet is an entity's formal, written means of introduction, used for targeted media contacts. Press packets should be assembled for any event to which the media is invited. This advance information gives reporters the necessary background to cover the event. Press packets are most often submitted within a two-pocket folder, the outside cover of which is usually embossed with the entity's logo or other identifying information. The inside of this packet contains the following components:

- Media liaison's business card
- Agenda or media advisory with information about the event
- Brochure or fact sheet about the entity
- Press release about the upcoming event
- Biographies of principal participants, often also containing their photos

When not distributed in advance, press packets should be available for distribution at a press registration table by the media liaison, who should also be available to assist reporters by facilitating interviews with spokespersons and handling any inquiries.

Maintaining Media Contacts

Media relations is about building and maintaining awareness about your business or organization through continuing communications. Initially, you'll build your media list by consulting current directories and, perhaps, polling those within your organization for suggestions as to their preferred vehicle for distributing your communications. Once you've established initial contact, it is in the best interest of your business or organization to maintain your relationships with the news media by doing such things as:

- Keeping them abreast of developments by ensuring they have a current list of section officers and issue experts, or at least a year-in-review report.
- If appropriate, hosting an annual informal media luncheon, or inviting individual media contacts to lunch.
- Sending interim media updates by e-mail.
- Sending a thank-you note to a reporter after you receive good coverage.
- Familiarizing yourself with the other work done by your media contacts, mentioning and complimenting them for recent stories if you have the occasion to speak with them, or sending an appropriate congratulatory note.
- Maintaining a clip, transcript, video, and audiotape file to help you establish a record of your media efforts. (Don't rely on your memory.)

It's bound to happen someday: Somebody from the media makes a mistake when presenting the information you submitted. Don't be afraid to point out erroneous coverage; just be sure you restrict your polite "suggestions" to draw attention only to instances of significant error, which is especially important if you need the media to issue some sort of correction (such as correcting a print error of your phone number or Web site URL).

Other Publicity

Other forms of obtaining publicity for your business's developments include newsletters, trade publication articles, and/or Web sites:

- **Newsletters:** A newsletter is an effective way of notifying others about your business's or organization's developments. The length and style will be dictated by your budget and by the type of information you need to distribute. (It isn't necessary to go to the expense of printing a full-color, glossy publication if your only content is a press release–style update without pictures. One less expensive way to use color is to distribute newsletters via e-mail: Colors can be used within the newsletter if you opt for HTML e-mail; otherwise, include your Web site URL to provide the option of viewing photos or other illustrations at the newsletter reader's discretion.)

- **Trade publication articles:** Rather than providing the "basics" about an event or product via a press release, a meatier trade publication article is an effective way to ensure that the targeted audience sees your message when it requires more coverage.

- **Web sites:** Unless it's essential that you offer some sort of online ordering option, a Web site doesn't have to have all the latest "bells and whistles" to be effective. A Web presence does add another layer of credibility to an organization, so even a site with only the company logo and basic "about" information is an easy way to keep up-to-date information instantly available for those who may need or want it.

Announcements

Announcements are another way to maintain essential contact with your customers or those in the media. Such contact also helps you get new business (new customers!). A loyal base of people familiar with your business helps ensure a healthier bottom line.

New Acquisition

Customers like assurance that those with whom they do business are successful. Announcing a new acquisition not only gets your name in front of them again (and overcomes your "out of sight, out of mind" fears), it is also a subtle way for your business to boast about its successes.

New Acquisition Announcement

Dear Customer:

It is with pride that ABC Widgets announces our recent purchase of XYZ Industries. This acquisition of one of the nation's most respected manufacturers of sprockets will not only help ensure we have a reliable supplier for this necessary component of an efficient widget, it also adds an additional 5,000 employees to the ABC Widgets family.

For the past ten years, our goal at ABC Widgets has been to manufacture and distribute the most reliable widgets in the industry. We value your ongoing business and continued faith in our company, and recognize that as proof that you have trust in our abilities to meet our objectives.

If you have any questions, please contact your sales representative.

Thank you for your continued business and support.

Sincerely,

[Name]

If you anticipate that there will be any industry concerns about a recent acquisition (loss of jobs, relocation of employees, etc.), address those in your acquisitions announcement letter. Taking the offensive lets you put your spin on how the news is presented, rather than having to go on the defensive if that news gets unfavorably filtered through negative press or other coverage.

New Hours and Services

Your customers need to know when they can reach you and what services you provide. Don't assume this information is common knowledge. Make use of every opportunity to remind them of these essential details about your company.

Change of Service Announcement

Dear Customer:

You spoke and we listened!

As of Sunday, September 29, 2002, we're expanding our business hours:

Bethany's Bakery will now be open 24 hours a day, 7 days a week.

Bethany's Bakery will continue to be closed on Thanksgiving and Christmas; however, we're confident that our otherwise widely expanded hours will help make sure you have time to place your orders and get what you need in plenty of time before those busy holidays.

We're also expanding the information available on the Bethany's Bakery Web site. Now when you visit us online, you'll find news about our specials and current prices, plus pictures of our newest specialties and traditional favorites. (We challenge you to take a look at pictures of our new Chocolate Truffle Cheesecake and see if it doesn't make your mouth water!) We're providing this service to make it easy for you to know what's available at the shop. We can also now ship most selections to anywhere in the continental United States, so you can have Bethany's Bakery send your family's traditional holiday treats to anyone who can't make it to your home to enjoy the dessert in person.

Thank you for being an important part of Bethany's Bakery's success.

Best wishes,

[Name]

Sales Letters

Sales letters do more than just "sell." By including essential components of information within each letter, you alert and inform your customers. It's these letter components that also help you persuade the recipient to respond in the intended manner. These components act as the gentle nudging incentive to provide that response. In other words, you present this information in a way that grabs the recipient's attention, increases the desire to listen to your message, and encourages them to act. The most common components include the following:

Benefits

When somebody reads a sales letter, it's the benefits you present in that letter than converts someone's "want" into a "need." When that person can see how a product or service will benefit him or her, that person is sold! Always keep these benefits in mind when organizing your letter, presenting first the feature you anticipate will provide the best benefit. Make sure you are describing that which will motivate. Features (like size, color, and price) are important eventually, but they aren't what you're selling. You're selling the value of those features and how they will benefit the customer.

Features-based writing: "It only weighs . . ."
Benefits-based writing: "You get the convenience of a lightweight . . ."
Features-based writing: "It has surround-sound . . ."
Benefits-based writing: "You get the pleasure of being enveloped by luxurious sound coming from <description of> speakers positioned to . . ."

Offers

An effective offer must be one that is about more than special prices or services. An effective offer is one that motivates the letter recipient to act. To do so, an offer must convey value and scarcity.

Every time a sales letter recipient reads your offer, he'll be subconsciously asking himself: "Why do I need this now?" Anticipate that question and phrase your offer accordingly.

To the first three clients who respond to this cell phone upgrade service, we'll provide a hands-free headset at absolutely no cost!

To the next three clients who upgrade their service, we'll provide a free leather carrying case.

Testimonials

People do buy based on the influence of others. (That's why so many television commercials feature celebrities as company spokespersons. Other times the commercial characters—like the M&Ms candy "people" or the fictitious Maytag repairman—become recognized enough that that recognition alone adds credibility to the message.)

People also like to know that others like themselves have profitably or successfully used your product or service: They want to know how others benefited so they can see how they'll benefit as well.

Being able to provide testimonials requires some prep work on your part: You first have to "ask" satisfied clients for that information. One way to increase the odds that you'll get what you need is to offer a free gift or service in exchange for completing a survey form. If your product has been reviewed in a leading publication, you can pull a favorable quote from the review and use that. Try to include a validating testimonial for each benefit you're including in the letter.

Adapting Your Writing Skills

There are times when you'll need to write something that isn't for your audience to read. So, whether you need to stand in front of your audience to give a speech or a presentation, or if your audience is a captive one on the phone, the basics of writing remain the same.

ALERT!

The most important proofreading technique you can employ when checking the text of a speech or a script is to read it aloud. That's the only way you'll learn whether or not the words easily "roll off your tongue" and aren't ones that cause you to stammer or trip up.

Speeches

The format for a speech will depend on the purpose and the occasion. You can record your speech in one of four ways:

1. **Word for word:** Having your entire speech in front of you means you know in advance exactly what you're going to say. What you read aloud when you rehearse your speech is what you'll be saying in front of your audience. The disadvantage is that, especially if you're a beginner, the temptation will be to stick to the script and keep your eyes on the page the entire time. This is especially true if you're afraid you'll lose your place. Losing your place won't be a problem if you adjust the formatting for your speech. Use a font that's large enough for you to see easily. Double-space the text. Put transitions or keywords in bold text so they'll be easy to find. If your speech is well rehearsed and you're confident about what you're going to say, you can use one of the remaining three formats.
2. **Outline:** Include enough information to keep yourself on track.
3. **Key word:** Include the words that will be sure to trigger those things you need to include in your talk.
4. **Graphics:** Sometimes called a pictograph outline, your images will usually already be in the order you need if you're giving your speech as part of a presentation for which you're using a flip chart or overhead projector.

Nobody should rely on memory for the entire text of a speech. However, it is a good idea to memorize the first few sentences or your speech introduction. Knowing your opening lines helps build confidence, and lets you establish initial eye contact with your audience.

Phone Scripts

Phone scripts can be used for sales presentations. In fact, that's what probably first comes to mind when you think of the term "phone script"— the voice of a pesky telemarketer. Preparing a phone script can also be a way to help you know in advance what you want to say to another person once you reach him or her on the phone. Having that information on hand will also help you know what you should say if you have to leave a voice mail.

Such preparedness leads to confidence. It's also courteous because it helps you keep the conversation brief, an important consideration when you reach a busy person (which pretty much means anyone you call).

CHAPTER 15

Job Search and Employment-Related Writing

The biggest—if not the most obvious—fact about business writing is that, before you can get into doing most of that writing, you first have to get into some sort of business! To do that, chances are you'll need a resume—to start. This chapter covers all the materials you'll need to write for work, from letters of recommendation and follow-up letters to letters of resignation.

Resumes

Job-search time is a stressful time. You can alleviate some of that stress by preparing an effective resume. While the order in which the information given may vary, and additional information (such as a work summary or professional licensing information) is sometimes included, any resume will include essentially the same five key elements:

1. Your name, address, and phone number; e-mail address is optional (Note: Because it's now so easy to do using word-processing software, this information is usually put in "letterhead" format.)
2. Your work experience
3. Your education
4. Your related activities (Note: The key word here is "related." Unless these experiences highlight your work experience, omit this category.)
5. Your references

The way that information is organized and presented will depend on the resume format you choose. That format depends on a number of factors that will become apparent as you progress through this chapter.

Show Your Energy and Resourcefulness

You don't intend to find a job just so you can be lazy once you do. Don't "slack" while you write your resume either. That's the impression you'll give if you oversimplify your previous job responsibilities and accomplishments. Now is the time to toot your own horn. Be descriptive. Use action verbs. Your resume is your advertisement for you.

Use the Appropriate Format

Keeping in mind that your resume is an advertisement, determine which format will best showcase the talents you wish to emphasize for the position for which you're applying: chronological, skills, experience, or CV (curriculum vitae). Choose the format that best lets you prioritize your information so that your prospective employer can see that you possess the skills needed for the job.

Use the Appropriate Style

Most occasions call for a resume that is direct and to the point, including the paper (white twenty-four pound bond or better) and font style (nothing fancy, black ink in Times New Roman, Courier New, or Bodoni). As in anything in life, there can be exceptions—such as if you're applying for a position for which you're expected to showcase your creative personality. In such instances, you can be a bit more daring and go with some colored paper or fancier fonts. Just be sure that whatever style you do use, your information is presented in that all-important "easy- and quick-to-read" format. A potential employer faced with a huge stack of resumes in front of him or her will only spend about twenty seconds scanning each one. Your objective is to make sure yours stands out in that amount of time!

Proofread, Then Proofread Again

You want your resume to be free of spelling and grammatical errors, and formatting inconsistencies.

Fiction has no place in a resume. Stick to the facts. Avoid the temptation to embellish your skills or the scope of your education. Misrepresenting your credentials can be grounds for an employer to terminate your employment.

Stick to One Page

Most human resources directors say they prefer a short, concise resume. (Remember: That first "glance" at your resume is only going to be a twenty-second one!) If you have lots of experience, list the pertinent details and then summarize by highlighting one key accomplishment per position. If you have less experience, you can include as many important details as it takes to fill the page. A one-page resume provides enough information to pique the prospective employer's interest, while letting you hold back additional details with which you can razzle-dazzle during the job interview. However, if you're submitting a CV or resume geared toward garnering an education-related job, two or more pages are acceptable—or even expected.

When your resume goes beyond one page, use the name line from your "letterhead" and the page number at the top of each subsequent page:

Pamela Rice Hahn–Page 2

Resume Action Verbs

In any situation in which they are used, action verbs convey more impact. Impact is especially important in a resume, the purpose of which is to command attention. Here's a list of some good verbs to use:

accommodated	determined	maintained	reported
achieved	devised	managed	selected
acquired	directed	mentored	separated
advertised	distributed	merged	served
advised	edited	minimized	shaped
applied	enforced	modified	sold
approved	enhanced	monitored	sponsored
arranged	established	negotiated	strengthened
assembled	founded	observed	studied
assisted	gathered	operated	summarized
built	generated	oversaw	supplied
collected	guided	photographed	tested
compiled	handled	presented	trained
completed	illustrated	promoted	translated
coordinated	implemented	proofread	treated
delivered	improved	purchased	updated
designed	initiated	recommended	utilized
detected	labeled	reduced	verified

Chronological Resume

In a chronological resume, you start with your current work position and work your way backward. Likewise, you list your most recent education first.

Jodi Cornelius

1234 River Road
Country Corners, PA 16727

Phone: (555) 555-5555
E-mail: jodi@isp.net

OBJECTIVE

Entry-level management position in Social Services or Human Resources

EDUCATION AND LICENSURE

2002:   MS, Human Resource Management, Ohio State University
2000:   MS, Counseling Psychology, Ohio State University
1998:   BS, Social Sciences, Ohio State University
Licensed Professional Counselor
Licensed Chemical Dependency Counselor

EXPERIENCE

2000–present: Shelter Coordinator
Families in Transition—Columbus, OH
Handled all budgetary and daily management aspects of shelter, including coordinating on-staff and volunteer assignments.
Created and implemented at-risk families support groups.
Acted as liaison between the shelter and local funding organizations.
Researched funding grants availability and completed applications.

1998–2000:   Social Service Assistant
Derrick Crisis Center—Columbus, OH
Counseled chemical dependency victims in coping skills, providing information on overcoming self-destructive tendencies.
Provided case management, budget preparation, community outreach, and individual and group counseling.

MEMBERSHIPS

American Psychological Association (APA)
Society of Professional Counselors (SPC)
Society of Human Resource Managers (SHRM)

References and supporting documents available on request.

Also notice in the following example that the name of the state is spelled out instead of abbreviated. Either format is okay, as long you consistently use the same format throughout your resume.

Shelter Coordinator:	Families in Transition
	Columbus, Ohio, 2002–present
	Handled all budgetary and daily management aspects of shelter, including coordinating on-staff and volunteer assignments.
	Created and implemented at-risk families support groups.
	Acted as liaison between the shelter and local funding organizations.
	Researched funding grants availability and completed successful applications.

"Skills" is another optional category often included in a chronological resume. When used, it's most often added at the end of the resume, immediately above the "available upon request" line:

SKILLS

Draft budgets for annual corporate and government sponsorship and complete grant proposals for third-party funding sources. Oversee office, supervise and train personnel. Publish case study and other articles in professional journals, such as *Journal of American Social Service Directors* and *Sheltered Needs*. Possess strong mathematical and analytical skills, plus mastery of all Microsoft Office and other business-related programs.

Skills Resume

A skills resume works well when, as the job applicant, you want to stress your skills and accomplishments over current or previous job titles or education.

Jodi Cornelius

1234 River Road
Country Corners, PA 16727
Phone: (555) 555-5555
E-mail: jodi@isp.net

OBJECTIVE
Position that will allow me to utilize my computer skills, with both hardware and software.

RELEVANT SKILLS
Created a program for a disabled vet for a specific inventory requirement.
Taught adult computer courses at a local vo-tech school.
Built all the computers and programmed them for a local federal prison.

KEY QUALIFICATIONS
- Incorporate communication skills by writing and editing technical documentation and training manuals for local business and national publishers.
- Experience using all major software.
- Install, troubleshoot, and repair individual and networked computer systems.

EMPLOYMENT
1988–present: Technical Support Manager
Computer Store, Bradford, PA
Deal with all problems with computers sold, teach basic and advanced computer usage classes, build and install computers for both personal and business use.

1980–1988: Freelance Game Tester and Programmer

EDUCATION
Bradford Area High School, Bradford, PA, 1980
National Honor Society President, Library Club Secretary, Computer Club President

Experience Resume

Anthony Rice

1234 West East Street, Celina, Ohio 45822, (555) 555-5555, tony@isp.net

OBJECTIVE
A challenging career as a company administrator

PROJECTS AND ACTIVITIES
- Responsible for staff recruiting and interviewing.
- Supervises all corporate human resources needs.
- Coordinates all permanent and temporary staff.
- Authorizes regulatory provisions.
- Arbitrates employee disputes.
- Implements market strategies.
- Facilitates business and government relations.

AREAS OF EXPERTISE
- Management and leadership skills
- Effective written and verbal abilities
- Proven ability to reach a targeted goal
- Strong organizational skills
- Detail-oriented and accurate
- MS Word (75 wpm)

EXPERIENCE
Office Administrator—Lenny and Mercury, Inc. Celina, Ohio, 1997–Present
Coordinate daily human resources activities, including staff recruiting, hiring, and benefits. Facilitate all staffing numbers and evaluations with company president. Conduct all personnel interviews and testing. Administer six departments. Provide for all office needs.

Assistant Office Administrator—Dennis and Ann. Montezuma, Ohio, 1990–1997
Designed and implemented efficient mailroom procedures. Coordinated word-processing team. Supported Office Administrator in executive board meetings: took minutes, distributed reports, and executed client notification procedures.

EDUCATION
Wright State University
B.A., Liberal Arts, Minor: International Relations, 1990

REFERENCES
Available upon request

Additional Considerations When Writing Your Resume

Do not list current or past salaries on your resume. Only include such information when specifically asked for it, such as on a job application. (Even then it's appropriate to list a salary range, rather than a specific hourly, monthly, or annual rate.)

If you have a college or advanced degree, do not list your high school information. In fact, only include high school information when that information includes credentials you believe will help establish your qualifications for a job. Never show middle- or grade-school data.

ALERT!

Your resume is not the place to include personal information such as height, weight, hobbies, number of children or grandchildren, or marital status. Such information can inadvertently lead to discrimination, and is unprofessional.

Online Resumes

The objective of getting your resume in front of a perspective employer is to convert yourself from a perspective employee to an actual employee. Therefore, the easier you can make that employer's chore of perusing your resume, the better your chances of getting hired. That's why it's no surprise that in today's electronic world, online resumes are becoming an efficient way to submit your information to each perspective employer.

An online resume is one that is designed to be:

- Readable from a computer screen
- Convertible into another electronic file type, such as a database file
- Searchable by keywords so it can be located via search engines
- Sent over the Internet
- Stored on an electronic medium, like a computer hard drive or portable disk

It is up to an employer's discretion whether or not an electronic resume is printed out on paper, so an online resume is an eco-friendly option, too. Online resumes are generally done in one of three formats:

1. **Text file:** Either ASCII text pasted into an e-mail (or into the forms on online sites like Monster.com) or sent as a .doc-file attachment
2. **HTML:** Either pasted into an HTML-format e-mail or put on a Web page
3. **PDF:** Either sent as an e-mail attachment or used as a way that preserves special formatting when posting a resume on a Web page

Rather than pasting directly from your word-processing program into an online text entry form, when submitting an ASCII text resume make sure that you first paste and save your resume in a text editor (like Notepad); this ensures that the special formatting codes added by a word processor no longer remain in the document. You'll also want to replace other special formatting such as bullet points with a text equivalent, like an asterisk.

Letters of Recommendation and Reference

Whether you need to write a letter of recommendation or provide a reference, or your purpose is to write to request one or the other, it's essential that you make things as easy as possible for the letter recipient.

- Be as direct and truthful as possible; only give a glowing recommendation if that's truly how you feel.
- State the purpose of the letter up front.
- Give enough details so the letter recipient can make a connection between you and the requested or included information.
- If you can—and are willing to—offer to provide additional information, and then include an invitation for the letter recipient to contact you if that information is needed or wanted.

Now take a look at some samples.

Request for Letter of Recommendation

Dear Ms. Sutton:

I plan to submit an application for one of Mendon University's five leadership scholarships. I'm hoping you'll be willing to write one of the letters of reference I need to submit with my application.

The scholarships are to be awarded to those who best exhibit academic excellence and leadership skills. As both my political science professor and faculty advisor for my work as intern in Senator Hahn's office, you're someone I believe can offer an objective perspective on my abilities in those areas.

The deadline for submission of my scholarship application is May 15. I've included a self-addressed, stamped envelope for you to use to send the requested letter to me; however, if you feel we should discuss this in person first, please contact me so we can set up a time for me to stop by your office

Thank you for your time and consideration.

Sincerely,

Request for Letter of Reference

Dear Mr. Cornelius:

I'm under consideration as a technical writer for Bradford Electronics. Because I've completed several similar (but noncompeting) writing projects for your company, I'm hoping that you'll be willing to provide me with a reference.

I'll give you a call at the end of the week so that we can discuss how you prefer to proceed with my request.

With thanks,

Writing a Letter of Recommendation

Dear Mrs. Murphy,

I'm pleased to have this opportunity to provide you with this letter of recommendation for David Hebert. I've worked with David on several tech writing projects, done for my department at CJ Software, and I hope I get the opportunity to work with him again in the future, too. David does a professional job, always meeting or exceeding my expectations. Just as important, if not more so, David completes his work on or before deadline.

Feel free to contact me at (555) 555-5555 if you need any additional or specific information.

Sincerely,

References

Similar to a recommendation request, a reference is usually a request for somebody to provide information about character as well as work habits. Take a look at the following samples.

Requesting Permission to Use as a Reference

Dear Ms. Cornelius:

I plan to send copies of my resume to a number of local businesses with the intent of soliciting more writing assignments. Should I receive any positive responses from that effort, I'm wondering if I could have your permission to use you as a reference.

[If there is any chance the recipient of this letter may not recall on which projects you've worked together in the past, list some examples here.]

Regardless of your decision, I thank you for your time and consideration.

Sincerely,

Reference Permission Granted Letter

Dear Mr. Hebert:

By all means, feel free to use me as a reference. I am more than happy to help in any way that I can.

Good luck in your search for more work.

Sincerely,

Reference Permission Denial Letter

Dear Mr. Hebert,

It is with regret that I need to inform you that I am unable to grant permission for you to use me as a reference at this time. You may recall that the work you did for this company was done under a confidentiality agreement; company officials advise that any mention of that work would violate that agreement.

Good luck in your search for more work.

Sincerely,

When you must refuse someone's request, do so gently and with tact. While it isn't necessary to state your reason for doing so, giving your reason is the polite thing to do if (and only if) you can do so in a positive manner.

Checking References Letter

This letter is one that could be used to request information from an applicant's former employer or named references. Such letters should include the following:

- Applicant name and position for which he or she is under consideration.
- Information about the applicant's association with the reference.
- Specific areas about which you'd like the reference information.
- A deadline for the receipt of the requested information.
- A thank-you for the reference giver's time and consideration.

Letter to Reference

Dear Mr. Ehlers,

We are in recent receipt of an application from Erin Indiana Klitzke for the position of professor and archaeology researcher at our university. It is our understanding that Ms. Klitzke works for your publication as a contributing editor.

We would appreciate any information you can provide regarding Ms. Klitzke's work habits—specifically her ability to meet deadlines, her attention to detail, and her attitude regarding her work. Please feel free to provide any other details about your association with Ms. Klitzke that you believe to be pertinent.

If possible, we need your reply to this request by the beginning of next month. We will respect your wishes to keep any information you provide confidential, if that's what you prefer.

Thank you for your time in considering this request.

Sincerely,

Job Acceptance and Other Important Employment Letters

When writing any employment-related letter, it is best to be direct and to the point, including any information pertinent to confirm your understanding of the terms offered.

Applicant Refusal Letter

Dear Mr. Jones:

Thank you for submitting your resume. While your qualifications are impressive, the position has already been filled. Unfortunately, at this time we don't have any other positions open that would take advantage of your skills and experience.

We appreciate your interest in Hahn Haberdasheries.

Sincerely,

Job Offer Letter

Dear Mr. Brown:

I am pleased to offer you the position of Managing Editor with Blue Rose Publishing. Your qualifications and experience will be the perfect complement to our mission and goals for the company.

I enjoyed the chance to meet with you during your recent interview and sincerely hope we get the opportunity to work together.

Please contact me within the next week to advise whether or not you're willing to accept this position—at the terms we discussed during that interview.

Sincerely,

Employment Acceptance Letter

Dear Ms. Emans:

To say I was happy to receive your call today would be an understatement.

It is with pleasure that I accept your offer to begin employment as Managing Editor with Blue Rose Publishing at an annual salary of $150,000. It is my understanding that in addition to full employee benefits (health, dental, and vision insurance), I will receive six weeks vacation my first year. (As you are aware, the vacation is an important consideration because it will allow me the time necessary to finish my own book.) In addition to standard office equipment of a personal, networked computer, your company agrees to provide me with an appropriate notebook computer and cell phone to use on business trips.

Other terms of my employment as I understand them include a private office. In addition, I will have my own personal administrative assistant.

My starting date is to be Monday, September 16. Blue Rose Publishing also agrees to reimburse me for mover's fees and other miscellaneous expenses involved in my relocating to Boston.

On a personal note, I look forward to having you as my boss during what I am certain will be a long, productive working relationship.

Best,

Applicant Acceptance Letter

Dear Mr. Brown:

It is with great joy that I acknowledge your acceptance of employment with Blue Rose Publishing. We look forward to having you as an employee.

Please accept my best wishes for a successful career with our company.

Sincerely,

Employment Refusal Letter

Dear Ms. Stone:

It is with deep regret that I must decline your offer to work for Blue Rose Publishing.

Thank you for your time and consideration during my recent interview. Perhaps we'll have the opportunity to work together in the future, but at this time I've decided to accept a position that provides me with the opportunity to work according to a more flexible schedule.

Sincerely,

ALERT!

It's often a good idea (and a way to provide you or your company with legal protection) if you spell out the terms of any contract in a job offer or job acceptance letter. Even routine correspondence can serve to prove certain elements, such as starting dates or the fact that certain information was conveyed at the start of the employment or contract relationship.

Follow-Up Letter

Writing a follow-up letter can often make the difference between accepting or completing a job or making that job the first step in the beginning of a long-term working relationship. While such letters include a "thank-you" for the opportunity, they also provide you with the opportunity to refresh your client's memory about your other skills and abilities. This is also true if the letter is sent to acknowledge a first sale or other first association. A follow-up letter helps ensure a lasting, productive association.

Follow-Up Letter

Dear Mr. Brown:

Thank you for the opportunity to write Blue Rose Publishing's annual report.

At your convenience, I'd like to get together soon to discuss other work I might do for your company. In addition to my writing work, I also work with a team of graphic artists. In addition, I've done book formatting, indexing, and editing work for other publishers and can provide examples and references should you be interested.

I'll call you within the next week to see if we can schedule a meeting.

Thank you again. It was a joy to work with you.

Sincerely,

A follow-up letter can also be sent to inquire whether or not a potential customer or client received information you sent them.

Letters of Resignation

Whenever you find it necessary to move from one job to another, a consequence of such a change is to notify your current employer of that change. A letter of resignation should include the following information:

- The actual notification of your resignation
- The exact ending date of your employment
- An offer to help train a replacement, if appropriate
- A sincere, positive statement about your employment with the company, unless you're leaving on unfriendly terms
- Your reason for leaving (optional)

Letter of Resignation

Dear Mr. Capshaw:

This letter is to notify you that I have accepted a position with Everhart Electronics. I am therefore resigning from my position here with Case Computer Technology. My last day will be November 30. By giving this six weeks notice, please accept my willingness to help with finding and training my replacement.

I have thoroughly enjoyed my position here at Case, and it is with deep regret that I leave; however, Everhart—being a much larger company—is in a position to pay me a far greater salary and provide greater benefits. Were Case in a position to match their offer, you know I'd be willing to continue in my current capacity; however, as we recently discussed, that isn't possible at this time.

Sincerely,

If your resignation is on less than friendly terms, be direct and to the point in your resignation letter:

Less Friendly Letter of Resignation

Dear Mr. Capshaw:

This letter is to notify you that I am resigning from my position with Case Computer Technology, effective in two weeks. My last date will therefore be November 30.

Sincerely,

If you are in a position to provide for longer notice, then do so. Likewise, if you wish to soften the effects of those "less than friendly terms" and offer to train your replacement, do so. Use your judgment. Two weeks is generally accepted as the minimum notice.

CHAPTER 16

Grant Writing

Community interest groups or other organizations are often called upon to submit proposals or grants to access funding. You will also find firms that charge a fee to find appropriate funding programs. A reputable firm may very well help you secure funding. Be careful, however. Investigate the firm's claims, and make sure that it isn't a fly-by-night organization that simply collects consulting fees and then disappears without a trace.

Seeking Grants

Naturally, nothing comes free. The money you're applying for has to come from a source somewhere, and there may sometimes be strings attached. Determine up front what the requirements will be; this is an important step in any grant application.

ALERT!

Some organizations offer to help you find funding—for a fee. Many of these organizations advertise on the Internet. Just do your homework first. Make sure that the firm is reputable; read up on the firm as much as you can, and check any references that are available. Don't throw your money after the first opportunity you find. If it looks too good to be true, it probably is.

There is no rule of thumb to grant applications. Every funding program will be a little different, due to the scope of funding agencies that exist. Even some tobacco companies have special funding bodies that provide grants to artistic or sports groups. All funding programs will have specific requirements that must be met in order to qualify for funding. If there is an eligibility requirement you don't meet, don't give up hope too soon! Ask yourself if you can modify your program to make it fit the requirements.

Just meeting the basic criteria, however, will not guarantee your success. Anytime free money is involved, there will be a number of groups clamoring for it. Use your proposal to demonstrate that your group is capable of managing the program and achieving the results, and can do it as outlined in your proposal.

The Strategic Assessment

Because of the diversity of arrangements, some funding will carry with it certain conditions that must be met, and this brings up some questions that must be addressed. Will you have to include sponsorship information?

- On your letterhead?
- In any newspaper ads you produce?
- In radio or TV advertising?

If these things are considered early in the proposal writing process, you can go a long way toward ensuring that surprises don't pop up later. Wouldn't it be terrible to have your funding pulled because you didn't comply with an advertising provision?

It's your job to know about these things in advance. All of the funding agency's requirements will help guide you through the submission process. Make a list, and ensure that the important points are emphasized in the proposal by including them in your strategic assessment.

The best way to start is to review the criteria for the particular grant or program. Guidelines provided by the funding agency will dictate the eligibility requirements. Some programs may only be open to disabled persons, females, or people of a particular ethnic background. Before you take the time to fill out any paperwork, make sure that you qualify.

In the strategic assessment stage, you will identify all of the areas you must address. Some of these were outlined above, with the qualification requirements. You must also consider your plan of attack in securing this funding, including a determination of the specific funding programs you plan to access. From that point, you can come up with a list of specific actions that must be performed in order to follow the procedure through from start to finish.

Defining Your Goals

Make a wish list. Grab a piece of paper and write down everything you'd like to see accomplished. If you're working with a group, brainstorm all the ideas you can come up with. The sky's the limit on this one—just keep writing down ideas, no matter how ludicrous or bizarre they seem. This is a great way of generating ideas.

Once your mind is free, and not worrying about whether or not an idea will be okay, you tend to come up with some fairly innovative ideas. The parameters are simple: You just think of absolutely anything you can accomplish. As long as you can see a way to accomplish the goal, it can go on the list. If the idea must have some special development occur before the idea can be implemented, then include that too.

The only trick is to let your imagination go absolutely wild. Even if you tend to come up with silly ideas, they can still help. Often components of what seems like one silly idea can be used with components of another "silly" idea to make up one really good idea that can be easily implemented.

Once you have your ideas, cull them. Delete them one by one, but don't delete them from your list too easily. Before you decide not to include something, ask yourself if the idea might work. And, when you delete them from your list, include them on a list of ideas you didn't consider—because you never know when that idea might come in handy later.

Concept Paper

You can use a concept paper to determine the feasibility of a project or program. In it, you investigate the opportunities that could be accessed; you also identify the areas that will have to be addressed to make the project work. In a sense, it's like a preliminary proposal in that both a proposal and a concept paper contain very similar information.

Some funding agencies will require that a concept paper be submitted along with the proposal, but most will not. Nevertheless, doing work on the concept paper or preliminary proposal in the early stages will make the job less tedious later. Treat the concept paper as the initial draft of your proposal, and begin it even before you've begun to investigate funding agencies. Try to get as much of the work done as you can beforehand. Then, you can just use the information in the concept paper to draft your proposal.

A concept paper may have budget information in it, but usually only in a preliminary sense. Ballpark figures are acceptable. Formal budgets and cash flow statements should be tailored to the program and the requirements of the funding agency; they will ultimately be attached to your proposal, but it is not necessary to go into a great deal of detail at this early stage.

Letter of Inquiry

Before you do anything with your proposal, you may be required to submit a letter of inquiry. This is simply a preliminary letter that inquires as to the nature of the funding available, such as its availability and eligibility requirements. There is no need to go into any great detail about the proposal you wish to submit, but feel free to include some basic information about your organization.

Letter of Inquiry

Project title: SkaterSpace

Our organization is currently investigating ways to address the ongoing problem of teen skating activity in unauthorized areas, such as busy parking lots, parks, and malls. We believe we have a solution that will assist in reducing the amount of citations issued to teens caught skating in these unauthorized areas.

We would like to know if your agency is able to offer any financial support, and would appreciate any information regarding funding opportunities that you can provide.

Yours truly,

Fred J. Esquire

Letter of Intent to Apply

Some funding agencies follow certain procedures, which you must also follow. A letter of intent to apply is a simple preliminary letter that notifies the agency that a proposal will be forthcoming. You should include a little bit of basic information about your organization and the nature of the things you will be proposing.

If a letter of intent to apply is required by the funding agency, the agency should also be able to provide you with a list of the items that must be addressed by the letter of intent. If no guidance is forthcoming, it's a good idea to make sure that your letter of intent includes the following:

- Name of organization
- Contact person, title
- Address
- Telephone (and extension, if applicable)
- Fax number
- E-mail address
- Web site address
- Project title
- Brief project description
- Amount requested

Your project description should be brief—no more than three or four lines. The purpose of its inclusion in the letter of intent to apply is only to make the staff at the funding agency aware of the program. Your proposal will outline how you plan to achieve the goals.

This is also the place to include questions about eligibility, the application process, or any other questions or concerns you may have. While the letter of intent often is not even considered by the actual decision-makers, it provides invaluable information to the staff and evaluators, and aids them in their case management.

Letter of Intent to Apply

Coalition for Community Involvement
Fred J. Esquire, Coordinator
123 Fake Street
Needsfunding, OH 59119
Telephone: (419) 555-9877
Fax: (419) 555-9876
FredEsq@communitycoalition.not
http://www.communitycoalition.not
Project title: SkaterSpace

Our proposal will address the current problem of teen skating activity in unauthorized areas, such as busy parking lots, parks, and malls, and will assist in reducing the amount of citations issued to teens caught skating in these unauthorized areas. The Coalition for Community Involvement has developed an approach that will benefit the community, both by providing a place for teens to skateboard while also removing the problem of unauthorized activity in other areas.

We anticipate that our proposal can be implemented for a cost of $5,000. We will submit a full budget and cash flow forecast along with our proposal.

The Coalition for Community Involvement is not yet a body corporate; it is a nonprofit association of interested individuals from the community. If Magma Funding requires that sponsored agencies are incorporated, we will undertake to meet your qualifications; however, we would hope that any required incorporation could be done concurrently with the execution of the proposal, so as not to delay this season's proposed program.

Should you have any questions, please don't hesitate to call. We will forward our full proposal within the next thirty days.

If you are sending your letter on letterhead, the name of your organization and the address should be obvious. If the funding agency asks for the information in a specific format, however, follow that! Do not assume that the address on the letterhead will suffice; some places are sticklers for detail, and the slightest deviance from their standard form will often result in delays.

Completing the Grant Application Packet

Some funding agencies provide their own forms and insist that they be used for all applications. This is quite common with government agencies. Don't let the paperwork daunt you—it might look complicated, but it's actually your opportunity to provide all the information you can.

ALERT!

When completing a grant application form, answer every question and fill in every space, unless it clearly says "office use only." If a particular question is not applicable, write "N/A" under the heading. This shows the evaluator that you read, understood, and answered the question. Leaving it blank might indicate that you missed the question, therefore making your application incomplete.

For the applicable questions and requests for information, fill in the appropriate information. Do not write "see attached proposal"; pull the relevant information out of the proposal and write it in on the application.

The Proposal

Your proposal is the main source of information for the people who evaluate requests on behalf of the funding agency. Always remember that your proposal gets considered faster when you make the evaluator's job easier. If your proposal addresses every point, the evaluator doesn't have to do any additional research.

By doing your homework, you will emphasize to the evaluator that your organization is capable of completing the tasks you propose. If you include all relevant information, you make the evaluator's job that much easier, because the evaluator will not have to hunt down additional information in order to make his or her recommendation. If the evaluator has to do a lot of detective work, this may not reflect favorably on your proposal.

Introduction

The introduction should inform the evaluator about the gist of your proposal, touching only briefly on the points raised there.

The Coalition for Community Involvement has been active in the community since 1975. Our volunteer members have come up with a solution to the problem of teen skateboarding and would like the Acme Funding Agency to sponsor our innovative program.

In order to make your introduction most effective, avoid including too much information. Save that for the balance of your proposal. Some organizations now ignore the "introduction" entirely, instead submitting an "executive summary" at the beginning of the proposal.

Needs Statement

The needs statement identifies the needs of your organization. In it, you simply characterize the problem you are trying to address, showing the problem as it exists. Then, in your analysis, you can offer solutions to the problem.

Needs Analysis

You also need to demonstrate how your needs will be addressed by the actions your group plans to undertake.

In a needs analysis, you should show how your needs will be fulfilled by the activities put forth within your proposal. While you don't need to make a separate "needs analysis" section, somewhere within your proposal you do have to show how your needs will be met by implementing the goals you propose.

The needs analysis provides you with a very effective technique: addressing how your goals will be achieved. This operates on two levels:

1. It shows that you have put the foresight into identifying how your needs will be met, so it gives an indication of the dedication and thought your group has put into the project.
2. It also provides the evaluator with a concrete example of how particular goals will be met. It shows the evaluator that your plan is concrete and is capable of evaluation.

Even after your proposal has been completed, its effects will live on. Ideally, you will achieve all of the goals you suggest. When evaluating a proposal, an evaluator must be able to determine ways to establish whether or not your proposal is succeeding. Including your goals in the proposal gives the evaluator an identifiable means of evaluating the success of a particular provision.

Additional Information

In addition to your basic proposal, you may wish to attach additional information. You can add these as appendices, labeled either by letter or number.

Appendix I   Cash flow forecast
Appendix II   Budget breakdown
Appendix III   Letters of support

You can use "schedule" instead of the word "appendix," if you prefer. If the funding agency has a preferred format, use that.

The Management Plan

The management plan ties in closely with the strategy you adopt, but its elements should be considered separately. While you should keep them in mind, it is not necessary to include these headings in your proposal.

Methods

Methods dictate the means you plan to use to achieve your goals. Within your proposal, you should demonstrate the methods you will implement to ensure that your goals are accomplished.

Activities

In order for an evaluator to judge your proposal, he or she must have an idea of the activities you propose. The activities should be broken out independently, showing exactly what your group plans to do with the funding allocated to it.

Timeline

The proposed timeline is one of the most important aspects of your proposal. You need to be able to tell the funding agency when certain activities will take place. The funding agency will also need an idea of when you'll require a cash influx to make sure your proposal sees its way to fruition.

An important complement to your timeline is your cash flow forecast. You need to show the funding body when certain expenditures will be made, so that they can make arrangements to have the correct amount of cash forwarded to you before you need to spend it. Your cash flow forecast is simply a calendar of when certain budget items must be spent. To make a cash flow forecast, simply take all of the budget items from your budget and break down the monthly (or quarterly) costs.

Remember that doing a good job on the timeline and cash flow forecast instills confidence and convinces the funding agency that you will be able to accomplish the task.

Reports

Once a funding agency gives you money, you can expect that they will want to see how it's being spent. It will be necessary to provide progress reports, and it's a good idea to make sure that you address this in the initial proposal. Define what information is important, and demonstrate how you will show your sponsors that you are making progress. Success must be measurable, so define up front how you plan to measure it.

Once this task is completed, reporting is simply a matter of filling in the blanks. Provide the information promised in the proposal. Your funding agency may have special requirements for reporting, including special forms you may have to fill out. If no forms exist, a report in a letter format is fine, as long as it includes a summary of the measurable goals you have identified.

Persuasive Writing Techniques

In a sense, much of grant writing involves making sure that the Ts have been crossed and the Is have been dotted. Another thing to consider is the language itself that is used to identify the objectives outlined in your proposal. Make sure that your writing is positive and upbeat. Instead of using wishy-washy words like "should," "think," or "might"—use instead strong, definite words like "will," "believe," or "know." Here are some guidelines to follow:

- **Marshall your information.** Each paragraph should have only one main point. You'll find your job much easier if you start with an outline; then, you can focus each paragraph of your proposal to drive home the points you wish to make.

- **Structure your argument.** Coming up with a persuasive argument is not difficult; it just takes an organized approach. To begin, break your argument down into its basic components. This ensures that you won't miss anything along the way.

- **Start with your proposition.** Your proposition identifies the problem you plan to address. For your own purposes, structure it in the form of a question. While you may not use it this way in the proposal, forming this as a question in the planning stages helps you come up with the analysis.

- **Follow up with facts and evidence.** What information is important to address the problem you've identified in your proposition? When appropriate, include the evidence you are using to back up the facts.

- **Provide a thorough analysis.** Don't jump to conclusions. Even though you may understand the rationale for your argument, within the proposal you must demonstrate to the evaluators that your argument reaches a logical conclusion. Demonstrate how the proposition will be addressed. Use the facts to show the evaluator what the positive effects of the implemented proposal will be.

- **State your conclusion.** At the end of your analysis, your conclusion should demonstrate how the proposition is addressed and how its needs are met. Ultimately, this is the answer to the question you formed when coming up with your proposition. The facts and analysis simply show your work, illustrating how you reached your conclusion, as in this example:

Last summer, our county issued 175 citations to teenagers riding skateboards in unauthorized areas. The secondary parking area at the community college receives no traffic in summer; in addition, it is paved and includes a number of access ramps that would be of interest to these teenagers. Allowing this area to be used by summer skateboarders would provide teens with an appropriate place to participate in their sport, while saving the general public from the inconvenience of having to beware of teenagers whizzing by on skateboards. This action may also reduce the number of infractions that occur during the season. Therefore, allowing the community college's secondary parking area to be used as a skateboarding area would benefit the community at large.

While the proposition doesn't appear overtly stated in the passage, it can be inferred. Stated as a question, the proposition would read: "How will allowing summer skateboarders to use the community college secondary parking area benefit the community?"

Structuring your argument following these guidelines aids the evaluator in making a decision. Keep in mind that because you've helped him or her along the way by showing how the needs will be addressed, you're actually making the evaluator's job easier, which increases your chance of success.

Final Review

Your proposal will appear more persuasive if you check it closely for spelling, grammatical, or factual errors. Misspelled words, especially if the proposal is rife with them, can make an evaluator believe that you don't have attention to detail. To enhance the professionalism of your proposal, ensure that all words are spelled correctly and that proper grammar is used. Have someone else give it a final read before you submit it.

CHAPTER 17

Technical Writing

The ability to write clear and concise documents can be an asset for any professional. When it comes to writing technical or scientific documents, it's essential. Whether your intent is to translate technical terms and instructions into language that anyone can understand or to explain a scientific process to another scientist, there's no room for ambiguity in technical writing.

Parts of a Technical Document

The standard model of technical writing is a style and structure that has been widely used for about fifty years. This documenting method, which is usually taught in schools, is how most professional scientists, engineers, and other technical writers choose to write. The main features of a document that follows the standard model include the following:

- **Abstract or summary:** A brief overview of the document, including its conclusions and recommendations if there are any. An average length for an abstract is about 300 words; however, some scientific journals actually specify the required number of words. The abstract of a scientific paper or document should be capable of standing alone to be published separately.

- **Acknowledgments:** A brief note of thanks to those people who directly helped in the work the document describes. In a novel or less formal technical documents, authors often thank their friends and family; many scientists and engineers consider it slightly pretentious to do this. Instead, research assistants and others who assisted with the preparation of the paper normally appear in this section. Also, if the document is destined for publication and describes work supported by a grant, the grant-awarding body may insist that it be acknowledged.

- **Introduction:** The introduction explains what the document is about, and its role in relation to other work in the field. In most technical documents, the introduction will say something about the context of the document—how the work it describes forms part of the overall body of work in that subject area. When describing an investigation, the introduction will state explicitly what the investigators set out to find.

- **Objectives:** This optional section states what the work being documented was expected to accomplish, why it was undertaken, and at whose instigation.

- **Theory:** A description of any background theory needed to understand the document. For example, such a section might be used to describe a mathematical process that the lay reader may not know.

- **Method or methodology or procedures:** A description of the way the work was carried out, what equipment was used, and any problems that had to be overcome. For example, if the document describes a survey, this section would explain how the subjects were selected and checked for bias, and how the results were analyzed.

- **Results:** A brief explanation, sometimes accompanied by tables and graphs, that includes enough data to show that you have done what you said you would do, and that your conclusions are valid.

- **Discussion or interpretation:** An interpretation of the results, sometimes including comparisons with other published findings and mention of any potential shortcomings in the work. The discussion section of a traditional document is the place where the author is allowed to be less objective than usual. It is acceptable to mention opinions, and to speculate about the significance of the work. In particular, if your findings are unusual or very different from other people's conclusions, you should explain why you think this might be.

- **Conclusion:** The overall findings of the study. Conclusion does not just mean "summary." In this case, your conclusions are statements that can be concluded from the rest of the work.

- **Recommendations:** The author's advice to the reader. (If, for example, the document is about making some sort of business decision, the recommendation is usually what the author perceives as the appropriate course of action. The recommendations section can also include suggestions for further work.)

- **References and/or bibliography:** The purpose of giving references is to allow the reader to follow up on your work. The bibliography is the set of publications referred to in a general sense during the writing of the document or in carrying out the work it describes. These publications will not usually be cited explicitly in the text. References, on the other hand, are given in support of some specific assertion, and are always mentioned explicitly in the text. Normally, this citation would be given after the statement the author wants to support.

- **Appendices:** Additional supporting material, such as mathematical proofs, diagrams or style examples, troubleshooting information, listings of abbreviations and technical terms, and so forth.

Doc Plan

A doc (documentation) plan, often called a project plan, is a written explanation detailing all components of a technical writing process. To understand how best to approach preparing this plan, it's necessary to understand some specifics about any technical writing project.

The main purpose of a technical document is to convey information. The document should place as few hindrances as possible between the mind of the writer and the mind of the reader. A secondary function is to stimulate and entertain. There are people who can inform and entertain at the same time. Like most people, however, you will have to make a choice between the two. And this means you need to inform rather than to entertain. Of course, if you were writing a novel the priorities would be reversed; but in document writing it is the information that is paramount.

A good document needs careful planning. As part of the planning stage you should try to answer the following two questions:

1. What is the document about?
2. What are you trying to say?

You need to arrange things so that the key facts and conclusions are accessible. Not everyone will read the entire document, so make sure that your message gets across even if a person only skims the document.

So, just who is it you are writing for? It is impossible to write a technical document that will be equally easy for everybody to read: the level of explanation you need for an expert audience is totally different from that needed for readers who are unfamiliar with the subject. It is essential that you identify the potential readers before you start working. If you are writing for computer scientists you don't need to explain, for example, what a modem is, nor the World Wide Web, but you may need to explain what "baseband" is, and what "ppi" stands for. If you are writing for people who have no knowledge whatsoever about your topic, you'll have to go into greater detail; you may need to define terms within the text, which also provide the context, or provide an all-inclusive glossary at the end of your text. Regardless of your audience, keep the level of knowledge in mind and try not to wander too far from that level.

FACT

Tech writing references are not, as many people seem to think, a written list of related publications used to convince your audience that you have read a lot. They are additional sources of relevant information.

Once you know the exact nature of the job ahead and have an understanding of when your written documentation is to be completed, you're ready to begin preparing your doc plan. One way to do this is to begin with a "Preliminary Project Plan" to help organize information as it's gathered and considered. In order to complete such a project, you'll need to be able to determine the following:

- **Project description:** Think of this as the "mission statement" for the project, a one- or two-sentence description of what your document should accomplish.
- **Title:** At this point, you can use a working title; as long as you have something that serves to designate the particular project, it should suffice.
- **Project incidentals:** Notes about the purpose, scope, and limitations of the document.
- **Audience:** This is probably the most important aspect at this point. To know how to proceed, you need to know who will be reading what you write. You'll need to know your audience's education level and technological expertise—as it applies to the project.
- **The why and the what:** The reasons why the documentation will be used by the intended audience, and for what purpose.
- **Proposed table of contents:** Often referred to as a "fluid document," this draft table of contents is the map that details the direction your document should take. It will be modified as you go along, but it helps to plot out your objective and to ensure that you're marshalling your information in the best way possible.
- **Deliverables:** Unless you're writing a technical document on assignment from a publisher, you'll often handle other details beyond just writing. Deliverables can include printed copies (how many?) and details like whether disk copies are to be supplied, disk and file

formats (including software versions), and where and when they are to be delivered.

- **People and other resources:** Who and what resources will be available to help you? How many work-hours will be required? At what cost?
- **Change control:** This would cover procedures in place for passing information about program changes to the documenter during the development of a software manual, for example.
- **Milestones:** A schedule showing appropriate milestones, such as when the documentation plan was approved; the preparation, review, and approval of each draft; the index completion; the usability testing; the camera-ready artwork preparation; and the printing, binding, and distribution.
- **Source material:** What written information is already available?
- **Standards and specifications:** Is the documentation to be written to a particular standard or specification?
- **Technical edit:** Who will check the technical accuracy of the manual? Whose responsibility is it to hire (and pay) the technical editor(s)?
- **Editorial control:** Who has editorial control?
- **Budget:** An estimate of what it will cost—in time and out-of-pocket expense—to complete the project.
- **Copyright:** Who will own the copyright and any other proprietary rights? Usually, the author of a commissioned document is the first owner unless a specific work-for-hire or other agreement states otherwise. (See Chapter 10 for more information.)
- **Translation responsibility:** Provisions for the translation into other languages, if applicable.

Getting answers to these questions allows you to develop a suitable project plan. One scenario is that once you have your preliminary project plan, you'd then discuss it with the project manager. After any amendments that might arise from those discussions have been added, it should be signed off on or otherwise formally agreed to by both parties.

Project Outline

Once you know the specifics for a technical writing project, you can develop a schedule showing the milestones necessary for the project's completion. This outline will include items such as the following:

- Blueprint
- Research
- First draft
- Language edit (also known as the copyedit)
- Technical edit
- Beta test
- Final review date
- Master copy ready
- Printed copies ready for delivery

Identify Your Audience

The audience of a technical document, or any piece of writing for that matter, is the intended or potential reader(s). For most technical writers, this is the most important consideration in planning, writing, and reviewing a document. As discussed in Chapter 1, you "adapt" your writing to meet the needs, interests, and background of the readers.

Types of Audiences

One of the first things to do when you analyze your audience is to identify its type(s). The common audience categories are as follows:

- **Experts:** These are the people who know the theory or product inside and out. They designed it, tested it, and know everything about it. They usually have advanced degrees and operate in academic settings or in research and development.
- **Technicians:** These are the people who build, operate, maintain, and repair the stuff that the experts design and theorize about.

Theirs is a highly technical knowledge as well, but of a more practical nature.

- **Executives:** These are the people who make business, economic, administrative, legal, governmental, and political decisions on the things that the experts and technicians work with. If it's a new product, they decide whether to produce and market it. If it's a new power technology, they decide whether or not it should be implemented. Executives are likely to have as little technical knowledge about the subject as nonspecialists.

- **Nonspecialists (lay audience):** These readers have the least technical knowledge of all. Their interest may be as practical as those of the technicians, but in a different way. They may want to use the new product to accomplish their tasks, for example, or they may want to understand the new power technology enough to know whether to vote for or against it in the upcoming bond election.

Audience Analysis

It's important to determine to which of the four categories just discussed the potential readers of your document belong, but that's not the end of it. Audiences, regardless of category, must also be analyzed in terms of characteristics:

- Background, knowledge, experience, and training
- Needs and interests
- Other demographic characteristics, such as age groups, type of residence, area of residence, gender, political preferences, and so on

Audience analysis can get complicated by at least two other factors:

1. **More than one audience:** You may find that your document is for more than one audience. For example, it may be seen by technical people (experts and technicians) and administrative people (executives). How you handle this will be dictated by your project, but one solution is to write each section strictly for the audience that would be interested in

it, then use headings and section introductions to alert the reader to the intended audience for those areas.

2. **Wide variability in an audience:** When you have such an audience, you have the choice of writing for the expertise level of the majority of readers (at the sacrifice of the remaining minority that needs more help) or, of using the safer method of putting supplemental information in appendixes or inserting cross-reference suggestions to books or materials for beginners.

Writing to your audience may seem to have a lot to do with in-born talent, intuition, and even mystery, but there are some devices you can use to have a better chance of connecting with your readers. To make technical information more understandable for nonspecialist audiences, you need to make sure your writing includes easily understood steps and definitions of key terms. Also, stick to the facts. Include basic instructions, examples, and graphics, but omit theoretical discussions about the topic.

Defining the Project and Preparing a Proposed Table of Contents

The integral part of the front matter of any published book—the table of contents—is also the technical writer's best tool for organizing the document itself. Your proposed table of contents not only shows your editor or project manager that you have grasped the material well enough to know how to organize it into effective sections, but it also gives your editor or project manager a chance to see whether or not you've included every important aspect of the project.

Most often an initial table of contents is considered to be a fluid document. That's because new information that arises during the research and writing phases may result in sections being added to cover the new material. Your editor or project manager may decide on a different focus for the project after viewing your initial drafts. You may later realize that additional subheads are needed to explain something within the context of the document itself rather than relegating that information to an appendix.

Most editors or project managers can provide examples of previous tables of contents used for other projects. This documentation can show you the preferred format for inserting supplemental notes or comments.

A proposed table of contents should contain your outline of the numbered chapters, parts, or sections and the heads and subheads within those parts. Depending on the style guidelines provided for submitting your table of contents, you'll probably also need to include an estimated total page or word count.

In short, your proposed table of contents is the tangible expression for your vision on how the document should be organized and what it will say.

Publisher Style Guides

Many publishers that produce technical manuals require that their writers follow their particular style guides. Style guides address linguistic style as well as formatting issues.

Style guides help maintain consistency. A dissimilar spelling and punctuation convention makes for disjointed writing. Guidelines help keep the stylistic choices consistent. Consistency improves writer efficiency and therefore lowers the cost to produce technical information. Such consistency also makes it easier to maintain the project over time as it is revised by different writers.

Consistency can be considered even more important for online information than paper documents since the reader has less physical structure to maintain his or her orientation in the project. Because online help systems rely on both screen design and language to communicate ideas, both are usually covered in an online style guide.

Writing to a Publisher Template

Many times a publisher will have its own specific way of putting together a document. This is sometimes done with macros that the writer will use in the word processor of choice. It is simply a matter of downloading the macros, then using them when writing the assignment. Such templates save the publisher from having the additional step of "formatting" the document for publication. The template macros are usually set to insert the necessary differences in font size and styles used for such things as chapter titles, heads, subheads, and body text.

White Papers

A white paper is a document that states a position, or proposes or explains a draft specification or standard. It can be very technical or hardly technical at all, depending on its intended audience. For example, a company might have a white paper on its Web site that examines obstacles associated with a particular new technology and explains why its approach to this problem is better than other solutions. (Many Web sites for specific software products include a white paper that gives product specifications and usage information.)

A white paper can also be an article that states an organization's philosophy or position about a political or social subject. Other times, a white paper might be used to explain the conclusions resulting from a design or research collaboration or development effort.

An important area where many technical writers are employed is in producing a white paper as supplemental sales and marketing material. For example, a white paper can be released after a new product or service is already on the market. In that case, a problem is presented and a solution (the product or service) given. Target audiences range from investors and vendors to potential customers. Often, because what you are "selling" in such a white paper has already been released, you can usually safely assume that your reader will have some background information. Such white papers are distributed through many channels, including the Web, trade shows and conferences, and sales representatives.

The first step in creating an effective white paper is the treatment. Give a brief description of the problem and solution. This can be done by giving a history of the problem and the proposed solution, a summary of the technology involved and why it is better than others, how it can be best used, and the action you want from the reader.

A white paper is usually organized in three sections:

1. A summary of the history of the problem.
2. Details about the solution, how it can be best employed, and why it is better than those of competitors.
3. A summary of what is expected from the reader. (This is the most important part of your paper because it is the "sales pitch" that you have been leading up to. Make it clear and persuasive.)

Next, develop an outline by expanding on each of the topics in your problem-solution treatment with subsections and bullets that summarize the main points in each subsection. Determine approximately how many paragraphs and pages each subsection will need so you can get an idea of the length. Once these steps are completed and approved, you're ready to start writing.

CHAPTER 18

Humor, Reviews, and Other Specialized Writing

Anecdotes and other forms of humor, reviews, and personal essays and memoirs are ways you can personalize your writing. An understanding of these forms and how to write them can add further dimension to your skills. This chapter not only provides descriptions to help you learn about the writing choices available, but also gives suggestions about how to adapt your personalized stories to meet your writing needs.

Humor

Everybody likes to laugh. It's therapeutic. It's nonfattening. It's fun! Even more satisfying than laughing yourself is the ability to make others do so. If you're ready to make an artistic statement as well, you may be ready to write your own material.

This chapter will describe some of the humor theories that will help you when you're ready to slant your writing so that the world laughs with you—and how and where to use what you've learned.

Understanding What Makes People Laugh

Humor can be an effective (and sometimes less risky) way to show:

- Ambivalence
- Incongruity
- Surprise
- Superiority

This is done using wordplay that evokes emotion, uses exaggeration, conveys disguised hostility, creates a surprise twist, or employs humor aimed at popular targets such as authority, family, finances, sex, and technology. Other comedic formulas that make people laugh include double entendres (words with double meanings, the second of which usually has a sexual connotation); incongruity (using logical ideas that result in an unconventional conclusion); insult humor ("Your momma is so fat she __ __."); one-liners ("Take my wife, please!"); and paired phrases (complete-the-phrase jokes like: "Today it was so cold that _____.").

Comedy Genres

As already established, humor comes in all shapes and sizes, and there's something for everyone. Some of the most popular, and adaptable—as explained after the definitions and examples—are as follows.

Anecdotes

Anecdotes are short narratives about a humorous incident.

A few weeks before her fifth birthday, my niece Jemma ran through the room, picked up her mom's purse on the way, and grabbed the cordless phone. Her mother asked her, "What in the world do you think you're doing?"
Jemma answered: "I want to get you this mop I just saw on TV and the guy told me I only have five minutes to order it!"
Copyright © 1999–2007 Pamela Rice Hahn
Used by Permission

Cartoons

Cartoons are illustrated, single-thought jokes. They are among the most difficult types of humor to write, as it's quite a challenge to get your comedic point across in a single illustration accompanied by a sentence or two. Randy Glasbergen (*www.glasbergen.com*), whose *The Better Half* comic strip appears in many newspapers, is also well known for his cartoons, many of which run in corporate newsletters.

Comic Strips

Comic strips are similar to cartoons, but include more than one "scene." The standard format consists of three panels, but this is by no means a hard and fast rule. Comic strips give the creator the luxury of building the humor slowly, setting the reader up for the punch line in the final panel. They also allow for a greater variety of characters in a single work; because there's more space, there's more room to put them! Examples of the more well-known strips like Charles Schultz's *Peanuts* and Scott Adam's *Dilbert* can be seen at *www.comics.com*. Other writer-artists publish their works on their own sites, like *Squinkers* at *www.squinkers.com*, *Writing Woes* at *www.blueroses.com/writing/*, and *Chronic Illness Realities* at *www.chronic-illness.org/comic/*.

Humor Columns

Dave Barry is probably one of the best known, and widest read, humor columnists working today. Whether he's writing about current events or one of his personal experiences, he blends phrases his readers now come to expect like "I'm not making this up" and "a good name for a rock band" with his exaggerated style of reporting to make people laugh. Many writers take advantage of magazines and Web sites that publish similar columns to establish publicity for their other works. Southern humor book author Ed Williams (*www.edwilliams.com*) self-syndicates his column to a number of Georgia newspapers. The Blue Rose Bouquet (*www.blueroses.com*) reprints the works of newspaper columnists like Randy Shore, who writes about his children, and others, like Ron Collins, who writes about the challenges of establishing a writing career.

Parody

A parody is a work of humor that imitates the style of a particular source. Writers for *The Onion* (*www.theonion.com*) and *Scrappleface* (*www.scrappleface.com*) combine satire and newspaper article-style parody. Parodies on these Web sites range from such things as a human relations story about tenants in a building too polite to ask their on-site elderly maintenance man to fix anything, to ones that have fooled members of the foreign press, like *The Onion* "article" quoted as fact in a Beijing newspaper about Washington bureaucrats who are threatening to move the Capitol building to another city if they don't get a retractable dome.

Puns

These dual meaning wordplay jokes aren't the source of laugh-out-loud humor. These subtle—and sometimes not-so-subtle—plays on words usually cause groans. (They can also be the source of disagreements: Some people absolutely hate them; others love them.) A pun takes a common word or phrase and skewers it enough to change its meaning such as a review for a bad German restaurant that tells the reader he or she should only go there for the "wurst of times" or the headline that proclaims "Udder Relief for the Dairy Industry."

Puns can be one-liners:

Kiwifruit tart is a berry good dessert.

The answers to riddles:

Do you know what they call ushers at the Vatican?
Papal People Seaters

. . . or they can provide the punch line in a story:

From: The Blue Rose Bouquet
www.blueroses.com
Billions of dollars in research grants had already been spent for the studies conducted by the best and brightest physics, psychiatric, medical, and other scientific researchers across the country when a psychology professor at Harvard arrived at the conclusion that perhaps everyone was putting too much energy into the project. He argued that minds were too easily distracted by everyday life and other body functions. Therefore—at the conclusion of another grant-funded study, of course—it was determined that because extra bodies were unnecessary for the project, tenured professors everywhere severed the heads of all doctoral candidates, hooked them to life support systems, and assigned them the sole purpose of working on a solution to the problem. Still no one could arrive at the desired results. Finally, one scientist invited everyone to gather up the heads and bring them to a conference at Cambridge, because "I'm sure if we all put our heads together, we can come up with a solution."
Copyright © 1999–2007 Pamela Rice Hahn
Used by Permission

Satire

Satire is humor that uses sarcasm, irony, derision, and a sharpened wit to lampoon human experience. The more seriously a segment of society seems to take itself, the bigger a target it becomes for satirical skewering. Certain subjects lend themselves particularly well to satire: educational systems, politics, pop culture, and religion. Many "articles" on *The Onion* (*www.theonion.com*) and *Scrappleface* (*www.scrappleface.com*) also fall within this category.

A nationally recognized teachers union announced today that they'd oppose any legislation asking for teacher certification testing, stating that tests are not a reliable and accurate way to gauge proficiency. Students across the nation welcomed this news, adapting that philosophy as they put in a bid to establish their own union.

Targeted Humor

Niche market humor features jokes specifically geared to make fun of or parody a specific topic, such as religion, pets, and sports. For example, knowing that one popular target is overweight women, one of the newer niche humor markets turns the tables on the usual, run-of-the-mill fat jokes. Instead, the authors make fun of themselves, celebrating their abundance, so to speak. Rather than be the brunt of fat jokes, Dee Adams makes the brunt of her humor those who, shall we say, celebrate size in an unconventional way. Adams also takes that concept a step further and derives humor from another struggle for many older women, as illustrated by the title pun for her domain: *www.minniepauz.com.*

How and Where to Use Humor

Even in cases where the information is the main thrust, humor can be used to get the message across. Chris Pirillo's Lockergnome.com is a great example—it's a tech newsletter and Web site that dispenses technical, computer information with a humorous bent. Whether he's telling you about a step-by-step instruction that's "so simple, even Patrick Duffy and Suzanne Somers could use it" or ending the latest newsletter information with his usual "Yours Digitally" close, you know that the time spent reading what Pirillo told you helped you learn something new and offered a good time in the process.

Only limit your message when your purpose is to direct its meaning. For example, the anecdote example earlier in this chapter (about the young girl rushing to order the mop for her mother within the five-minute deadline imposed by the announcer) could be told as part of the introduction to an advertising promotion planning meeting. After sharing the anecdote, it could be followed by a transition like "that story illustrates both the good news and the bad news of one television advertising campaign," followed by: "An effective infomercial advertisement is one that reaches the target audience and convinces those within that audience to act, and to act now. The good news is that somebody who heard the message was motivated to act. The bad news is that five-year-olds are not the target audience."

The pun story about "putting our heads together" could be used as part of the introduction to a team-building exercise.

As long as you keep your audience in mind and target your humor so that it's in good taste and appropriate for the occasion, humor can be an effective way to get (and keep) that audience's attention.

ALERT!

Appropriate humor doesn't only mean that which is suitable for a business setting. Racial slurs or derogatory language aren't appreciated by any audience.

The Essentials of a Good Review

You already know that who, what, where, and when are important aspects of informative writing; however, when it comes to writing a review, the other two elements—why and how—are especially important. A review is your assessment about a product or service. You establish the first four elements when you explain who is reviewing the product (sometimes an unspoken understanding), what is being reviewed, and where and when the product was used. But describing those elements is only effective if you also give details about why and how you reached your conclusions.

Share your personal experiences. Why do you recommend a product? How has it made your life better?

Before you write your own reviews, first become a reviewer of other reviews. Study them to determine which ones you found most informative. Figure out what those authors did (or didn't do) to make the reviews effective.

Your review should be your opinion, supported by those facts that caused you to form that opinion. A statement like "I recommend you buy this book" is only effective if the reader knows why you feel that way.

Unless you're establishing your own review medium—like the game review site at *www.timewastersguide.com*—you'll need to follow the dictates of the publisher for whom you're writing the review. Some publications prefer reviews written in the first person ("I like this product because . . ."). Others prefer second person ("You will find this product helpful because . . .").

Personal Essays

Personal essays are the written equivalent of "reality TV." These opinion pieces include the author's personal perspective about the subject of the essay. Each essay is a personal narrative about how the author feels about a subject, and often his or her reactions and opinions about those feelings, too. Anything about which the author cares deeply is an appropriate subject for the personal essay. It's an essay about what you feel, written so that the reader recognizes what you believe and why you feel that way.

Personal essays range from political commentary (opinion pieces) to humor columns like those written by Dave Barry to anecdotal musings. Personal narratives are often as effective whether they're read by the reader or read aloud by the author in the form of a speech or radio commentary.

Begin with a Hook

The hook is the device you use to get your reader's attention, as in the following examples.

A Description of a Person or Setting

My computer monitor has a Winnie the Pooh Band-Aid on it.

The opening line to "Life's Bumps and Band-Aids"

From *Rhymes and Reasons* (Unpublished book of personal essays by Pamela Rice Hahn)

Copyright © 1999–2008 Pamela Rice Hahn

Used by Permission

A Description That Involves the Senses

In a nursing home, it's possible to get overwhelmed by the ever-present odors. Sweet citrus disinfectant does little to mask them. Chlorine scent clings to bleached linens. Perfumes and aftershaves worn by residents, visitors, and employees leave intermittent wafts of fragrance in their wake. And, always, worst of all, is the stench of functioning and malfunctioning body processes. Fluids and wastes. Their trail rises above all else. It permeates the air. It penetrates the very essence of that environment, becoming a fixture. Tangible.

The opening lines to "We Never Lose Hope"

From *Rhymes and Reasons* (Unpublished book of personal essays by Pamela Rice Hahn)

Copyright © 1999–2008 Pamela Rice Hahn

Used by Permission

A Question or Questions

Men. And what about those eyelash-batting, collagen-injected, vacuumed-thighed, plunging necklined, surgically augmented jiggle machines who make them feel like boys? Don't they just make your butt dimple with envy?

The opening lines to "The Seduction Samba"

From *Rhymes and Reasons* (Unpublished book of personal essays by Pamela Rice Hahn)

Copyright © 1999–2008 Pamela Rice Hahn

Used by Permission

A Quotation

A friend's comment probably sums it up best: After the initial flames die down on the charcoal of the marriage, the real cooking is done on the glowing embers.

The opening lines to "The Comfortable Familiarity of Marriage"

From *Rhymes and Reasons* (Unpublished book of personal essays by Pamela Rice Hahn)

Copyright © 1999–2008 Pamela Rice Hahn

Used by Permission

A Statement Intended to Introduce Controversy

The way I figure it, there are men out there overlooking the opportunity to find the perfect mistress.

The opening lines to "PWC*: An Untapped Market"

From *Rhymes and Reasons* (Unpublished book of personal essays by Pamela Rice Hahn)

Copyright © 1999–2008 Pamela Rice Hahn

Used by Permission

A Statement That You Will Either Support or Dispute

Today, it seems, everybody wants to be a victim.

From the Introduction to *Rhymes and Reasons* (Unpublished book of personal essays by Pamela Rice Hahn)

Copyright © 1999–2008 Pamela Rice Hahn

Used by Permission

Ensure Accuracy

If your commentary is supported by what you're presenting as facts, make sure those facts are accurate. One "quote" gaffe that made the news occurred in Barbra Streisand's spoken commentary at a fundraising concert; she cited quotes she attributed to Shakespeare, only to receive negative publicity later because the quotes she cited were actually fictitious ones from a perpetrated Internet fraud. If you make such an error, your mistake may not be as highly publicized, but you still want to avoid any negative publicity that affects your credibility and thereby destroys your intended message.

Establish Connections

Even if you're writing about global issues (e.g., terrorism, women's rights), introducing a personal example—or at least one "closer to home"—helps the reader relate better to the issue. If the opposite is true and you're writing, say, your opinions about the increase in local spousal abuse statistics, citing a wider range of statistics helps establish a broader perspective.

Include Fictional Elements

Dialogue, characterization, and setting details are ways to introduce constructive changes into your essay. They increase the readability of your essay by giving you a way to alter the pace, and providing you with devices to use to avoid beginning every sentence with "I."

Involve the Reader

An essay in which you only state your opinions about something in order to get it off your chest is just a rant. Instead, find ways to introduce elements that will connect with your reader.

FACT

Academic essays (like those discussed in Chapter 12) include more facts than opinion. Personal essays, on the other hand, generally include more opinions than facts.

Memoir

Similar to a personal essay, a memoir is an author's autobiographical description of events—usually associated with the longer, extended book-length format. (One of the more famous recent such books is Frank McCourt's *Angela's Ashes*.) A memoir is something written as a way to revisit parts of the past and record those events as a means of self-discovery, or to preserve those memories for future generations.

Memoirs aren't necessarily always written with publication in mind. Nor are they always lengthy pieces.

A memoir, however, does differ from an autobiography, which is a factual telling of an entire life. A memoir doesn't necessarily focus on a chronological description of an entire life, but rather on the author's impressions of his or her life, often limiting that description to a single event. A memoir allows for some leeway, if not creative license, on the author's part, and therefore isn't something that's heavily researched. A memoir is more about the author's recollections and perceptions about details and relationships than it is about specifically recorded events.

A memoir can be something as simple as a written impression about a memory evoked by a photo in a scrapbook (and inserted into the book to be preserved along with the photograph), ranging from a one-sentence description that begins with "I remember that on the day this photograph was taken . . ." to something as long as the author feels is necessary to record the event.

CHAPTER 19

Electronic Age Writing

Writing in the electronic age has undergone some changes as a result of new technology. This chapter will show you the ins and outs of writing with such technology. From faxes to e-mails to instant messages, it is becoming increasingly easy to send off quick messages to one another.

19

Fax Facts

Faxing continues to be an important part of communication today. It remains a cheap, quick, convenient, and easy way to correspond, without having to worry about delays associated with the various postal services around the globe.

Business

Despite the recent increase in popularity in e-mail, faxes are still an integral part of the business world. Many government agencies and corporate interests rely on faxes for the quick dissemination of information, such as proof of signed contracts.

For the most part, your fax transmission should follow the suggestions in other chapters for the writing of business correspondence. It is important to include a cover page, described later in this section.

Personal Correspondence

The business world isn't the only place faxes are used. Many people use faxes to send letters quickly to family and friends, especially when a family member doesn't having keyboarding skills and prefers to write out such correspondence in longhand. Faxes send the message quickly and easily, while allowing family members and close friends to keep in touch, especially if those loved ones are halfway around the world.

Because a fax merely reproduces the original page at another destination, you can send anything you like, as long as the letter or item is legible and will be able to be read once it is printed out on the receiving fax machine.

The Fax Cover Page

The cover page ensures that your fax is delivered to the person for whom it is intended, and gives your fax transmission a little bit of privacy—people don't have to read through the entire document to see where it's supposed to be going.

The fax cover page should clearly indicate the following:

- **The intended recipient.** It's a good idea to list the person's name, title, and department in case the fax gets misdirected.
- **The intended recipient's fax number.** If your fax does not go through, and it must be sent again, this will save you (or your personal assistant) from having to find the fax number to re-send the message.
- **The sender.** You should include your name, your title, your department, and both your fax and voice numbers so that the recipient can respond.
- **Instructions on what to do if the fax is received in error.** Sometimes, fax numbers get mixed up, and documents go to the wrong machine (or even the wrong company). Most companies will have a standard clause on their fax cover sheets instructing people to notify the sender and destroy the fax or return it to the sender at the sender's expense. If no such instructions exist, it's acceptable to attempt to call the company collect to advise of the fax error.

(Refer to Appendix B for an example of a Fax Cover Page.)

E-mail

E-mail is a fast, convenient, and easy method of communication, but it, like all other forms of writing, has its own conventions.

Because of the fast nature of e-mail, people often don't consider the ramifications of what they're sending. Messages can be interpreted differently, and some unintentional meanings can arise. Simple messages can be seen as being terse or impertinent, which probably isn't your intention. Therefore, you have to be careful that your message won't be taken in the wrong way once it's received.

It's considered bad form to quote the entire original e-mail in your response with a one or two word reply, such as "I agree" or "okay." Take a second and summarize the point you're agreeing with. This is common courtesy, and it makes the other person feel as if you're giving him or her due attention, rather than just banging off a quick reply.

Business E-mail

Business e-mails should be concise and to the point. People in the business world receive many e-mails per day, and the amount of time it takes to wade through these e-mails can put a severe dent in that person's work day, taking time away from other tasks that must be accomplished.

ALERT!

The language you use in your business e-mails should not be overly colloquial—remember that you're corresponding with business associates who expect certain levels of decorum. The use of "emoticons"—typographic characters used to represent facial expressions like smiley faces—should be avoided in business correspondence.

Personal Correspondence E-mail

With personal e-mails, you have a great deal more flexibility in your approach. You don't have to be as careful with getting your point across as you might with business correspondence, but an upset friend can be just as bad as an upset business colleague, so try to be equally careful with the language you use.

One of the ways you can personalize your correspondence is to add *emoticons*, which is Internet-speak for small typographical symbols that represent facial expressions.

Common Emoticons	
Smiley face	:)
Smiley face with glasses and a nose	8~)
Sad face	: (
Perplexed look	: /

E-mail Subject Line

Many people receive upwards of a hundred e-mails per day, and the subject line is often used as a form of triage to help the recipient decide which e-mails need an immediate response, and which can be left for later in the day or week.

Make sure that you use a descriptive subject line to indicate what is contained in the body of the e-mail. Otherwise, you risk having your message pushed back or ignored completely if the recipient doesn't recognize it as requiring attention or a response.

The Salutation

In the business world, you will want to use a regular salutation line, such as *Dear Fred*, or *Dear Mr. Brown*. In a personal setting, you can use something more colloquial, such as, "Hi, Lisa!" Of course, in an informal personal message, you may also want to ignore the salutation entirely and simply start out with the body of your message.

Your Signature

You can't actually sign an e-mail, but you can include information about yourself, such as your name, your job title, your contact information, and any other information you consider relevant.

If you wish, you can also specify a "signature line" that will be tacked onto the end of every e-mail you send, so that you don't have to worry about "signing" each message as you send it.

Sig Lines

Almost all e-mail programs provide the ability to specify a line or two that will be attached at the end of every message, known as a signature line. In the professional world, people often use these to indicate their name, profession, address, and contact information, in addition to other information such as book titles published, areas of specialization, or associated Web sites. Others (like the Fawnn'sFriendsList at *http://groups.yahoo.com/group/Fawnns Friends*) use pithy, cute quotes, such as "Save our planet—it's the only one with chocolate!" However, if you're writing for business, you may want to avoid such quotes.

FACT

Another electronic form of communication is the instant message. An instant message, or "IM," is a short message sent over the Internet to another user who is actively reading on the other side. Basically, it is like a written phone conversation. The rules for IMs are about the same as those for e-mail—the more familiar you are with the recipient, the more informally you can write.

E-mail Cover Letter with Attachment

When you send an e-mail with an attachment, it's always a good idea to inform the recipient about what the attached file contains. Your approach will be slightly different depending on whether it's a business or personal communication.

Business

If you are sending a letter as an attachment, you don't need to reproduce the entire letter; you must simply convey the salient points of what it contains, so that the recipient has some idea about what he or she will find inside. If you're sending other types of documents, make sure you identify what the attached file is, so that the recipient knows what to expect when he or she opens the file.

Personal Correspondence

You can be more lax in your approach with personal correspondence, but it's still a good idea to give your friend an idea of what's inside. Even a quick note like "Hey, check out this picture; it's really funny!" will convey the necessary information.

ALERT!

If you're sending an e-mail that contains questionable material, such as adult jokes, it's a good idea to put a note in the subject line to warn people—so that the message doesn't get opened when the boss or small children are present.

E-mail Courtesy

Because e-mail is such a new form of communication, new rules are developing. Keep the following "e-mail etiquette" points in mind when sending out messages.

Forwarding Messages

When dealing with e-mail, it's very easy to click the forward button to send to others when you want to share what you've received. Very likely you already get a number of these kinds of e-mails per day from friends who want to share jokes and other messages.

Be considerate of other people's busy schedules. Take a few moments before you forward the e-mail, and edit it for the following considerations:

- **Delete the past e-mail addresses from the text of the e-mail.** There's no reason to forward the complete history of the e-mail along with the message; this only serves to annoy people when they must scroll past pages of forwarded "from" lines that have nothing to do with the message itself. It also broadcasts e-mail addresses that some people may wish to keep confidential.
- **Don't "comment out" the text.** Follow this suggestion closely, especially if the message already has a number of comment characters at the beginning of the lines. This only serves to clutter up the message and contribute to the file size, without adding any value.
- **Edit the subject line.** A great deal of e-mail programs insert a "fwd:" comment at the beginning of the subject line. If a message is forwarded many times, these comments can quickly fill up the line.

One "fwd" comment is sufficient to indicate that this is a forwarded message.

- **Use the blind cc: option when forwarding to multiple people.** There's no reason to include 200 e-mail addresses of your friends in the "To:" line. If you're sending something to a large number of people, use the bcc: option to suppress the listing of those e-mail addresses that aren't necessary for everyone to see.

Recently, e-mail viruses have caused companies to re-evaluate how they accept messages from outside sources. Some have gone to the trouble of denying all attachments, stripping away the attached files at the server before it hits the recipient's inbox, or deleting the e-mail altogether without delivering it. Therefore, it's always a good idea to obtain permission to send an attachment before you send it.

Blogs and Blogging

Some writers are beginning to use the innovations of the Internet to create new writing forms that incorporate sound files and other elements. Other writers simply use the Internet to publish their works, but use the technology in an innovative way to display the stories.

Of course, you don't need a specific purpose to incorporate elements of multimedia into your writing. One of the current trends on the Internet involves something known as Web logs—or "blogs."

You can find links to blogs online at Blogger (*www.blogger.com*), a site started by Pyra Labs in August of 1999 and now owned by Google. Some bloggers use Blogger to power blogs they host on their personal domains. Blogger is also the home of a wide variety of blogs, where others like the winner of the 2007 Weblog Awards (Bloggies) for the best food Weblog—Help! I Have A Fire In My Kitchen—appear directly on that site at addresses prefaced by a part of the blog name, like *http://firein mykitchen.blogspot.com/*.

Using a blog, you can easily publish your writing on the Web, uploading your work using a simple template. The server will then do the rest of the work for you. Blogs are an easy-to-access publishing forum that can provide visitors with current and topical information.

Because it's informal, you can take whatever approach you like. Some people write full essays and upload them; others simply make short comments and observations, much like an online journal.

Online Forums

An Internet forum is a site on the World Wide Web for holding discussions by posting user-generated content. Each such discussion is commonly referred to as a thread. Generally, unless they are deleted by a forum administrator or moderator, these threads are saved on the Web site hosting the forum where they remain available for future reading. Computer games, health, politics, and technology topics (such as specific software help) are popular forum themes.

FACT

Because Internet forums evolved from early, pre-Internet dial-up bulletin boards (where users would connect directly with a bulletin board via their modem), some still refer to them as such. Internet forums are also commonly referred to as electronic bulletin boards, discussion boards, discussion groups, discussion forums, message boards, Web forums, or simply forums.

Most forums require some sort of registration process which then allows only registered members to post threads or replies to threads.

It's a good idea (and the polite, courteous thing to do) to read over other posts before you post to a forum. Doing so will help you become familiar with what constitutes appropriate behavior for that forum. Most forums also have some sort of FAQ (Frequently Asked Questions) page that gives the rules for the forum. Posting information or using language that is contrary to those rules can cause a user to be banned from posting further messages.

CHAPTER 20

New Horizons in Web Writing

By now, you should realize that the appropriate style of writing is defined by your purpose. New rules have surfaced since the advent of the Internet; it, too, requires its own unique approach. With high-speed Internet access more widely available, keeping page-loading times short isn't as important as it once was, but readers still expect information to be presented in much smaller segments. That's why in most cases, short paragraphs and clear and concise language are a must.

20

Nonlinear, Multimedia Writing

With much writing, ideas are introduced gradually and are used as building blocks to form the basis of what is to come later. The traditional print novel is a very good example of linear writing. You have to read what's at the beginning before the stuff in the middle will start to make sense.

Nonlinear writing simply means that you don't have to start at the beginning and go to the end to understand everything that is being presented. This really is just a complicated way of saying that each section should stand on its own. With nonlinear writing, you should be able to start reading at any point and learn what you need to know, without having to digest what's in the entire document.

When writing multimedia, never assume that your readers will start reading at the same place and follow a particular pattern. The very nature of the technology allows readers to wander anywhere, so you may not want to bury a critical piece of information in an audio file. If you're conveying important information, make sure it's in more than one place.

Each individual section, then, must contain all of the relevant information when writing for a nonlinear purpose. This means that you'll have more work to prepare for a nonlinear manuscript, but you'll find that the actual writing will go much easier because you'll have a comprehensive outline. In addition, your writing usually ends up being more concise and polished because of the extra time spent with organizing the information.

Interactive Writing

With most writing, your words will appear on the page in a linear format. It used to be that the interactive nature of printed documents was limited to looking at the table of contents or index and choosing a page number. Multimedia writing differs in that the components can be accessed through different ways. For example, visitors may link from a site index to see only the specific page they want. This ability to choose is what makes multimedia so dynamic. The reader gets to choose what comes next, instead of the author. It allows the user to interact with the information, rather than just read it.

The only thing that has heightened the new multimedia wave is the technology available to create it. With the advent of more powerful computers, new applications have greatly expanded the presentation formats available. The applications are not limited to just the printed word, either; multimedia can be presented on video or in other formats. The scope of applications is almost limitless.

On the Web, this new technology means that people can jump from place to place by following links that connect two relevant bits of information. But it doesn't stop there. The links can take visitors to relevant pictures, or sound files, or video files, or virtually anything else that can be displayed on a computer. For this reason, much of the Web has taken on a new flair.

The Web certainly went through its growing pains as people experimented with this new medium. Pages started out simply, due to technological limitations. Soon, the technology evolved, and Web page designers were then able to implement different elements, such as colored text or background images.

The concept of "multimedia" can be taken further. Even office presentations using software such as Microsoft PowerPoint use a similar approach to convey information. (The interactivity is just sometimes more limited, that's all.) Corporations can use interactive brochures to provide information to their shareholders, or as reference materials for staff training initiatives. The application combinations of multimedia writing are seemingly limitless.

In the years since, the technology has evolved further, providing a dynamic medium that can be used to disseminate virtually any kind of information. For example, news sites like *www.cnn.com* or *www.foxnews.com* use the Web as a publishing medium to provide news-related stories and information that complement the broadcasts of their respective networks, providing visitors with more in-depth information that they just don't have time to convey on the air. Television networks and stations also use their sites to provide broader information, such as viewing schedules and information about upcoming episodes. Sites like the Food Network (*www.foodnetwork.com*) post supplemental information, including the recipes featured on the shows.

Multimedia Formats

Multimedia is not really that new of a concept. Silent movies are an example that incorporated video, sound, and text to convey meaning. Educational filmstrips from the '60s and '70s also used similar elements, with accompanying cassette tapes for the classroom environment.

The principles of multimedia can be applied wherever information is being conveyed to make the presentation more interesting or easier to understand. While effective presentation can augment the way information is absorbed, don't think that it can ever replace relevant and topical information. A multimedia presentation, including one on a Web page, can incorporate any of the following elements:

- Animations
- Music
- Pictures
- Sounds
- Speech
- Text
- Video

In designing an online presentation, you must decide which of the above factors will help you to convey your information in the most effective fashion. Be careful, however, not to use elements just because they're available. Your online presentation doesn't have to have sound, for example, unless it's integral to your goals. As an example, you could publish the lyrics to a song you wrote, and then include the melody in a sound file that the visitor can play. Be careful, however, to give the user a choice and not start things like sound or video files automatically. It's best to leave it as an option. Some users don't have the best computers, and things like sound files playing in the background can take up a lot of resources and are distracting. (In fact, some people will skip viewing a page altogether if it doesn't offer the option of turning off the background sound.)

ALERT!

Remember—all the fancy and flashy presentation in the world won't help your cause if you're not also presenting relevant information along with the glitz.

In most cases, your emphasis will be on the information that you're presenting, not on the way you present it. A scrolling marquee may seem like a wonderful idea to you, but visitors may not want to sit through the whole thing. Others may be upset that they can't scroll back and forth in the marquee to read what they may have missed. Never use a presentation format just because you think it's cool.

QUESTION?

What things should I take into consideration when exploring multimedia formats?
When incorporating elements, take into consideration the technological challenges your readers may face. For example, if you use special technology like Macromedia Flash Player, not all visitors may have it installed. If you use such special technology, make sure it isn't the only source of the information you're trying to present. Also offer the option of viewing your Web page as a standard HTML file.

Start with the information you want to present, and then ask yourself how it can best be conveyed to the visitor. If it's text, then use writing. If it's sound, then use sound files. If only a video will do, then use that. Remember that all of these technologies require a certain degree of expertise. If you plan to incorporate elements and you don't know how to create the files, give yourself ample time to figure out how to do it before your project must be completed—or subcontract such work to someone else, if necessary.

Instructional Multimedia Writing

Because of its dynamic ability to display different forms of information, many multimedia projects are created for educational or introductory purposes. Multimedia elements can enhance the learning process by increasing the learning potential of the participants.

Normally, instructional materials consist of written information, audio presentations, or video presentations. Multimedia, whether on the Web or in a cross-linked file, can encompass all three of these elements.

No matter which formats you choose to use in your multimedia presentation, the presentation must achieve the following three objectives:

1. Explain all concepts, terms, and other information the user will need to know.
2. Illustrate the principles and practical aspects of the information you're presenting.
3. Inform the user about new concepts, aspects, or new material.

High-Impact Online Presentations

As stated earlier, it's important to ensure that you're presenting important and relevant information as your first step. After you've identified that information, though, you can begin to think of the way you'd like the information conveyed.

Often, when it comes to writing for online presentations, the axiom "less is more" is appropriate. You don't need to incorporate all elements; rather, use only those which will enhance the presentation of the information. Here is a small selection of design tools that can be used to enhance the presentation of a site:

- Embedded sound files
- Embedded video files
- Flash

Java
JavaScript
Shockwave

You may need to do some research to figure out how to use these tools. A great deal of online resources exist to assist you in finding answers to questions about Web design tools. There are also many sites that provide free automated Web scripts that will complete certain tasks for you. Identify what it is you want your site to do, and then set out to find the appropriate tool. If you're lucky enough to be working with a production team, hopefully you will have access to people experienced in using these tools. (You'll learn more about production teams later in this chapter.)

Remember, any time you try to enhance your site using specialized tools, you run the risk of losing a part of your audience who may not have the appropriate software or browser plug-ins installed.

Incorporating Text into Graphics

It's very likely that with your online presentation, you'll want some aspects of your site to appear stylized, rather than just using the simple default fonts displayed by a browser. Some Web page editors allow you to specify certain fonts, but the page will not display properly if the visitor does not have the selected font installed. In order to ensure browser compatibility, you can create graphics for headers and icons that contain the text you want to display.

If you use graphics to display text, remember that search engines can't index what they say. Therefore, it's a good idea to repeat the text in the image's <alt> tags to ensure that there's something there for search engine spiders to grab.

If you choose to do this, you can use just about any graphic editing software. However, it's important to keep a log of the following information:

- Background color
- Font point size
- Font type
- Graphic size
- Style (i.e., boldfaced? italicized?)
- Text color

You'll want to have this information if you ever need to modify or add any additional headings to your site. There is nothing more frustrating than having to figure out which font was used or ascertain other uncertain information in order to re-create the look and feel of images you created months (or years) before.

Choosing Your Presentation Format

The first rule of thumb when writing anything for online presentation is to use short paragraphs; this is more conducive to online reading because short paragraphs are easier to skim. Visitors probably won't read every word you write; they'll certainly read sections, but the majority will be looking for specific information. Make it easy for people to find.

ALERT!

Remember to consider visitors with disabilities. Site design with poor color choices and font size can alienate some users because they create a host of problems: Not all monitors—nor all users—interpret colors in the same way, some font colors can blend into the background color for someone who's colorblind, and fonts that are too small or contain unusual design elements can be difficult for someone with vision problems to read.

No matter what you do, keep the following guidelines in mind whenever writing material that will be displayed on a computer:

- **Use proper contrast between the background and the text color.** Some combinations can be impossible to read. Make your Web pages as easy to read as possible; this helps ensure people will take the time to digest your message.
- **Use a proper size font.** If you use smaller fonts, make sure that your HTML code doesn't preclude users from making the text larger. You don't want to risk limiting the readability of your site to those who suffer from physical disabilities such as poor eyesight.
- **Use short paragraphs.** Not only is this what an online user expects, it also reduces eyestrain for those who read computer monitors for long periods of time.
- **Break up your pages.** Long pages make scrolling and printing cumbersome. Keep your pages short; split long ones into smaller sets of two or three.
- **Verify your links.** It is maddening for users to click on a link, thinking that they have found the perfect answer to a question, only to find that the page does not exist. In addition, update your links promptly when you find out that one has changed.
- **Cross-index your site.** Make sure that you can access the index pages from any page in the site, or you may find that you lose some visitors who might land at your site via a middle page. If there is not an indication of other information available, the user may just close the window or move on to another site.

If you're looking for a Web style guide, you can find one at *www .webstyleguide.com*. This will give you an indication of online style usage. Information is also available from the Columbia Guide to Online Style at *www.columbia.edu/cu/cup/cgos2006/basic.html*.

Determining Your Audience

As you've seen elsewhere in these pages, you must always be attentive to your prospective audience. If you write beyond their comprehension level, they simply won't understand your message. On the Web, that means that people will simply click off the page and find something a little easier for them to understand.

You must do a little bit of investigation, then, and try to figure out some demographics for your ideal audience. Do some research on the Web and look for sites that appeal to the same kinds of users. How specific is the information they offer? Will a broad approach suffice, or will you have to break your ideas down into further specialized categories?

Once you have an idea of who your visitors will be, you can start to tailor your approach for them. You'll have an indication of the expected content and the readership level you should aim for when you're writing. Once you know who you're writing for, you can start to figure out how to present it to them.

Establishing Your Content Outline

Once again, a good outline will save you a lot of wasted time and effort. Outlines force you to plan out your presentation so that you don't end up spending a lot of time on extraneous things that don't (or won't) contribute to your final product.

Plan out the information for the following headings: An example of a Web design outline is provided. Of course, much of the same information will help you with other forms of multimedia presentations, too. If you're not writing for the Web, you still need to address all of these concerns, but you will not need a domain name.

FACT

A Web site to which people return is known as a sticky site, and is the objective of any Web presence intended to build customer loyalty or a following.

- **Domain name:** Do you want a special domain name for visitors to type in? (A Web site name like CookingWithPam.com is easier for somebody to remember than a lengthy URL.)
- **Objective:** What kinds of things do you plan to achieve with your online presentation?

- **Target audience:** Who do you anticipate will read or participate in your online presentation?
- **Resources:** What do you plan to offer visitors, and what things can you offer that will keep people coming back?
- **Layout notes:** How do you plan to present your information?
- **Tree structure:** How do you plan to categorize and link your Web pages (or the individual components in your non-Web multimedia presentation)?

The following content outline shows one way to answer all of these criteria. It was used in the site design for the Cookingwithpam.com domain.

Sample Content Outline for a Web Site

Domain Name: *www.cookingwithpam.com*

Objective: Provide a free recipe resource to promote cookbooks and other titles authored by Pamela Rice Hahn

Target Audience 1: Visitors who like to cook

Target Audience 2: Visitors who don't like to cook but want quick and easy recipes

Resources—Target Audience 1

Recipe pages

Reviews: Products and ingredients—generic, and also from specific suppliers
Utensils and cookware from specific suppliers
Appliances—general instructions and reviews of specific brand names
Cookbooks—written by Pamela Rice Hahn and other authors

Resources—Target Audience 2

Quick and Easy Recipe pages

Reviews: Products and ingredients—generic, and also from
                      specific suppliers, with emphasis on time-saving
                      and not sacrificing quality for time
                      Utensils and cookware from specific suppliers, with
                      emphasis on time-saving benefits
                      Appliances—general instructions and reviews of
                      specific brand names, with emphasis on time-sav-
                      ing benefits
                      Cookbooks—Provide additional tips along with any
                      reviews, plus links to related information

Layout Notes: For the purposes of continuity, all Web pages will
                      follow a template. Each page will follow a hierarchi-
                      cal structure based on the Tree Structure.

Tree Structure

                      Main title page: Featured recipes, featured tips, nav-
                      igation guide

                      Categories: About, Bread, Baking, Chocolate, Equip-
                      ment, Cookbooks, My Books, Grilling, Diabetes,
                      Enabled, Whey Low/Sugar-Free, Tips & Tricks

Individual recipes and related information: Linked from categories

                      Resources: Site index, category index, alphabetical
                      index, search page

   Once you have all of these elements addressed, you can get down to
the real work of creating the content without having these little details stop
you along the way.

Storyboard Styles

Using a storyboard can be a very effective tool for planning your online presentation. In essence, a *storyboard* is simply an outline that incorporates pictures that indicate the steps that will be taken along the way. The beauty of storyboarding is that it allows you to plot your presentation out visually so that you can see how it will look at all stages.

Storyboards are often used in film or television production to provide the crew with a visual example of how the final shot should look. This way, the director's vision is represented in a graphic format that can be easily seen by the props people, lighting technicians, and everyone else involved in the process. When working with a team, these storyboards are very effective in getting everyone focused toward a common goal.

Even if you're not working on a team, a storyboard is still effective because it makes you think about how your presentation will be viewed graphically. It gives you the opportunity to figure out how you want each screen to look; then, using the tools at your disposal, you can figure out how to make the resulting screen look like you want it to.

Of course, your storyboard won't contain only pictures. It will also contain a written description to accompany each picture and describe the elements that pertain to that particular section. Similarly, you won't want to have a picture in the storyboard for each and every screen of your online presentation. You'll merely want to plot out the major elements, and then elaborate upon them in the accompanying text. You can use hand-drawn stick figures and written notes or Microsoft PowerPoint-style presentation storyboard pages.

Your first step is to break down your presentation into individual components. If you've already been working from an outline, this should be relatively simple; you can just follow the outline you've created, with slight modifications to incorporate the visual aspects. If you haven't already started your outline, now is the time. Follow the instructions for making a general outline, and simply note where you plan to include the pictures as the visual element of your storyboards. Then, elaborate upon the descriptions.

This also gives you the ability to see how your final product will be displayed and gives you the opportunity to realize what problems may arise in the implementation stage. This can also save countless hours later. If you catch them early, you have the chance to fix design challenges before they become very difficult to change.

It also gives you the opportunity to experiment with a number of different formats without having to go through all the work of carrying each design through to its full implementation. You can create a number of different versions of storyboards and then choose which is the best representation for your online presentation. By far its best benefit, however, is that it provides you with a step-by-step guide that will assist in the implementation of your idea.

Script Formats

If your multimedia piece will use sound bites or small audio clips, you'll need to script them.

Remember that the written word and the spoken word are two completely different forms. Writing usually conveys information in a different manner than speech. Often, grammatical rules are bent (or ignored entirely) when people are speaking. You want your sound bites to sound natural and appealing, not stilted and artificial. So when you're writing scripts for the spoken word, you need to take a slightly different direction.

For example, using the above Web outline for Cookingwithpam.com, say you wanted to incorporate some light conversations to go along with the recipes. A script for some "Editorial Commentary" for a basmati rice recipe might be:

Man: Why do you like basmati better, out of curiosity?
Woman: It's plumper. It cooks up fluffier.
Man: Okay. Well, since your answer wasn't "grittier," I'm gonna let this cook a bit longer.

You'll notice that the grammar indicated in the script wouldn't be acceptable in formal writing. That's because it's being scripted for speech. The voices would be recorded and broadcast to visitors, who will expect it to sound like spoken conversation, not written words being read aloud. The example illustrates the inconsistencies of the spoken word, making it sound more natural.

What would be the purpose of "light" conversation on a formal Web site?
Humor can be used in many ways. By its very nature, light conversation can break up the tension in an otherwise tense moment. (A salesperson might time the telling of a joke in the sales presentation so that it occurs shortly before the sales close.)

Working with a Production Team

If your multimedia presentation is going to be very large, you probably won't be the only person working on it. It's very likely that you'll be working with an entire production team to achieve your goal of an effective online multimedia presentation.

A production team will often consist of the following:

- A team leader who oversees the group
- Design specialists who are familiar with Web publishing technology
- Writing staff, including writers, proofreaders, and copyeditors
- Financial management staff for very large projects
- Production assistants who ensure that day-to-day tasks are completed

The design and makeup of a production team will depend on the actual scope of the project being created. For very large projects, the above roles may be carried out by a number of people. For smaller projects, team members may find themselves wearing multiple hats.

The production team will break up the necessary tasks and assign them to individuals within the group. Often, frequent production meetings will be held to discuss progress and challenges. Be forthright in your dealings with the group, as you may find that they are able to offer invaluable assistance if you are having problems. By the same token, offer your assistance when others require it.

CHAPTER 21

Considerations When Writing for Publication

Whenever you're writing for publication, there are certain rules to follow. Manuscript style preferences and submission standards vary from publisher to publisher—and by imprint within larger publishing conglomerates. Submission standards for fiction also vary from those for nonfiction. The content needs and expectations for general interest publications differ significantly from those of academic, literary, religious, and scientific periodicals.

Letter to Obtain Publisher Guidelines

Almost all publishers have a guideline sheet available on request. Such publisher guidelines contain specific information about the kinds of work the publisher buys from authors. In addition, the guidelines will also contain important information about how your manuscript should be formatted and submitted for consideration. Obtaining such guidelines requires a simple, straightforward letter. There's no reason to go into detail about your writing project in this letter. Your only purpose is to obtain the guidelines.

Query Letter to Publisher

Ms. Janet Worth
Acquisitions Editor
ABC Publisher
12115 5th Ave.
New York, NY 10112

Dear Ms. Worth:

Enclosed please find a SASE. I would like a copy of your writer's guidelines.

Thank you,

Whenever you send a letter to a publisher, you should always include a self-addressed, stamped envelope, known as a SASE. The SASE is an expected courtesy from the author. Without it, there is a chance that your letter will hit the garbage instead of the "response" pile—publishers cannot afford to respond to all mail they receive from prospective writers.

The Query Letter

A query letter is used to introduce you and your work to a publisher or an agent. Pay close attention to each publisher's requirements (as outlined in the writer's guidelines from that publisher) to determine whether the publisher wants a complete manuscript, an outline with sample chapters, or only a query letter outlining your proposed manuscript. Any of these are submitted to gauge the publisher's interest in your project; you'll be asked to submit more if the publisher wants to consider your book for publication or if an agent is willing to represent your work.

Publisher Query Letter

When a publisher doesn't publish specific submission guidelines, it's acceptable to send a query letter to inquire as to what the publisher prefers—the complete manuscript or a synopsis and sample chapters.

Query Letter

Ms. Janet Worth
Acquisitions Editor
ABC Publisher
5555 Fifth Avenue
New York, NY 10112

Dear Ms. Worth:

I have recently completed a mystery novel titled "Lurker@Heart." It is a cyber-thriller that investigates the recent popularity of online chat rooms and the potential problems that can arise from visiting them.

I can provide you either with the complete manuscript or with a synopsis and sample chapters, whichever you prefer.

Enclosed please find a SASE for your reply.

Thank you,

Agent Query Letter

Some publishers will not accept submissions from unrepresented authors, so you may need to find an agent first.

Query Letter to Agent

Mr. A. Dealmaker
XYZ Literary Agency
555 Fifth Avenue
New York, NY 10116

Dear Mr. Dealmaker:

I have recently completed a mystery novel titled "Lurker@Heart." It is a cyber-thriller that investigates the recent popularity of online chat rooms and the potential problems that can arise from visiting them.

I am currently seeking representation for this work. May I forward the manuscript to you? Or do you prefer a synopsis and sample chapters?

Enclosed please find a SASE for your reply.

Thank you.

Sincerely,

David L. Hebert

Manuscript Format

Manuscripts should always be double-spaced. This makes it much easier to read, and also allows room for changes or comments to be made in the margins. Your manuscript should be single-sided as well; photocopying a double-sided manuscript can be tedious. Don't try to save paper by squeezing out your margins or by printing on both sides of the page. Remember, editors are people who read for a living. Make it easy on their eyesight by following these rules.

Each page should have a one-inch margin on all sides. Check your word processor's default settings; you may need to modify them to meet a particular publisher's requirement.

The first page of your manuscript should contain the title, your byline, and your real name. If you write under your real name, then you don't need to include a byline; however, if you plan to use a pseudonym, you must let the publisher know this by indicating the byline.

Your title page should also have your contact information on it, and your agent's contact information, if applicable. The body of your manuscript can start on page one, after you list the contact information; it's not necessary to start your story on page two.

Each subsequent page should also have a header that includes your last name, the manuscript title, and a page number. If you have a very long title, you can put a portion of it instead of the whole thing, as long as what you choose to put there will help to trigger an editor's memory if the pages get separated in the office. It's sometimes sufficient to list only your last name, rather than your entire name. If you're using a pseudonym, unless the guidelines state otherwise, show the last name in your byline followed by your actual last name in parenthesis.

Winglethorp (Hahn)

Some publishers like the page numbering to appear centered at the bottom of the page; however this is the exception to the rule and seldom used. (Manuscripts submitted electronically as a word-processing program file often don't require page numbering, either as a header or footer, at all.) If the guidelines do not give page header or page numbering specifics, use this format, flush right, at the top of the page:

Hahn/*The Everything Improve Your Writing Book*/Page 2

Also, you should not hole-punch, staple, or otherwise bind the manuscript. A large butterfly clip is sometimes fine (unless specifically prohibited in the publisher guidelines), but the manuscript pages themselves should remain unmarred.

Here is a checklist for manuscript preparation. Use it when preparing your manuscript to make sure you haven't missed anything.

- ❑ One-inch margins on each side
- ❑ Double-spaced
- ❑ Header (author name, book title, page number)
- ❑ Unbound
- ❑ Single-sided

Some publishers will require variations. For example, if the publisher uses a "blind" editorial evaluation team, editors will read manuscripts without knowing who has submitted them or who the authors are. If this is the case, the publisher will request that your contact information go on a separate title page, and also require that your name appear in no other place on the manuscript. (Your header, then, would contain only the title of the work and the page number.)

Manuscript formatting usually follows a specific standard, but some publishers require that the manuscript be presented differently. All publishers will have a spec sheet that lists their individual requirements; all you have to do is write and ask. For a sample, see "the letter to obtain publisher guidelines" earlier in this chapter.

Your Author Bio

Many publishers will ask that you send along a short biographical statement with your manuscript. This gives them a bit of background as they're reading your work, and it can also be used for promotional purposes (or even to draft the bio blurb that will appear on the back of your book).

Your bio should include the following information:

- **Your background experience:** What kinds of relevant things have you done in your life? What can you include in your bio that will show the publishers and the editors your background and past experiences?
- **Your educational experience:** Do you have a Ph.D. or other titles that lend credibility and demonstrate your expertise on a subject that will help sell books for you? Have you completed any training programs relating to the field you're writing about? Even if your educational experience is unrelated, include it—it provides good background for the people who must publicize and market your book.
- **Past writing credits:** It's a good idea to include any information you have about past writing jobs that you've done. This shows the editors, publicists, and publishers that they're working with someone who has experience.

Your bio should be short; a page—or about 250 words—is a good length. (It's permissible to use 1½-line spacing instead of double spacing on the biography only, if that's what it takes to achieve that one-page goal.) Some publishers may request more detailed information, while others will want a bio of no more than a few sentences. If the publisher has required specifications, follow those closely. Write your biographical statement in the third person.

The following introductory lines from a biographical statement come from the Web site of a Canadian colleague. Unless it's accompanying a humor submission, it might be a little too tongue-in-cheek to send to a publisher; however, it shows you how one author conveys his information:

David L. Hebert came into this world on December 24, 1970, and just like Gracie Allen, was so surprised he didn't speak for almost two years. It was a burst of enthusiasm from which he still hasn't quite recovered.

When submitting it with a book proposal (see information later in this chapter), keep the style of your author biography appropriate for the style of the book you're pitching—humorous, if appropriate, or cerebral for more serious works.

Other details you can include in an author biography being submitted with a book proposal include the following:

- Any awards or fellowships you've received
- Background information directly relevant to your book, such as professional organization affiliation
- Significant sales information or review quotes on previous works

Fiction Basics

Writing fiction can be a fun and rewarding pastime; it can also be a rewarding career. The following sections will give you an idea about writing for this interesting and potentially lucrative market.

Genre

Much of today's fiction is written in a particular genre, like mystery or science fiction. Genres have special style considerations that make them appeal to a certain type of reader.

Each genre has its own rules to follow. Some, like romances, are very stringent; publishers expect the story to follow a certain structure. Others give you more room to move. A mystery, for example, must always have a crime to solve, but there is a great deal of latitude as to how the story progresses. Science fiction and fantasy are often lumped together, although there are different sets of rules for each.

There are a number of genre categories available in the current publishing market:

- Action/adventure
- Chick Lit
- Horror
- Mystery
- Romance
- Science fiction and fantasy
- Thrillers
- Westerns

Some have categories within the categories, such as the techno-thriller genre for which Tom Clancy is known. A solid market exists for all of these categories, although different categories enjoy different levels of popularity at different points in time. There's also a solid body of reference material dedicated to each genre. For information about specific titles, consult *The Everything® Writing Well Book* resource at *www.ricehahn.com/books/*.

Each genre also has its own rules about length. Some romance novels, for example, are relatively short, with as few as 56,000 words. Horror and mystery novels tend to be longer, on average, coming out somewhere around 80,000 words, while fantasy novels surpass 100,000 words. Consult publishers for current word length requirements for your particular genre.

Viewpoint

There are three basic kinds of viewpoints (also known as points of view or POV) that are commonly used in fiction:

First Person

Written in the first person, this viewpoint creates instant identification between the reader and the narrating character. It's more personal and intimate, but it can have its drawbacks. While it gives you the ability to climb inside your main character's head and share his or her thoughts directly with the reader, it also limits the interaction your reader will have with your other characters. It also places limits on the way you tell your story, because you can never tell anything to the reader that the character doesn't already know. In a mystery, for example, you cannot fill the reader in on clues without having them known by the main character. By contrast, with the third-person viewpoint, this is done by shifting the point of view from one character to another.

Third-Person Omniscient

With third-person omniscient, the reader is not limited to the thoughts of the narrator. Indeed there is no narrator, and the story is told in the third person, using third-person pronouns like *he* or *she* to describe the actions of the characters involved in the scene. The omniscient part means that the unseen narrator can jump inside the heads of whichever character it wants. You must be careful, however; jumping from one mind to the next can disorient the reader. It is sometimes better to limit your viewpoint to one character per scene. Shifting the viewpoint takes skill.

Third-Person Limited

The third-person limited viewpoint is like an amalgam of the previous two, and is much more common in today's literary marketplace. It limits the reader's exposure to one mind, as with the first person, but the story is simply told without a narrator. Romance novels were once limited to this viewpoint, told only from the heroine's perspective.

Second Person

Although the second-person viewpoint does technically exist, it is seldom used in fiction. Instead of using first-person or third-person pronouns, the second-person pronoun *you* is used.

You walk through the doorway into a dimly lit passage. Dusty air floods your nostrils as you slowly creep along the passageway, passing by the bare timbers holding up the soil. Your feet scrape on the rough hewn stone floor, creating echoes throughout the chambers. You find it spooky.

If you have an idea that would adapt itself well to the second-person viewpoint, feel free to use it, but remember that it's not often done. It is a hard POV to master, as the misuse of it will quickly alienate the reader (who would never do the things you're telling the reader that he or she is doing).

Plot

Your plot is simply the progression of your story. It is how the story develops. It starts at point A, progresses to point B, and then on to point C. Think of the plot as the building blocks for your story.

Anton Chekhov, master playwright and short-story writer, supposedly once said, "If you have a gun on the stage in Act I, it had better go off by Act III." This is simply a short way of saying that your story must develop, and if you set up something early in the story, that setup must be essential to the story. Also, if you plan to use something toward the end of the story, it's usually more effective that you set it up early so that the groundwork is laid.

By thinking this way, you'll avoid plot inconsistencies that will jar the reader. Anything you try that isn't properly set up will seem out of place or contrived. Worse, the reader will think you're cheating by taking shortcuts like having the character win a lottery and never having a care in the world again. Don't be seen as taking the cheap way out.

Using an outline will help your plotting. Simply write yourself a list of what happens in the story. If you decide to change anything later, you can easily see how it will affect the flow of your story.

Some writers don't like to worry about plot when they first start writing. They'd rather see where the characters take them and see what kind of story unfolds. That's fine if you choose to take this route; it can be a very fun way of writing, as you're actively using your imagination as you write. Basically, you're playing "what if?" with yourself and recording the answers that come out of your mind.

This stream-of-consciousness process, however, requires extensive editing later. The odds are against your being able to write an entire novel off the cuff without putting any planning into the plotting or scheduling time for massive rewrites later.

The other way, of course, is to concentrate on the outline and figure out where your plot is going to go before you actually sit down and do any substantive writing. This way, you have a clear indication of what should happen and where you will be going with the story when you start writing.

Premise

In addition to your plot, you should always have a premise. While a plot is simply the progression of your story, the premise is the culmination of it. In a way, it's like the moral or the point of the story.

The premise is just a short way of encapsulating everything that goes on with your story. But it also provides you with a yardstick by which you can measure how effectively your story line is developing.

FACT

The premise need only be a one-sentence line about the outcome of your story, such as: "Drinking and carousing leads to a loss in career." You don't need to include anything character-specific, as that will be addressed in your plot. The premise is there only for you to measure the effectiveness of your individual scenes, to make sure that they are contributing toward the plot.

Conflict

Conflict is the glue that holds your story together. Conflict is what causes characters to develop and change. It is these changes that are interesting to the reader, who likes to see character evolution from the beginning of the book to the end. It also creates more identification, so that the reader can relate to the characters better.

There is no magic to conflict. It is simply the challenges that your characters must face along the course of your story. Conflict is inextricably tied to plot; your plot will actually progress on the basis of conflict.

Your story will also have a major conflict, which is often known as the climax or the crisis of the story. This will be covered in a later section of this chapter.

Characters and Dialogue

Dialogue is important when one character is learning information from another. It's a great technique you can use to convey new facts and information to the reader. Rather than dumping a ton of detail into your narrative, you can introduce information gradually, while letting the reader participate in the action of how the characters uncover the information.

"What's this?" Roger asked, holding up a sheet of paper.

Dr. Harvey looked up from his work. "Those are the final lab analysis results."

Roger scanned the list. The report meant nothing to him. "What's it say?" he asked.

"Well, it says that there were very high levels of lead in the water." The doctor took the sheet from Roger and consulted the figures. "More than four times what is considered acceptable, actually."

"Wow, that's a lot," Roger said. "Any idea what might have caused that?"

The doctor shook his head. "Not yet. But we've ordered another series of samples. I've got technicians out there gathering them right now—from multiple sources all along the stream."

"You think it's from the Axendale plant?"

The doctor nodded slowly. "I don't see where else it could have come from."

This short little scene gives a lot of information to the reader. It shows that a chemical investigation is underway to try to determine why lead levels are so high. It also sets up the next part of the story, where the supplemental samples are obtained and analyzed. In addition, it reveals the doctor's suspicions about the origin of the poisoning. While much of the same could have been done using plain narrative, the use of dialogue engages the reader and lets him or her participate in the story, rather than just being told information. (This is part of that "show, don't tell" you'll hear about often from those giving fiction-writing instructions.)

Character Traits

You can use character traits to demonstrate quirks about your characters. For example, someone who always tells the truth will be put in an interesting position if he or she, through the course of the story, finds that he or she absolutely must lie (for a very good reason).

Any time you can pit a character trait against the character's need for change, you'll end up with gripping, emotional reading, because the reader can see the inner struggle that the character is going through. This is where reader identification comes from.

Speech Patterns, Not Dialect

As a cautionary note, be very careful not to make characters speak in dialects. If they speak in one, that's fine; you just should not convey that in the actual dialogue, that's all. It will do nothing but confuse the reader.

Keep your dialogue simple. If you're writing about country bumpkins, convey that in the words they choose to use, like short simple phrases, rather than trying to cut off the ends of words, which only serves to make the manuscript look choppy.

Setting

Your setting is where the story takes place. While your story can probably happen almost anywhere, you may want to evaluate how different settings will change the mood or the tone of your piece.

It's always a good idea to try to make your setting resonate with the other events in your story. This adds depth and also a layer of emotional texture to your piece, as the reader will experience the story on more levels.

For example, if you are writing about a character in a depression, it might be a good idea to set that character in a drab, dreary place to start out with. Later, as the character changes, you can place this character in more exciting surroundings to augment the emotional mood you're creating.

Flashbacks and Other Devices

When you want to fill the reader in on parts of the story that have occurred prior to the present action, you can use a flashback to convey the information. A flashback is merely jumping back in time to convey information.

Be careful not to use jargon that your readers won't understand. It's perfectly acceptable to have one of your characters be a rocket scientist from NASA, but if the reader doesn't understand anything the character says, the character probably isn't contributing very much to your story.

As a word of caution—never use a flashback in the middle of an important, exciting scene. You'll only detract from the emotional impact of the fast pace. Save your flashbacks and other literary devices for lulls and low points in the story, where they make the most sense.

Crisis

The crisis is the major climax point of your story. It's where everything you've been writing toward happens. In action-adventure movies, this is often in some dramatic location, where all the cards are on the table and the characters have everything to lose. The major conflict is the deciding factor (where good will triumph or evil will win out).

Crisis will usually cause the characters to undergo some sort of major transformation.

Resolution

The resolution is what happens at the end of your novel or story. After the crisis or conflict, the resolution is how everything gets resolved. This is where your happy (or not-so-happy) ending comes in. The resolution gives the reader emotional satisfaction in knowing that everything is nicely wrapped up (but not too much so).

Nonfiction Basics

With nonfiction, there is a different thrust. Your objective is to convey information in a simple and forthright manner. It is necessary that you thoroughly understand your topic. This doesn't mean that you can't write about things you don't already know (as mentioned earlier in this book when William Zinsser's *Writing to Learn* was cited); it simply means that you must be willing to do the necessary research to learn all about the subject.

The market for articles is extensive. Newspapers and magazines need articles, both local and national, general audience and trade. Also, there are a number of Web sites that pay for articles on various subjects. You can search online for Web markets.

The word length for each will vary depending on the market. Consult the publisher guidelines to determine how long each piece (or each book) should be.

Features

Features will normally be for newspapers or magazines, although it is possible to extend an idea for a feature into a book-length project. Included among features are short biographies.

How To

There is a huge market for instructional books if you are able to convey information clearly and in a concise and logical, easy-to-understand format. Get into the habit of creating an outline for everything you write, and you'll find that your overall writing is much more on point and focused—a talent especially important when writing this type of book.

There is also a healthy demand for how-to articles that will show people how to accomplish a particular task. Naturally, these won't be covered in as much depth as they would in a book, but it is still possible to convey a lot of useful information in a thousand words.

Biography

Biographies are writings about a particular person's background. It is an exposé of the trials and tribulations that person has undergone, studying the factors and events that made this person who he or she was or is.

The Essentials of a Book Proposal

Be sure to consult the publisher or agent guidelines before you submit a proposal. Some expect to first receive a query letter. There are several proposal formats that are acceptable.

The Cover Letter

A cover letter that accompanies a book proposal can be longer than the standard one-page cover letter because it includes the "pitch" for your book. Format this letter as you would a formal business letter, using single spacing with two-line feeds between each paragraph. Introduce your proposal by giving your proposed book title, followed by a one-sentence description of your proposed book. Next, introduce other essential information about the book in synopsis format, explaining such things as:

- The potential audience for the book
- The tone of the book (humorous, instructional, exposé)
- The type of book (hardcover, trade paperback, etc.)
- Your expertise (why you're the perfect person to write the book)
- Any other experience (e.g., media) that will help market the book
- A brief description of the supporting documents you're including with the proposal

Cover Letter

Ms. Regan
555 Fifth Avenue
New York, NY 10112

Dear Ms. Regan:

More than a million people now work with widgets on a daily basis and that number is growing with each passing day. *The Wonderful Widget* is a book that would be appropriate in either hardcover or as a trade paperback. The book will address the phenomena of America's fascination with the widget, defining the many aspects of what makes the widget an essential part of so many households. The book will walk the reader step-by-step through the information necessary to know, appreciate, and then use the widget.

I worked as Mr. Michael Bishop's personal assistant for more than ten years and have observed the evolution of the widget—from concept to working model to marketing phenomena. Now, as marketing director for the company, I have appeared as his spokesperson on news programs on all major networks, when Mr. Bishop has been unable to appear himself because of scheduling conflicts. Mr. Bishop promises his full cooperation on the development of this book. I'll have full access to his notes and supporting documents.

I'm including my proposed table of contents for this book (along with chapter descriptions), plus information on competing titles, my author biography (this isn't my first book), a sample chapter, and publicity and promotion suggestions for the book.

Thank you for your time and consideration. I look forward to discussing this project with you at your convenience.

Sincerely,

FACT

If you work with an agent who will be submitting the book for you, unless your agent requests it (so she or he can adapt it for when your book is submitted), you can forego the cover letter and just use the cover page and book pitch proposal format.

Some authors prefer to forego doing a cover letter and begin with a cover page, followed by a two- to three-page "pitch" for the book. This book pitch contains essentially the same elements that go into a cover letter, except rather than showing the editor and publisher (or agent) information and greeting, it begins by immediately repeating the proposed title for your book, followed by a one-sentence description of your proposed book. The book pitch, like the rest of the proposal, is double-spaced.

The Cover Page

Your first task is to write a great title for your proposed book. Once you've done that, to prepare the cover page, print that title in all upper case letters, centered in the upper third of a blank page; use double-spacing if the title is more than one line. Centered and double-spaced below the title, print your name in capital and lowercase letters. In the bottom third of the page, and tabbed over so that the information appears near the right margin, type your name, address, and phone number (or your agent's name, address, and phone number). If you include both, be sure to identify the agent information. This information can be single- or double-spaced, depending on the amount of information you include.

The Book Pitch

When you work with an agent who'll be submitting the work to the potential publishers for your book, write your book pitch in third person.

The Wonderful Widget is a book that will walk the reader step-by-step through the information necessary to know, appreciate, and then use the widget.

More than a million people now work with widgets on a daily basis and that number is growing with each passing day. *The Wonderful Widget*, whether as a hardcover book or as a trade paperback, will address the phenomenon of America's fascination with the widget, defining the many aspects of what makes the widget an essential part of so many households.

The author for this work, Jodi Cornelius, worked as Mr. Michael Bishop's personal assistant for more than ten years. During that time she observed the entire evolution of the widget—from concept to working model to marketing phenomenon. Now, as marketing director for the company, she has appeared as his spokesperson on news programs on all major networks, when Mr. Bishop has been unable to appear himself because of scheduling conflicts. Mr. Bishop promises his full cooperation on the development of this book. Ms. Cornelius will have full access to Mr. Bishop's notes and supporting documents.

As you'll see from Ms. Cornelius's author bio, her experience with the Wonderful Widget Corporation, as well as her prior writing experience, makes her the perfect author for this work.

If you have published articles on the subject of your book, include those along with your sample chapter. Such published works add to your credibility, and they illustrate an interest in your topic.

The Proposed Table of Contents

The proposed table of contents essentially involves working the concept for your book into an outline of sorts, only in this instance you'll list chapter titles, followed by one-paragraph descriptions of what you intend to cover in that chapter. A well-written table of contents description demonstrates to the editor that you know how to organize a book.

Initial Part of a Table of Contents

The Everything Improve Your Writing Book
Chapter 1: The Basics
This chapter will cover the *who, what, when, where, why,* and *how* of effective formal and informal writing, including information on how the writer goes about determining the audience for a work and establishing a voice in that writing. It will conclude with a discussion on how to begin a work, how to decide what should go in the middle, and how to wrap things up.

CHAPTER 22

Dealing with Writer's Block

Writer's block can occur for any number of reasons. Sometimes, there's a simple reason, like you're bored with your topic. (In that case, switch topics—even if only temporarily. If you don't have time for that, try to see if you can come up with some ways to personalize your topic to make it more interesting.) Whatever the reason behind it, writer's block is no fun. In this chapter, you'll learn how to deal with it and move forward.

Anti–Writer's Block Calisthenics

When you find you're suffering from writer's block, the agonizing thought of coming up with a sufficient amount of organized content can seem like an intimidating chore. Rather than becoming overwhelmed by the task ahead of you, there are writing exercises that might help.

Lead with Your Best Shot

The lead is the bait. It's the carrot you dangle in front of the reader. The purpose of the lead is to entice the reader, and make him or her want to read more.

A good lead can act as your incentive, too. It can entice you to want to write more. If it falls flat, it fails to do that. Sometimes, something as simple as rewriting the lead can provide the impetus to get your productivity back on track.

Sample Uninspiring Lead

Chronic Fatigue Syndrome and fibromyalgia advocate Pamela Rice Hahn spoke to the Celina Chamber of Commerce last night about things local businesses can do to help make shopping a friendlier experience for those in the community who suffer from illnesses or deal with disabilities.

Lead, Rewritten as a "Visual" Lead

With slow, deliberate movements, the woman—her ankles swollen, her dress a bit too tight across her wide hips—lumbered to the podium. Facing the audience, she took a deep breath and said, "In a nation that celebrates physical fitness and supermodel beauties, it's difficult for someone with challenges like mine to be taken seriously. You see: I don't look sick; I just look fat." Thus began what proved to be an hour-long, insightful speech by author and Chronic Fatigue Syndrome and fibromyalgia advocate Pamela Rice Hahn.

Edit for Sensitivity or Other Problems

Sometimes, your subconscious (or conscious) can do a number on you, especially if you've written something that, while accurate, may cause discomfort for another person or introduce unnecessary controversy that distracts from the intent of your message. Other times, your concern may just be overly long descriptions, verbose passages, or maybe a word that doesn't sound quite right.

ALERT!

Perfectionism is a form of procrastination. Don't get hung up on honing each and every word to make it perfect, if that's keeping you from completing your assignment. You want your writing to be the best it can be, but you don't want editing to become your excuse for not finishing.

If you suspect that might be the case, read over what you've written thus far and highlight or underline any passages about which you feel the least bit uncomfortable. (It isn't necessary at this point to make a decision as to whether or not to cut or replace those passages. The exercise is to make them stand out in such a way that you know you'll remember to address such issues when you do your final draft.)

With slow, deliberate movements, the woman—her ankles swollen, her dress a bit too tight across her wide hips—lumbered to the podium. Facing the audience, she took a deep breath and said, "In a nation that celebrates physical fitness and supermodel beauties, it's difficult for someone with challenges like mine to be taken seriously. You see: I don't look sick; I just look fat." Thus began what proved to be an hour-long, insightful speech by author and chronic fatigue syndrome and fibromyalgia advocate Pamela Rice Hahn.

Give Yourself Permission to Fill In the Blanks Later

Your most important task while you write your first draft is to "get your story down"—something that's difficult to do if you keep interrupting yourself to look up facts or search for the perfect word. To avoid such disruptions to the flow of your writing, adapt a "code" or place marker (that's easy for you to remember and one that won't be confused with any other part of your manuscript, such as publisher formatting codes) to insert into your paragraphs. Make this identifier unique so that it's easy to search for later.

Shortly before leaving office, in a January 2002 press release Surgeon General Dr. David Satcher put the number of people diagnosed with Chronic Fatigue Syndrome at one million. The local health department estimates that number locally is ***xxx, with another ***xxx locally who must cope with other disabling conditions like MS and arthritis.

Hone Your Outline

If you're still struggling with decisions about what shape your writing should take, there are steps you can take to help you further develop your outline. One method is to pick a word or term specific to your topic and write out a definition for that word. Then do another. Starting with the simplest, more elementary terms and progressing to the more complex, place those terms in the order in which you think they should be introduced in your paper.

For longer works, like a novel, chances are you already have an idea about some of the scenes you plan to include. For a romance, for example, write up the first meeting and first kiss scenes. Perhaps write another scene that includes a description of one of the places where you intend for your hero and heroine to spend some time. Once you have several such scenes written, decide where you think you should place them in the book and write your outline around those scenes.

Coming Up with Ideas

One of the most common questions asked of writers is: Where do you get your ideas? Some authors get incredibly frustrated with the question, because the simple answer is: All over the place! (In fact, once you begin writing on a daily basis, you may eventually ask yourself, "How do I get the ideas to stop long enough so I can decide which one I want to write about next?")

There is no set formula to use to come up with ideas for stories, or non-fiction articles—or any form of writing, really. What you'll find is that the more you exercise your creativity, the more ideas just tend to pop into your head. Sometimes, you'll get a partial idea, and a few days later a slightly different idea will come. Your subconscious may combine the two and come up with a completely innovative third idea that you'll find absolutely brilliant, and that will get you motivated to write.

The simple trick is to be open to these ideas as they come along. Your imagination is like a muscle. The more you allow your imagination to play, the fitter it will become at generating interesting ideas.

Immediate Ideas

For short-term ideas, there are a variety of tricks you can keep in your magic imagination bag. The following list provides some examples, but don't think of it as an exhaustive list. The more you play, the more you're likely to come up with ideas that work for you. As mentioned above, the trick is to be open to ideas as they come along.

On the Bus

As you ride around waiting to get to your destination, covertly observe other people on the bus. Where do you think they might be going? What kind of mood are they in? What kind of story can you weave about the people, coming up with the history of how they got here and where they are going now? What are they wearing? Are they dressed shabbily, or are they dressed immaculately? Use these as a springboard, and let your imagination run wild. Do you think that any of the people on the bus actually know each other, but are pretending not to for some strange reason? All of these questions can give you traits for characters that you can use in your own stories.

In the News

What's happening in your community? What's happening across the country? In the world? One little element of a news story or a human interest feature can tweak wonderful ideas. Keep a notepad beside you and jot down ideas as they come. Play a game, and pull one element from one story (such as a break-in at the doughnut shop) and combine it with an element from another story (like the purchase of a winning lottery ticket by a little old lady). How can you combine these into an interesting story?

On Your Bookshelf

You can do the same thing with the books on your bookshelf. Flip through them and look for things that trigger your imagination. Sometimes, a simple short phrase is enough to do it. Just pick a page at random and see what lies there waiting for you. Any book works, too. A book on prescription drugs might give you a great idea for a murder mystery.

On Television

This can work too, but be careful with it. You don't want to get caught becoming engrossed in what you're watching. Grab your remote, and flip through channels at random. Maybe an ice bucket you see on the shopping channel will give you some sort of idea. Combine that with the tube of lipstick you see a couple of channels later, and you might end up with the image of the evening after a celebration with smeared lipstick and a little too much champagne.

The Yellow Pages

Sure, it seems absurd, but the Yellow Pages offer a concise encyclopedia of the businesses and services that are available in your area. Each one is a potential idea for the location of a story. If you're having trouble coming up with names for your characters, try the phone book. There's a big list of names there. Choose a first name from one page, then choose a last name from a different page. Just be careful to pick and choose and not name your characters after someone who already exists.

Long-Term Ideas

Long-term ideas are really just an extension of the short-term idea generating strategies. The only trick is to come up with some way to remember what all of these ideas are when you don't have time to work on them. Using the story-generating ideas in the short-term section, you'll soon find that you'll have more ideas than you know what to do with.

It's a great idea to keep an ideas folder. When your ideas come, write them down—don't count on being able to remember them later. Whether you write your ideas on scraps of paper and keep them in a file folder, or whether you use a notebook dedicated to that purpose, record the idea at the time you get it so it'll be there later. Never count on your memory when it comes to story ideas, because they tend to be fleeting things that disappear if they don't get used.

When you're making your notes, make sure that you include enough information so that you'll remember it later. You may not come back to the idea for months or years, so you'll want to have as much information as you can to trigger your memory.

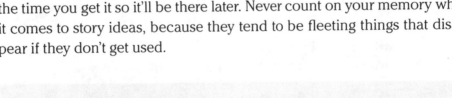

Bad Idea Notes Example

Ice cream parlor—chocolate sprinkles

While the above example might give you enough to recall the idea a few days later, as time wears on, you're bound to forget about the details you didn't write down. If you make more extensive notes, however, the chances are much better that you'll be able to recall the entire scene, or at least be able to reconstruct it.

Good Idea Notes Example

Flashback: Little girl—in ice cream parlor—got money from grandmother to buy a cone—wants chocolate sprinkles—doesn't have enough money—nice old gentleman gives her the extra nickel—affects little girl for rest of life—she becomes compassionate remembering the kindness of the old man who helped her

Your ideas folder can also contain copies of magazine articles or newspaper clippings, but you may also want to attach a sheet outlining why this piece spoke to you and what kind of ideas it gave to you. As far as your notes go, write down everything you can. Personal observations, snippets of conversations you have overheard, and impressions about setting and mood are all important things to record. If you have ideas for dialogue, it's a good idea to elaborate in your notes a little bit, so that the dialogue has context, and you'll have an idea later about how you wanted to use the quote.

Keep yourself committed to maintaining these notes, and you'll always have a resource to consult when you're stuck for ideas.

Other Ideas That May Help

It's easy to overlook the obvious when you're under pressure. Facing a writing deadline can be a stressful time. Here are some other things you can do to help you get beyond writer's block:

- Break up the writing assignment into a series of tasks; promise yourself some sort of reward each time you complete one.
- Decide you need to get the job done, and just start typing.
- Make sure you understand the assignment.
- Talk to yourself. (Pretend you're verbally explaining your topic to somebody and write down what you say.)
- Write the ending. (This way when you go back to the beginning and start writing your paper, the end really will be "in sight.")

Probably the most important thing to remember when you encounter writer's block is that it isn't a fatal affliction. It's only a symptom that your mind is temporarily playing tricks on you, and for whatever reason is trying to interfere with your productivity. If one exercise you use to overcome your block doesn't work, try another. As long as you remain determined to get the (writing) job done and don't allow yourself to become overwhelmed by the task, you'll eventually determine your best writing process.

Writing is like any worthwhile endeavor: Persistence results in the reward of a job well done.

APPENDIX A

Further Reading

Academic Writing

Asher, Donald. *Graduate Admissions Essays: Write Your Way into the Graduate School of Your Choice.* (Berkeley, CA: Ten Speed Press, 2000)

Bolker, Joan. *Writing Your Dissertation in Fifteen Minutes a Day: A Guide to Starting, Revising, and Finishing Your Doctoral Thesis.* (New York: Owl Books, 1998)

Cuddon, J. A. *The Penguin Dictionary of Literary Terms and Literary Theory.* (New York: Penguin, 2000)

Germano, William. *Getting It Published: A Guide for Scholars and Anyone Else Serious about Serious Books* (Chicago Guides to Writing, Editing, and Publishing). (Chicago, IL: University of Chicago Press, 2001)

Hoffman, Gary and Glynis Hoffman. *Adios, Strunk and White: A Handbook for the New Academic Essay.* (Huntington, CA: Verve Press, 2003)

Lester, James D., Jr. *Writing Research Papers: A Complete Guide.* (New York: Longman, 2006)

Madsen, David. *Successful Dissertations and Theses: A Guide to Graduate Student Research from Proposal to Completion* (Jossey-Bass Higher and Adult Education Series). (San Francisco, CA: Jossey-Bass, 1991)

Markman, Roberta H., Peter T. Markman, and Marie L. Waddell. *10 Steps in Writing the Research Paper.* (Hauppauge, NY: Barrons Educational Series, 2000)

Oshima, Alice and Ann Hogue. *Writing Academic English.* (Upper Saddle River, NJ: Prentice-Hall Trade, Pearson Educational, 2005)

Page, Marti and Justin M. Cohen. *Yale Daily News Guide to Writing College Papers.* (New York: Kaplan, 2000)

Rudestam, Kjell Erik and Rae R. Newton. *Surviving Your Dissertation: A Comprehensive Guide to Content and Process.* (Thousand Oaks, CA: Sage Publications, 2007)

Stelzer, Richard J. *How to Write a Winning Personal Statement for Graduate and Professional School.* (Princeton, NJ: Petersons Guides, 1997)

Swales, John M. and Christine A. Beer Feak. *Academic Writing for Graduate Students, Second Edition: Essential Tasks and Skills.* (Ann Arbor, MI: University of Michigan Press, 2004)

Turabian, Kate L., Wayne C. Booth, Gregory G. Colomb, and Joseph M. Williams. *A Manual for Writers of Research Papers, Theses, and Disserta-

tions, Seventh Edition: Chicago Style for Students and Researchers (Chicago Guides to Writing, Editing, and Publishing). (Chicago, IL: University of Chicago Press, 2007)

Turabian, Kate L. *A Manual for Writers of Term Papers, Theses, and Dissertations* (Chicago Guides to Writing, Editing, and Publishing). (Chicago, IL: University of Chicago Press, 1996)

Business Style Guides

Alred, Gerald J., Charles T. Brusaw, and Walter E. Oliu. *The Business Writer's Handbook.* (New York: St. Martin's Press, 2006)

Cunningham, Helen and Brenda Greene. *The Business Style Handbook: An A-to-Z Guide for Writing on the Job with Tips from Communications Experts at the Fortune 500.* (New York: McGraw Hill, 2002)

Economist Staff. *The Economist Style Guide: A Concise Guide for All Your Business Communications.* (London: Profile Books, 2005)

Martin, Paul R., ed. *The Wall Street Journal Guide to Business Style and Usage.* (New York: Free Press, Simon & Schuster, 2002)

Business Writing Guides

Blake, Gary and Robert W. Bly. *The Elements of Business Writing: A Guide to Writing Clear, Concise Letters, Memos, Reports, Proposals, and Other Business Documents.* (New York: Longman, 1992)

Bly, Robert W. *The Copywriter's Handbook: A Step-by-Step Guide to Writing Copy That Sells.* (New York: Owl Books, 2006)

Bly, Robert W. *The Encyclopedia of Business Letters, Fax Memos, and E-Mail.* (Franklin Lakes, NJ: Career Press, 1999)

Bond, Alan J. *Over 300 Successful Business Letters for All Occasions.* (Hauppauge, NY: Barrons Educational Series, 1998)

Chase, Maureen and Sandy Trupp. *Office Emails That Really Click.* (Newport, RI: Aegis Publishing Group, 2000)

Hogan, R. Craig. *Explicit Business Writing: Best Practices for the Twenty-First Century.* (Bloomington, IL: The Business Writing Center, 2005)

De Vries, Mary A. *Prentice Hall's Complete Desk Reference for Office Professionals.* (Paramus, NJ: Prentice Hall Press, 2000)

Duncan, Melba J. *The New Executive Assistant: Advice for Succeeding in Your Career.* (New York: McGraw-Hill Professional Publishing, 1997)

Freed, Richard C. and Joe Romano. *Writing Winning Business Proposals: Your Guide to Landing the Client, Making the Sale and Persuading the Boss.* (New York: McGraw-Hill Professional Publishing, 2003)

Geffner, Andrea B. *Business English.* (Hauppauge, NY: Barrons Educational Series, 2003)

Griffin, Jack. *The Complete Handbook of Model Business Letters.* (Paramus, NJ: Prentice Hall Press, 1997)

Griffin, Jack and Tom Power. *How to Say It at Work: Putting Yourself Across with Power Words, Phrases, Body Language, and Communication Secrets.* (Paramus, NJ: Prentice Hall Press, 1998)

Hamper, Robert J. and L. Sue Baugh. *Handbook for Writing Proposals.* (New York: McGraw-Hill/Contemporary Books, 1995)

Harrison, Mim. *Words at Work: An Insider's Guide to the Language of Professions.* (New York: Walker & Company, 2007)

Munter, Mary. *Guide to Managerial Communication: Effective Business Writing and Speaking.* (Paramus, NJ: Prentice Hall Press, 2005)

O'Donnell, Michael. *Writing Business Plans That Get Results: A Step-by-Step Guide.* (New York: McGraw-Hill/Contemporary Books, 1991)

Piotrowski, Maryann V. *Effective Business Writing: A Guide for Those Who Write on the Job.* (New York: HarperCollins, 1996)

Porter-Roth, Bud. *Request for Proposal: A Guide to Effective RFP Development.* (Reading, MA: Addison-Wesley Professional, 2001)

Sant, Tom. *Persuasive Business Proposals: Writing to Win Customers, Clients, and Contracts.* (New York: AMACOM, 2003)

Copyediting

Einsohn, Amy. *The Copyeditor's Handbook: A Guide for Book Publishing and Corporate Communications.* (Berkeley, CA: University of California Press, 2005)

Judd, Karen. *Copyediting: A Practical Guide, 3rd ed.* (Menlo Park, CA: Crisp Learning, 2001)

Rooney, Edmund and Oliver Witte. *Copy Editing for Professionals.* (Champaign, IL: Stipes Publishing Co., 2000)

Stoughton, Mary. *Substance & Style: Instruction and Practice in Copyediting.* (Redway, CA: Editorial Experts, 1996)

Copyright

Bunnin, Brad and Peter Beren. *The Writer's Legal Companion: The Complete Handbook for the Working Writer.* (Cambridge, MA: Perseus Publishing, 1998)

Fishman, Stephen. *The Copyright Handbook: How to Protect & Use Written Works.* (Soquel, CA: Nolo Press, 2005)

Fishman, Stephen. *The Public Domain: How to Find & Use Copyright-free Writings, Music, Art & More.* (Soquel, CA: Nolo Press, 2006)

Jassin, Lloyd J. and Steve C. Schecter. *The Copyright Permission and Libel Handbook: A Step-by-Step Guide for Writers, Editors, and Publishers* (Wiley Books for Writers). (New York: John Wiley & Sons, 1998)

McSherry, Corynne. *Who Owns Academic Work: Battling for Control of Intellectual Property.* (Cambridge, MA: Harvard University Press, 2003)

Stim, Richard. *Getting Permission: How to License and Clear Copyrighted Materials Online and Off, 2nd ed.* (Soquel, CA: Nolo Press, 2004)

Editing and Proofreading

Anderson, Laura Killen. *McGraw-Hill's Proofreading Handbook.* (New York: McGraw-Hill, 2005)

Browne, Renni and Dave King. *Self-Editing for Fiction Writers, 2nd. ed.: How to Edit Yourself into Print.* (New York: HarperCollins, 2004)

Camp, Sue C. *Developing Proofreading and Editing Skills.* (New York: Glencoe McGraw-Hill/Irwin, 2004)

Cook, Claire Kehrwald. *Line by Line: How to Edit Your Own Writing.* (Boston: Houghton Mifflin Co., 1986)

Ryan, Buck and Michael O'Donnell. *The Editor's Toolbox: A Reference Guide for Beginners and Professionals.* (Ames, IA: Iowa State University Press, 2001)

Essays

Learning Express Editors. *Write Better Essays in Just 20 Minutes a Day, 2nd ed.* (New York: LearningExpress, LLC, 2006)

Gutkind, Lee. *The Art of Creative Nonfiction: Writing and Selling the Literature of Reality* (Wiley Books for Writers Series). (New York: John Wiley & Sons, 1997)

Gutkind, Lee, ed. *The Essayist at Work: Profiles of Creative Nonfiction Writers.* (Portsmouth, NH: Heinemann, 1998)

Grammar and Usage Guides

Davidson, Mark. *Right, Wrong, and Risky: A Dictionary of Today's American English Usage.* (New York: W. W. Norton, 2005)

Feierman, Joanne. *Action Grammar: Fast, No-Hassle Answers on Everyday Usage and Punctuation.* (New York: Fireside, 1995)

Garner, Bryan A. *Garner's Modern American Usage.* (New York: Oxford University Press, USA, 2003)

Hahn, Pamela Rice and Dennis E. Hensley. *Alpha Teach Yourself Grammar and Style in 24 Hours.* (East Rutherford, NJ: Alpha, Penguin Group (USA) Inc., 2000)

O'Conner, Patricia T. *Woe Is I: The Grammarphobe's Guide to Better English in Plain English.* (New York: Riverhead Trade, 2004)

Princeton Review. *Grammar Smart: A Guide to Perfect Usage* (Princeton Review Series). (New York: Princeton Review, 2001)

Shertzer, Margaret. *The Elements of Grammar.* (New York: Longman, 1996)

Stilman, Anne. *Grammatically Correct: The Writer's Essential Guide to Punctuation, Spelling, Style, Usage and Grammar.* (Cincinnati, OH: Writer's Digest Books, 2004)

Straus, Jane. *The Blue Book of Grammar and Punctuation, 9th ed.* (Mill Valley, CA: Jane Straus, 2006)

Tarshis, Barry. *Grammar for Smart People: Your User-Friendly Guide to Speaking and Writing Better English.* (New York: Pocket Books, 1993)

Thurman, Susan and Larry Shea. *The Only Grammar Book You'll Ever Need: A One-Stop Source for Every Writing Assignment.* (Avon, MA: Adams Media Corporation, 2003)

Walsh, Bill. *Lapsing into a Comma.* (New York: McGraw-Hill, 2000)

Grants and Fundraising

Ahern, Tom. *How to Write Fundraising Materials That Raise More Money: The Art, the Science, the Secrets.* (Medfield, MA: Emerson & Church, Publishers, 2007)

Barbato, Joseph and Danielle S. Furlich. *Writing for a Good Cause: The Complete Guide to Crafting Proposals and Other Persuasive Pieces for Nonprofits.* (New York: Fireside, 2000)

Blum, Laurie. *The Complete Guide to Getting a Grant: How to Turn Your Ideas into Dollars.* (New York: John Wiley & Sons, 1996)

Brewer, Ernest W., ed., Charles M. Achilles, ed., and Jay R. Fuhriman. *Finding Funding: Grantwriting from Start to Finish Including Project Management and Internet Use.* (Thousand Oaks, CA: Corwin Press, 2001)

Brown, Larissa Golden and Martin John Brown. *Demystifying Grant Seeking: What You REALLY Need to Do to Get Grants.* (New York: John Wiley & Sons, Jossey-Bass, 2001)

Browning, Bev. *Grant Writing for Dummies.* (New York: Wiley Publishing, Inc., 2005)

Burke, Jim and Carol Ann Prater. *I'll Grant You That: A Step-By-Step Guide to Finding Funds, Designing Winning Projects, and Writing Powerful Proposals.* (Portsmouth, NH: Heinemann, 2000)

Carlson, Mim and The Alliance for Nonprofit Management. *Winning Grants: Step by Step, 2nd ed.* (New York: John Wiley & Sons, Jossey-Bass, 2002)

Golden, Susan L. *Secrets of Successful Grantsmanship: A Guerrilla Guide to Raising Money* (Jossey-Bass Nonprofit Sector Series). (New York: John Wiley & Sons, Jossey-Bass, 1997)

Karsh, Ellen and Arlen Sue Fox. *The Only Grant-Writing Book You'll Ever Need: Top Grant Writers and Grant Givers Share Their Secrets.* (New York: Carroll & Graf, 2006)

Kuniholm, Roland. *The Complete Book of Model Fundraising Letters.* (Paramus, NJ: Prentice-Hall, 1995)

Mutz, John and Katherine Murray. *Fundraising for Dummies, 2nd ed.* (New York: Wiley Publishing, Inc., 2005)

Warwick, Mal. *How to Write Successful Fundraising Letters.* (New York: John Wiley & Sons, Jossey-Bass, 2001)

Humor

Carter, Judy. *The Comedy Bible: From Stand-Up to Sitcom—The Comedy Writer's Ultimate How-to Guide.* (New York: Fireside, 2001)

Helitzer, Melvin. *Comedy Writing Secrets, 2nd Edition: The Best-Selling Book on How to Think Funny, Write Funny, Act Funny, And Get Paid For It.* (Cincinnati: Writer's Digest Books, 2005)

Kachuba, John B. *How to Write Funny: Add Humor to Every Kind of Writing.* (Cincinnati: Writer's Digest Books, 2001)

Perret, Gene. *Business Humor: Jokes & How to Deliver Them.* (London, UK: Sterling Publications, 1998)

Perret, Gene. *The New Comedy Writing Step by Step.* (Sanger, CA: Quill Driver Books, 2007)

Rishel, Mary Ann. *Writing Humor: Creativity and the Comic Mind.* (Detroit, MI: Wayne State University Press, 2002)

Lateral Thinking

De Bono, Edward. *Lateral Thinking: Creativity Step-by-Step.* (New York: HarperCollins, 1990)

Sloane, Paul. *The Leader's Guide to Lateral Thinking Skills: Unlocking the Creativity and Innovation in You and Your Team.* (London, UK: Kogan Page, 2006)

Letter Writing

Booher, Dianna. *Great Personal Letters for Busy People: 501 Ready-to-Use Letters for Every Occasion.* (New York: McGraw-Hill Professional Publishing, 2005)

De Vries, Mary Ann. *The New American Handbook of Letter Writing, 2nd ed.* (New York: Signet, 2000)

Goodwin, Gabrielle and David MacFarlane. *Writing Thank-You Notes: Finding the Perfect Words.* (London, UK: Sterling Publications, 1999)

May, Debra Hart and Regina McAloney. *Everyday Letters for Busy People: Hundreds of Sample Letters You Can Copy or Adapt at a Minute's Notice.* (Franklin Lakes, NJ: Career Press, 2004)

Phillips, Ellen. *Shocked, Appalled, and Dismayed! How to Write Letters of Complaint That Get Results.* (New York: Vintage Books, 1998)

Shepherd, Margaret. *The Art of the Handwritten Note: A Guide to Reclaiming Civilized Communication.* (New York: Broadway Books, 2002)

Spizman, Robyn Freedman. *The Thank-You Book: Hundreds of Clever, Meaningful, and Purposeful Ways to Say Thank You.* (Atlanta: Active Parenting Publishers, 2004)

Marketing Guides

Brewer, Robert. *Writer's Market 2008.* (Cincinnati, OH: Writer's Digest Books, 2007)

Carroll, David. L. *A Manual of Writer's Tricks: Essential Advice for Fiction and Nonfiction Writers.* (New York: Four Walls Eight Windows, 2007)

Herman, Jeff. *Jeff Herman's Guide to Book Publishers, Editors & Literary Agents 2008: Who They Are! What They Want! How to Win Them Over!* (Stockbridge, MA: Three Dog Press, 2007)

Mosko, Lauren. *Novel & Short Story Writer's Market 2008.* (Cincinnati, OH: Writer's Digest Books, 2007)

Memoirs, Family History, Scrapbooking

Brown, Cynthia Stokes. *Like It Was: A Complete Guide to Writing Oral History.* (New York: Teachers & Writers, 2000)

Ives, Edward D. *The Tape-Recorded Interview: A Manual for Fieldworkers in Folklore and Oral History.* (Knoxville, TN: University of Tennessee Press, 1995)

Ledoux, Dennis. *Turning Memories into Memoirs: A Handbook for Writing Lifestories.* (Lisbon Falls, ME: Soleil Press, 2005)

Ritchie, Donald. *Doing Oral History.* (New York: Oxford University Press, USA, 2003)

Slan, Joanna Campbell. *Scrapbook Storytelling: Save Family Stories and Memories with Photos, Journaling and Your Own Creativity.* (Cincinnati, OH: Memory Makers Books, 1999)

Spence, Linda. *Legacy: A Step-by-Step Guide to Writing Personal History.* (Athens, OH: Ohio University Press, Swallow Press, 1997)

News Writing

Fox, Walter. *Writing the News: A Guide for Print Journalists.* (Ames, IA: Iowa State University Press, 2001)

Kershner, James W. *The Elements of News Writing.* (Boston, MA: Allyn & Bacon, 2004)

Knight, Robert M. *A Journalistic Approach to Good Writing: The Craft of Clarity.* (Ames, IA: Iowa State University Press, 2003)

Online and Electronic Writing

Angell, David and Brent Heslop. *The Elements of E-Mail Style: Communicate Effectively Via Electronic Mail.* (Upper Saddle River, NJ: Addison-Wesley Pub. Co., Pearson Educational, 1994)

Booher, Dianna. *E-Writing: 21st Century Tools for Effective Communication.* (New York: Pocket Books, 2001)

Garrand, Timothy. *Writing for Multimedia and the Web, Third Edition: A Practical Guide to Content Development for Interactive Media.* (Burlington, MA: Focal Press, 2006)

Korolenko, Michael. *Writing for Multimedia: A Guide and Source Book for the Digital Writer.* (Belmont, CA: Wadsworth Publishing Co., 1996)

Research Guides

Bass, Frank. *The Associated Press Guide to Internet Research and Reporting.* (Cambridge, MA: Perseus Publishing, 2002)

Berkman, Robert I. *Find It Fast: How to Uncover Expert Information on Any Subject Online or in Print* (Harper Resource Book). (New York: HarperCollins, 2000)

Booth, Wayne C., Gregory G. Colomb, and Joseph M. Williams. *The Craft of Research* (Chicago Guides to Writing, Editing, and Publishing). (Chicago, IL: University of Chicago Press, 1995)

Schlein, Alan M. *Find It Online, Fourth Edition: The Complete Guide to Online Research.* (Lanham, MD: Facts on Demand Press, 2004)

Speech and Speech Writing

Maggio, Rosalie. *How to Say It: Choice Words, Phrases, Sentences & Paragraphs for Every Situation.* (Paramus, NJ: Prentice-Hall Press, 2001)

McManus, Judith A. *How to Write and Deliver an Effective Speech.* (Princeton, NJ: Petersons Guides, 2002)

Style Guides

Siegal, Allan M. and William G. Connolly. *The New York Times Manual of Style and Usage: The Official Style Guide Used by the Writers and Editors of the World's Most Authoritative Newspaper.* (New York: Three Rivers Press, 2002)

Coghill, Anne M. and Lorrin R. Garson. *The ACS Style Guide: Effective Communication of Scientific Information.* (Washington, DC: ACS Books, 2006)

Dodd, Janet S. *The ACS Style Guide: A Manual for Authors and Editors.* (Washington, DC: American Chemical Society, 1997)

Gibaldi, Joseph. *MLA Handbook for Writers of Research Papers, 6th ed.* (New York: Modern Language Association of America, 2003)

Gibaldi, Joseph. *MLA Style Manual and Guide to Scholarly Publishing, 2nd ed.* (New York: Modern Language Association of America, 1998)

Goldstein, Norm, ed. *The Associated Press Stylebook and Briefing on Media Law.* (Cambridge, MA: Perseus Books, 2007)

JAMA & Archives Journals. *American Medical Association Manual of Style: A Guide for Authors and Editors (AMA), 10th ed.* (New York: Oxford University Press, USA, 2007)

Lynch, Patrick and Sarah Horton. *Web Style Guide, 2nd edition.* (Online edition: *www.webstyleguide.com*, 2005)

Lynch, Patrick and Sarah Horton. *Web Style Guide: Basic Design Principles for Creating Web Sites, Second Edition.* (New Haven, CT: Yale University Press, 2002)

Merriam-Webster. *Merriam-Webster's Manual for Writers and Editors.* (Springfield, MA: Merriam-Webster, 1998)

Sabin, William A. *The Gregg Reference Manual: A Manual of Style, Grammar, Usage, and Formatting, 10th ed.* (New York: McGraw-Hill Professional, 2004)

Schwartz, Marilyn. *Guidelines for Bias-Free Writing.* (Bloomington, IN: Indiana University Press, 1995)

Skillin, Marjorie E. and Robert Malcolm Gay. *Words into Type.* (Upper Saddle River, NJ: Pearson Educational, 1974)

Strunk, Jr., William, E. B. White, Charles Osgood, and Roger Angell. *The Elements of Style.* (New York: Longman, 1999)

Sutcliffe, Andrea, ed. *New York Public Library Writer's Guide to Style and Usage.* (New York: HarperCollins, 1994)

Trimmer, Joseph F. *A Guide to MLA Documentation: With an Appendix on APA Style.* (Boston: Houghton Mifflin Co., 1998)

University of Chicago Press Staff. *The Chicago Manual of Style: The Essential Guide for Writers, Editors, and Publishers, 15th ed.* (Chicago: University of Chicago Press, 2003)

University of Chicago Press Staff. *The Chicago Manual of Style: The Essential Guide for Writers, Editors, and Publishers, 15th ed.* (CD-ROM) (Chicago: University of Chicago Press, 2006)

Walker, Janice R. and Todd Taylor. *The Columbia Guide to Online Style.* (New York: Columbia University Press, 2006).

Williams, Joseph M. *Style: Ten Lessons in Clarity and Grace.* (Upper Saddle River, NJ: Addison-Wesley Pub. Co., Pearson Educational, 1999)

Williams, Joseph M. *Style: Lessons in Clarity and Grace, 9th ed.* (New York: Longman, 2006)

Technical Editing and Writing

Bremer, Michael. *Untechnical Writing—How to Write About Technical Subjects and Products So Anyone Can Understand.* (Concord, CA: UnTechnical Press, 1999)

Lindsell-Roberts, Sheryl. *Technical Writing for Dummies.* (New York: Wiley Publishing, Inc., 2001)

Microsoft Corporation. *The Microsoft Manual of Style for Technical Publications.* (Redmond, WA: Microsoft Press, 2003)

Pringle, Alan S. and Sarah S. O'Keefe. *Technical Writing 101: A Real-World Guide to Planning and Writing Technical Documentation.* (Research Triangle Park, NC: Scriptorium Press, 2003)

Tarutz, Judith A. *Technical Editing: The Practical Guide for Editors and Writers* (Hewlett-Packard Press). (Reading, MA: Addison-Wesley, 1992)

Writing and Communications Guides

Booher, Dianna. *Communicate with Confidence!* (New York: McGraw-Hill Professional Publishing, 1994)

Brown, Cynthia Stokes. *Like It Was: A Complete Guide to Writing Oral History.* (New York: Teachers & Writers, 2000)

Burroway, Janet and Elizabeth Stuckey-French. *Writing Fiction: A Guide to Narrative Craft, 5th ed.* (New York: Longman, 2006)

Condrill, Jo and Bennie Bough. *101 Ways to Improve Your Communication Skills Instantly, 4th ed.* (Beverly Hills, CA: Goalminds, 2005)

Flesch, Rudolf and A. H. Lass. *The Classic Guide to Better Writing.* (New York: HarperCollins, 1996)

Flesch, Rudolf and Salvatore Raimondo. *How to Write, Speak and Think More Effectively.* (New York: New American Library, 1994)

Gutkind, Lee. *The Art of Creative Nonfiction: Writing and Selling the Literature of Reality* (Wiley Books for Writers Series). (New York: John Wiley & Sons, 1997)

Heffron, Jack. *The Writer's Idea Book.* (Cincinnati, OH: Writers Digest Books, 2002)

Jacobi, Peter P. *The Magazine Article: How to Think It, Plan It, Write It.* (Bloomington, IN: Indiana University Press, 1997)

Kane, Thomas S. *The New Oxford Guide to Writing.* (New York: Oxford University Press, USA, 1994)

Knight, Robert M. *A Journalistic Approach to Good Writing: The Craft of Clarity.* (Ames, IA: Iowa State University Press, 2003)

Lamb, Sandra E. *How to Write It: A Complete Guide to Everything You'll Ever Write.* (Berkeley, CA: Ten Speed Press, 2006)

Lamott, Anne. *Bird by Bird: Some Instructions on Writing and Life.* (New York: Anchor, 1995)

Lederer, Richard and Richard Dowis. *The Write Way: The S.P.E.L.L. Guide to Real-Life Writing* (Society for the Preservation of English Language and Literature). (New York: Pocket Books, 1995)

Ledoux, Dennis. *Turning Memories into Memoirs: A Handbook for Writing Lifestories.* (Lisbon Falls, ME: Soleil Press, 2005)

McClanahan, Rebecca. *Word Painting: A Guide to Writing More Descriptively.* (Cincinnati, OH: Writers Digest Books, 2000)

O'Conner, Patricia T. *Words Fail Me: What Everyone Who Writes Should Know About Writing.* (New York: Harvest Books, 2000)

Rozakis, Laurie. *The Complete Idiot's Guide to Writing Well.* (Upper Saddle River, NJ: Alpha Books, 2000)

Skillin, Marjorie E. and Robert Malcolm Gay. *Words into Type.* (Upper Saddle River, NJ: Pearson Educational, 1974)

Slan, Joanna Campbell. *Scrapbook Storytelling: Save Family Stories and Memories with Photos, Journaling and Your Own Creativity.* (Cincinnati, OH: Memory Makers Books, 1999)

Spence, Linda. *Legacy: A Step-by-Step Guide to Writing Personal History.* (Athens, OH: Ohio University Press, Swallow Press, 1997)

Spizman, Robyn Freedman. *When Words Matter Most: Thoughtful Words and Deeds to Express Just the Right Thing at the Just the Right Time.* (New York: Crown Publishing, 1996)

Stein, Sol. *Stein on Writing.* (Irvine, CA: Griffin Trade Paperback, 2000)

Trimble, John R. *Writing with Style: Conversations on the Art of Writing.* (Paramus, NJ: Prentice-Hall, 2000)

Whiteley, Carol. *The Everything® Creative Writing Book: All You Need to Know to Write a Novel, Play, Short Story, Screen Play, Poem, or Article.* (Avon, MA: Adams Media Corporation, 2002)

Zinsser, William K. *On Writing Well: The Classic Guide to Writing Nonfiction.* (New York: HarperCollins, 2006)

Writing for Publication

Camenson, Blythe, Marshall I. Cook, and Marshall J. Cook. *Your Novel Proposal: From Creation to Contract: The Complete Guide to Writing Query Letters, Synopses and Proposals for Agents and Editors.* (Cincinnati, OH: Writers Digest Books, 1999)

Germano, William. *Getting It Published: A Guide for Scholars and Anyone Else Serious About Serious Books* (Chicago Guides to Writing, Editing, and Publishing). (Chicago, IL: University of Chicago Press, 2001)

Herman, Deborah Levine, and Jeff Herman. *Write the Perfect Book Proposal: 10 That Sold and Why, 2nd ed.* (New York: John Wiley & Sons, 2001)

Korolenko, Michael. *Writing for Multimedia: A Guide and Source Book for the Digital Writer.* (Belmont, CA: Wadsworth Publishing Co., 1996)

Lukeman, Noah T. *The First Five Pages: A Writer's Guide to Staying Out of the Rejection Pile.* (New York: Fireside, 2000)

Lyon, Elizabeth. *Nonfiction Book Proposals Anybody Can Write: How to Get a Contract and Advance Before Writing Your Book.* (New York: Perigee Trade, 2000)

Trottier, David. *The Screenwriter's Bible: A Complete Guide to Writing, Formatting, and Selling Your Script, 4th ed.* (Los Angeles, CA: Silman-James Press, 2005)

Common Formats

B

Letter: Block Style, Business, Justified Body

Company Name
Name (optional if company name given; name only for personal correspondence)
Address line
City, State Zip
Phone number (optional)

Month ##(date), #### (year) (Date; day of the week optional)

Mr.[First Name][Middle Initial][Last Name](Recipient information)
Address line
City, State Zip

Dear Mr.[Last Name]:

Body introductory paragraph: I agree we need to meet to discuss your concerns about my dog. However, I'm afraid there is more to the story about why my dog barks at your children than what you may be aware. You see, until you moved next door, Veener never had a barking problem. Now, before you think I'm being defensive or making excuses for my dog's behavior, allow me to explain.

Body paragraph: I myself couldn't understand the change in what used to be Veener's well-trained behavior until a neighbor pointed out that he'd seen your children throwing stones at my dog and poking sticks at him through the fence. I began to keep an eye on Veener when I let him outside, and sure enough, I saw this happen for myself. I talked to your boys about this one day when I was outside working on the yard, explaining to them how dangerous it is to throw rocks—that one could get caught up in the lawn mower, that sort of thing—and both boys promised it wouldn't happen again. However, while your boys have kept their promise not to throw anything, they still occasionally "pretend" like they're going to throw something, which gets Veener upset. I've seen this happen, as has my neighbor. Now when I hear my dog barking, I bring him inside.

Body paragraph: I do take some responsibility for this problem. I now realize that I should have spoken with you about what's been happening when I first learned of the problem, rather than take my "oh well, boys will be boys" approach and let it drop. I apologize for that error in judgment on my part.

Body closing paragraphs: Here's what I propose we can do to rectify the situation: I'm hoping that you, your wife, and the boys will join me outside at my picnic table some evening soon for some cookies, coffee (or milk), and conversation. I'd like to "properly introduce" your sons to my dog so they can get to know each other. I think this will help solve what is a problem for all of us. I'll give you a call tomorrow and see if we can schedule this meeting within the next few days.

I'm confident that together we can solve this problem and get our neighborhood back to being a nice, quiet pleasant place to live.

Sincerely,

(Signature)

[First Name][Middle Initial][Last Name]
Title, if appropriate

Letter: Block Style, Business, Reference Line, Justified Body, End Notations

(Note: This is the reply to the fax later in this appendix.)

Company Name
Name (optional if company name given; name only for personal correspondence)
Address line
City, State Zip
Phone number (optional)

Month ##(date), #### (year) (Date; day of the week optional)

Reference: (Phrase explaining purpose of letter)

Mr.[First Name][Middle Initial][Last Name](Recipient information)
Address line
City, State Zip

Dear Mr.[Last Name]:

Body introductory paragraph: Thank you for bringing the streetlight problem to my attention. The City of Celina's Utility Department recognizes that well-lit streets are an essential element of helping to keep our neighborhoods safe. Therefore, we always appreciate when people take the time to let us know when a light needs replacing.

Body paragraph: I dispatched crews to correct that situation today. All streetlights should now be working properly, illuminating your neighborhood once again.

Body closing paragraph: Please feel free to contact me in the future should you experience any similar problems.

Sincerely,

Company Name

(Signature)

[First Name][Middle Initial][Last Name]
Title

prh (Typist's initials)
appb\blockformal.doc (File Name Notation, which indicates where and how the letter is stored)
Enclosure (Enclosure Notation: used if letter accompanied by an enclosure)
By Priority Mail (Delivery Notation: used if letter sent via means other than standard mail)
cc: Ms.[First Name][Middle Initial][Last Name](Copy Notation: name or names of anyone receiving a copy of the letter)

Letter: Modified-Block Style, Business

(Condolences and Sympathy Letters: casual business associate)

Company Name
Name (optional if company name given; name only for personal correspondence)
Address line
City, State Zip
Phone number (optional)

September 30, 2007

Mr.[First Name][Middle Initial][Last Name](Recipient information)
Address line
City, State Zip

Dear Mr.[Last Name]:

Body introductory paragraph: I was saddened to hear of the death of your grandmother.

Body paragraph: I could tell you were close by the number of times you brought in cookies you'd baked together to share with the rest of the office. All too often people don't have a relative with whom they can share such moments and I hope you find comfort in your memories of those times you had together.

Body closing paragraph: Please extend my condolences to the rest of your family. I know all of you have suffered a great loss.

Sincerely,
Company Name

(Signature)
[First Name][Middle Initial][Last Name]
Title

Letter: Modified-Block Style, Business, Indented Paragraphs, Multiple Copy Recipients

(Condolences and sympathy letters: offer of specific assistance to a business associate)

Company Name
Name (optional if company name given; name only for personal correspondence)
Address line
City, State Zip
Phone number (optional)

September 30, 2007

Mr.[First Name][Middle Initial][Last Name]
Address line
City, State Zip

Dear Mr.[Last Name]:

Body introductory paragraph: I join the rest of the office in offering you sympathy on the death of your mother.

Body paragraph: There is never a convenient time for such tragedy, of course, but I was thinking that if you believe it'd help ease your burden during this time, I could edit this month's employee newsletter for you. I am in no way proposing that I take over your job. Everybody recognizes the fine job you do month in and month out on that publication. I count myself as one of your biggest fans. My hope is that temporarily easing your workload somewhat may help you as you deal with your grief. I'll check with you in a day or two to see if you'd like my assistance on the newsletter, or if there is any other way you prefer that I help.

Body closing paragraph: First and foremost, know that you have my heartfelt sympathy during this time of loss.

Sincerely,

Company Name

(Signature)

[First Name][Middle Initial][Last Name]
Title

cc: Mr.[First Name][Middle Initial][Last Name]
Ms.[First Name][Middle Initial][Last Name]
Mrs.[First Name][Middle Initial][Last Name]

Letter: Block Style, Personal, Formal, Justified Body

(Condolences and sympathy letters: Sent to a surviving spouse)

[First Name][Middle Initial][Last Name]
Address line
City, State Zip

Month ##(date), #### (year) (Date; day of the week optional)

Mrs.[First Name][Middle Initial][Last Name](Recipient information)
Address line
City, State Zip

Dear Mrs.[Last Name]:

Body introductory paragraph: Everybody here at Acme Corporation was saddened to learn of the death of your husband. Raymond was a valued employee and will be sorely missed.

Body paragraph: Once you feel up to it, please contact me and I will go over those company benefits you will continue to receive as a surviving spouse. We can discuss Raymond's 401(k) and other retirement funds at that time as well.

Body closing paragraph: I speak for everyone here when I let you know that you are in our thoughts during this difficult time.

Sincerely,

(Signature)

Ann M. Hibbard
Benefits Administrator
Human Resources Department

Letter: Modified-Block Style, Personal, Formal, Indented Paragraphs

(Condolences and sympathy letters: Loss of job)

[First Name][Middle Initial][Last Name]
Address line
City, State Zip

September 30, 2007

Mr.[First Name][Middle Initial][Last Name](Recipient name and address information)
Address line
City, State Zip

Dear Mr.[Last Name]:

Body introductory paragraph: Vicki and I just heard about your job loss.

Body paragraph: That has to have been a blow; we imagine that knowing that others were affected by the downsizing still doesn't begin to alleviate the stress you're feeling. We only hope that during this time of transition, you concentrate on your strengths—your experience and qualifications, of which there are many.

Body closing paragraph: If I can be of any help as a reference, please feel free to use my name. I'll give you a call soon. I'm hoping we can get together for lunch so that we can brainstorm your options, if you think that will be of any help.

Sincerely,

(Signature)

[First Name][Middle Initial][Last Name]

Informal Memo

Memo
(Date)
TO: Recipient First and Last Names, Recipient First and Last Names
FROM: Sender[First Name][Last Name]
SUBJECT: Phrase describing purpose of memo

Content paragraph

Closing paragraph

Memo
(Date)
TO: Marketing Department Employees
FROM: H. Baxter Grant
SUBJECT: Department Picnic

A decision was reached to hold our annual picnic a bit earlier than usual in the hopes that we'll avoid many of the vacation conflicts we've experienced in the past.

Rain or shine, that event will take place on Saturday, June 28, at 1:00 p.m. at the Grand Lake Shelter House on Bluegill Road. I've enclosed a map with complete directions.

All food and drink will be provided. We'll have door prize drawings, including gifts for the kids.

Please call my secretary at 555-2345 by Wednesday, June 25, to let him know if you can make it, and how many will be attending in your party. Spouse or guest and children are welcome.

Sincerely,

HBG
    prh
    Enc.

Formal Memo Format

MEMORANDUM

TO: [Recipient First Name][Recipient Last Name]

COPIES TO*:   [First Name][Last Name],[First Name][Last Name]

FROM: [First Name][Last Name]

DATE: September 30, 2007

SUBJECT: Phrase describing purpose of memo

Dear[First Name from "TO:" line only):

Content introductory paragraph

Body paragraph/paragraphs

Closing paragraph

*If there are too many names to fit on one line, use this format:

COPIES TO: [First Name][Last Name]
                [First Name][Last Name]
                [First Name][Last Name]
                [First Name][Last Name]

Formal Memo Alternative Multiple Recipients Format

MEMORANDUM

TO: See Distribution Below

FROM: [First Name][Last Name]

DATE: September 30, 2007

SUBJECT: Phrase describing purpose of memo

Dear[First Name from "TO:" line only):

Content introductory paragraph

Body paragraph/paragraphs

Closing paragraph

*If there are too many names to fit on one line, use this format:

Distribution:

[First Initial].[Last Name]
[First Initial].[Last Name]
[First Initial].[Last Name]
[First Initial].[Last Name]
[First Initial].[Last Name]

Fax Format Example

FACSIMILE TRANSMITTAL SHEET

TO:
[First Name][Last Name]

FROM:
[First Name][Last Name]

COMPANY:
[Company Name]

DATE:
09/30/2007

FAX NUMBER:
(555) 555-5555

PAGE TOTAL, INCLUDING COVER:
[Appropriate #]

PHONE NUMBER:
(555) 555-5554

SENDER'S REFERENCE NUMBER:
[###]

RE:
[Phrase describing purpose of fax] [###]

YOUR REFERENCE NUMBER:
[###]

__ URGENT   __ FOR REVIEW   __ PLEASE COMMENT   __ PLEASE REPLY
__ PLEASE RECYCLE

NOTES/COMMENTS:

Content paragraph: The streetlights at the corners of Vine and Elizabeth, Elizabeth and Baxter, and Baxter and Elm have been out for more than a week. There are also a few other streetlights in the middle of those blocks that are out as well.

Additional content paragraph: As you know, a well-lit neighborhood is a safe one. Please see that this problem is corrected within the next few days.

Additional content paragraph: Thank you for your time and consideration.

Optional: Sender Address Line

Index

THE EVERYTHING SERIES!

BUSINESS & PERSONAL FINANCE

Everything® Accounting Book
Everything® Budgeting Book, 2nd Ed.
Everything® Business Planning Book
Everything® Coaching and Mentoring Book, 2nd Ed.
Everything® Fundraising Book
Everything® Get Out of Debt Book
Everything® Grant Writing Book, 2nd Ed.
Everything® Guide to Buying Foreclosures
Everything® Guide to Mortgages
Everything® Guide to Personal Finance for Single Mothers
Everything® Home-Based Business Book, 2nd Ed.
Everything® Homebuying Book, 2nd Ed.
Everything® Homeselling Book, 2nd Ed.
Everything® Human Resource Management Book
Everything® Improve Your Credit Book
Everything® Investing Book, 2nd Ed.
Everything® Landlording Book
Everything® Leadership Book, 2nd Ed.
Everything® Managing People Book, 2nd Ed.
Everything® Negotiating Book
Everything® Online Auctions Book
Everything® Online Business Book
Everything® Personal Finance Book
Everything® Personal Finance in Your 20s & 30s Book, 2nd Ed.
Everything® Project Management Book, 2nd Ed.
Everything® Real Estate Investing Book
Everything® Retirement Planning Book
Everything® Robert's Rules Book, $7.95
Everything® Selling Book
Everything® Start Your Own Business Book, 2nd Ed.
Everything® Wills & Estate Planning Book

COOKING

Everything® Barbecue Cookbook
Everything® Bartender's Book, 2nd Ed., $9.95
Everything® Calorie Counting Cookbook
Everything® Cheese Book
Everything® Chinese Cookbook
Everything® Classic Recipes Book
Everything® Cocktail Parties & Drinks Book
Everything® College Cookbook
Everything® Cooking for Baby and Toddler Book
Everything® Cooking for Two Cookbook
Everything® Diabetes Cookbook
Everything® Easy Gourmet Cookbook
Everything® Fondue Cookbook
Everything® Fondue Party Book
Everything® Gluten-Free Cookbook
Everything® Glycemic Index Cookbook
Everything® Grilling Cookbook
Everything® Healthy Meals in Minutes Cookbook
Everything® Holiday Cookbook
Everything® Indian Cookbook
Everything® Italian Cookbook

Everything® Lactose-Free Cookbook
Everything® Low-Carb Cookbook
Everything® Low-Cholesterol Cookbook
Everything® Low-Fat High-Flavor Cookbook
Everything® Low-Salt Cookbook
Everything® Meals for a Month Cookbook
Everything® Meals on a Budget Cookbook
Everything® Mediterranean Cookbook
Everything® Mexican Cookbook
Everything® No Trans Fat Cookbook
Everything® One-Pot Cookbook
Everything® Pizza Cookbook
Everything® Quick and Easy 30-Minute, 5-Ingredient Cookbook
Everything® Quick Meals Cookbook
Everything® Slow Cooker Cookbook
Everything® Slow Cooking for a Crowd Cookbook
Everything® Soup Cookbook
Everything® Stir-Fry Cookbook
Everything® Sugar-Free Cookbook
Everything® Tapas and Small Plates Cookbook
Everything® Tex-Mex Cookbook
Everything® Thai Cookbook
Everything® Vegetarian Cookbook
Everything® Whole-Grain, High-Fiber Cookbook
Everything® Wild Game Cookbook
Everything® Wine Book, 2nd Ed.

GAMES

Everything® 15-Minute Sudoku Book, $9.95
Everything® 30-Minute Sudoku Book, $9.95
Everything® Bible Crosswords Book, $9.95
Everything® Blackjack Strategy Book
Everything® Brain Strain Book, $9.95
Everything® Bridge Book
Everything® Card Games Book
Everything® Card Tricks Book, $9.95
Everything® Casino Gambling Book, 2nd Ed.
Everything® Chess Basics Book
Everything® Craps Strategy Book
Everything® Crossword and Puzzle Book
Everything® Crossword Challenge Book
Everything® Crosswords for the Beach Book, $9.95
Everything® Cryptic Crosswords Book, $9.95
Everything® Cryptograms Book, $9.95
Everything® Easy Crosswords Book
Everything® Easy Kakuro Book, $9.95
Everything® Easy Large-Print Crosswords Book
Everything® Games Book, 2nd Ed.
Everything® Giant Sudoku Book, $9.95
Everything® Giant Word Search Book
Everything® Kakuro Challenge Book, $9.95
Everything® Large-Print Crossword Challenge Book
Everything® Large-Print Crosswords Book
Everything® Lateral Thinking Puzzles Book, $9.95
Everything® Literary Crosswords Book, $9.95
Everything® Mazes Book
Everything® Memory Booster Puzzles Book, $9.95
Everything® Movie Crosswords Book, $9.95

Everything® Music Crosswords Book, $9.95
Everything® Online Poker Book
Everything® Pencil Puzzles Book, $9.95
Everything® Poker Strategy Book
Everything® Pool & Billiards Book
Everything® Puzzles for Commuters Book, $9.95
Everything® Puzzles for Dog Lovers Book, $9.95
Everything® Sports Crosswords Book, $9.95
Everything® Test Your IQ Book, $9.95
Everything® Texas Hold 'Em Book, $9.95
Everything® Travel Crosswords Book, $9.95
Everything® TV Crosswords Book, $9.95
Everything® Word Games Challenge Book
Everything® Word Scramble Book
Everything® Word Search Book

HEALTH

Everything® Alzheimer's Book
Everything® Diabetes Book
Everything® First Aid Book, $9.95
Everything® Health Guide to Adult Bipolar Disorder
Everything® Health Guide to Arthritis
Everything® Health Guide to Controlling Anxiety
Everything® Health Guide to Depression
Everything® Health Guide to Fibromyalgia
Everything® Health Guide to Menopause, 2nd Ed.
Everything® Health Guide to Migraines
Everything® Health Guide to OCD
Everything® Health Guide to PMS
Everything® Health Guide to Postpartum Care
Everything® Health Guide to Thyroid Disease
Everything® Hypnosis Book
Everything® Low Cholesterol Book
Everything® Menopause Book
Everything® Nutrition Book
Everything® Reflexology Book
Everything® Stress Management Book

HISTORY

Everything® American Government Book
Everything® American History Book, 2nd Ed.
Everything® Civil War Book
Everything® Freemasons Book
Everything® Irish History & Heritage Book
Everything® Middle East Book
Everything® World War II Book, 2nd Ed.

HOBBIES

Everything® Candlemaking Book
Everything® Cartooning Book
Everything® Coin Collecting Book
Everything® Digital Photography Book, 2nd Ed.
Everything® Drawing Book
Everything® Family Tree Book, 2nd Ed.
Everything® Knitting Book
Everything® Knots Book
Everything® Photography Book
Everything® Quilting Book

Everything® Sewing Book
Everything® Soapmaking Book, 2nd Ed.
Everything® Woodworking Book

HOME IMPROVEMENT

Everything® Feng Shui Book
Everything® Feng Shui Decluttering Book, $9.95
Everything® Fix-It Book
Everything® Green Living Book
Everything® Home Decorating Book
Everything® Home Storage Solutions Book
Everything® Homebuilding Book
Everything® Organize Your Home Book, 2nd Ed.

KIDS' BOOKS

All titles are $7.95
Everything® Fairy Tales Book, $14.95
Everything® Kids' Animal Puzzle & Activity Book
Everything® Kids' Astronomy Book
Everything® Kids' Baseball Book, 5th Ed.
Everything® Kids' Bible Trivia Book
Everything® Kids' Bugs Book
Everything® Kids' Cars and Trucks Puzzle and Activity Book
Everything® Kids' Christmas Puzzle & Activity Book
Everything® Kids' Connect the Dots
**   Puzzle and Activity Book**
Everything® Kids' Cookbook
Everything® Kids' Crazy Puzzles Book
Everything® Kids' Dinosaurs Book
Everything® Kids' Environment Book
Everything® Kids' Fairies Puzzle and Activity Book
Everything® Kids' First Spanish Puzzle and Activity Book
Everything® Kids' Football Book
Everything® Kids' Gross Cookbook
Everything® Kids' Gross Hidden Pictures Book
Everything® Kids' Gross Jokes Book
Everything® Kids' Gross Mazes Book
Everything® Kids' Gross Puzzle & Activity Book
Everything® Kids' Halloween Puzzle & Activity Book
Everything® Kids' Hidden Pictures Book
Everything® Kids' Horses Book
Everything® Kids' Joke Book
Everything® Kids' Knock Knock Book
Everything® Kids' Learning French Book
Everything® Kids' Learning Spanish Book
Everything® Kids' Magical Science Experiments Book
Everything® Kids' Math Puzzles Book
Everything® Kids' Mazes Book
Everything® Kids' Money Book
Everything® Kids' Nature Book
Everything® Kids' Pirates Puzzle and Activity Book
Everything® Kids' Presidents Book
Everything® Kids' Princess Puzzle and Activity Book
Everything® Kids' Puzzle Book
Everything® Kids' Racecars Puzzle and Activity Book
Everything® Kids' Riddles & Brain Teasers Book
Everything® Kids' Science Experiments Book
Everything® Kids' Sharks Book
Everything® Kids' Soccer Book
Everything® Kids' Spies Puzzle and Activity Book
Everything® Kids' States Book
Everything® Kids' Travel Activity Book
Everything® Kids' Word Search Puzzle and Activity Book

LANGUAGE

Everything® Conversational Japanese Book with CD, $19.95
Everything® French Grammar Book
Everything® French Phrase Book, $9.95
Everything® French Verb Book, $9.95
Everything® German Practice Book with CD, $19.95
Everything® Inglés Book
Everything® Intermediate Spanish Book with CD, $19.95
Everything® Italian Practice Book with CD, $19.95
Everything® Learning Brazilian Portuguese Book with CD, $19.95
Everything® Learning French Book with CD, 2nd Ed., $19.95
Everything® Learning German Book
Everything® Learning Italian Book
Everything® Learning Latin Book
Everything® Learning Russian Book with CD, $19.95
Everything® Learning Spanish Book
Everything® Learning Spanish Book with CD, 2nd Ed., $19.95
Everything® Russian Practice Book with CD, $19.95
Everything® Sign Language Book
Everything® Spanish Grammar Book
Everything® Spanish Phrase Book, $9.95
Everything® Spanish Practice Book with CD, $19.95
Everything® Spanish Verb Book, $9.95
Everything® Speaking Mandarin Chinese Book with CD, $19.95

MUSIC

Everything® Bass Guitar Book with CD, $19.95
Everything® Drums Book with CD, $19.95
Everything® Guitar Book with CD, 2nd Ed., $19.95
Everything® Guitar Chords Book with CD, $19.95
Everything® Harmonica Book with CD, $15.95
Everything® Home Recording Book
Everything® Music Theory Book with CD, $19.95
Everything® Reading Music Book with CD, $19.95
Everything® Rock & Blues Guitar Book with CD, $19.95
Everything® Rock & Blues Piano Book with CD, $19.95
Everything® Songwriting Book

NEW AGE

Everything® Astrology Book, 2nd Ed.
Everything® Birthday Personology Book
Everything® Dreams Book, 2nd Ed.
Everything® Love Signs Book, $9.95
Everything® Love Spells Book, $9.95
Everything® Paganism Book
Everything® Palmistry Book
Everything® Psychic Book
Everything® Reiki Book
Everything® Sex Signs Book, $9.95
Everything® Spells & Charms Book, 2nd Ed.
Everything® Tarot Book, 2nd Ed.
Everything® Toltec Wisdom Book
Everything® Wicca & Witchcraft Book, 2nd Ed.

PARENTING

Everything® Baby Names Book, 2nd Ed.
Everything® Baby Shower Book, 2nd Ed.
Everything® Baby Sign Language Book with DVD
Everything® Baby's First Year Book
Everything® Birthing Book

Everything® Breastfeeding Book
Everything® Father-to-Be Book
Everything® Father's First Year Book
Everything® Get Ready for Baby Book, 2nd Ed.
Everything® Get Your Baby to Sleep Book, $9.95
Everything® Getting Pregnant Book
Everything® Guide to Pregnancy Over 35
Everything® Guide to Raising a One-Year-Old
Everything® Guide to Raising a Two-Year-Old
Everything® Guide to Raising Adolescent Boys
Everything® Guide to Raising Adolescent Girls
Everything® Mother's First Year Book
Everything® Parent's Guide to Childhood Illnesses
Everything® Parent's Guide to Children and Divorce
Everything® Parent's Guide to Children with ADD/ADHD
Everything® Parent's Guide to Children with Asperger's
    Syndrome
Everything® Parent's Guide to Children with Asthma
Everything® Parent's Guide to Children with Autism
Everything® Parent's Guide to Children with Bipolar Disorder
Everything® Parent's Guide to Children with Depression
Everything® Parent's Guide to Children with Dyslexia
Everything® Parent's Guide to Children with Juvenile Diabetes
Everything® Parent's Guide to Positive Discipline
Everything® Parent's Guide to Raising a Successful Child
Everything® Parent's Guide to Raising Boys
Everything® Parent's Guide to Raising Girls
Everything® Parent's Guide to Raising Siblings
Everything® Parent's Guide to Sensory Integration Disorder
Everything® Parent's Guide to Tantrums
Everything® Parent's Guide to the Strong-Willed Child
Everything® Parenting a Teenager Book
Everything® Potty Training Book, $9.95
Everything® Pregnancy Book, 3rd Ed.
Everything® Pregnancy Fitness Book
Everything® Pregnancy Nutrition Book
Everything® Pregnancy Organizer, 2nd Ed., $16.95
Everything® Toddler Activities Book
Everything® Toddler Book
Everything® Tween Book
Everything® Twins, Triplets, and More Book

PETS

Everything® Aquarium Book
Everything® Boxer Book
Everything® Cat Book, 2nd Ed.
Everything® Chihuahua Book
Everything® Cooking for Dogs Book
Everything® Dachshund Book
Everything® Dog Book, 2nd Ed.
Everything® Dog Grooming Book
Everything® Dog Health Book
Everything® Dog Obedience Book
Everything® Dog Owner's Organizer, $16.95
Everything® Dog Training and Tricks Book
Everything® German Shepherd Book
Everything® Golden Retriever Book
Everything® Horse Book
Everything® Horse Care Book
Everything® Horseback Riding Book
Everything® Labrador Retriever Book
Everything® Poodle Book
Everything® Pug Book

Everything® Puppy Book
Everything® Rottweiler Book
Everything® Small Dogs Book
Everything® Tropical Fish Book
Everything® Yorkshire Terrier Book

REFERENCE

Everything® American Presidents Book
Everything® Blogging Book
Everything® Build Your Vocabulary Book, $9.95
Everything® Car Care Book
Everything® Classical Mythology Book
Everything® Da Vinci Book
Everything® Divorce Book
Everything® Einstein Book
Everything® Enneagram Book
Everything® Etiquette Book, 2nd Ed.
Everything® Guide to C. S. Lewis & Narnia
Everything® Guide to Edgar Allan Poe
Everything® Guide to Understanding Philosophy
Everything® Inventions and Patents Book
Everything® Jacqueline Kennedy Onassis Book
Everything® John F. Kennedy Book
Everything® Mafia Book
Everything® Martin Luther King Jr. Book
Everything® Philosophy Book
Everything® Pirates Book
Everything® Private Investigation Book
Everything® Psychology Book
Everything® Public Speaking Book, $9.95
Everything® Shakespeare Book, 2nd Ed.

RELIGION

Everything® Angels Book
Everything® Bible Book
Everything® Bible Study Book with CD, $19.95
Everything® Buddhism Book
Everything® Catholicism Book
Everything® Christianity Book
Everything® Gnostic Gospels Book
Everything® History of the Bible Book
Everything® Jesus Book
Everything® Jewish History & Heritage Book
Everything® Judaism Book
Everything® Kabbalah Book
Everything® Koran Book
Everything® Mary Book
Everything® Mary Magdalene Book
Everything® Prayer Book
Everything® Saints Book, 2nd Ed.
Everything® Torah Book
Everything® Understanding Islam Book
Everything® Women of the Bible Book
Everything® World's Religions Book

SCHOOL & CAREERS

Everything® Career Tests Book
Everything® College Major Test Book
Everything® College Survival Book, 2nd Ed.
Everything® Cover Letter Book, 2nd Ed.
Everything® Filmmaking Book
Everything® Get-a-Job Book, 2nd Ed.
Everything® Guide to Being a Paralegal
Everything® Guide to Being a Personal Trainer
Everything® Guide to Being a Real Estate Agent
Everything® Guide to Being a Sales Rep
Everything® Guide to Being an Event Planner
Everything® Guide to Careers in Health Care
Everything® Guide to Careers in Law Enforcement
Everything® Guide to Government Jobs
Everything® Guide to Starting and Running a Catering
    Business
Everything® Guide to Starting and Running a Restaurant
Everything® Job Interview Book, 2nd Ed.
Everything® New Nurse Book
Everything® New Teacher Book
Everything® Paying for College Book
Everything® Practice Interview Book
Everything® Resume Book, 3rd Ed.
Everything® Study Book

SELF-HELP

Everything® Body Language Book
Everything® Dating Book, 2nd Ed.
Everything® Great Sex Book
Everything® Self-Esteem Book
Everything® Tantric Sex Book

SPORTS & FITNESS

Everything® Easy Fitness Book
Everything® Fishing Book
Everything® Krav Maga for Fitness Book
Everything® Running Book, 2nd Ed.

TRAVEL

Everything® Family Guide to Coastal Florida
Everything® Family Guide to Cruise Vacations
Everything® Family Guide to Hawaii
Everything® Family Guide to Las Vegas, 2nd Ed.
Everything® Family Guide to Mexico
Everything® Family Guide to New England, 2nd Ed.
Everything® Family Guide to New York City, 3rd Ed.
Everything® Family Guide to RV Travel & Campgrounds
Everything® Family Guide to the Caribbean
Everything® Family Guide to the Disneyland® Resort, California
    Adventure®, Universal Studios®, and the Anaheim
    Area, 2nd Ed.
Everything® Family Guide to the Walt Disney World Resort®,
    Universal Studios®, and Greater Orlando, 5th Ed.
Everything® Family Guide to Timeshares
Everything® Family Guide to Washington D.C., 2nd Ed.

WEDDINGS

Everything® Bachelorette Party Book, $9.95
Everything® Bridesmaid Book, $9.95
Everything® Destination Wedding Book
Everything® Father of the Bride Book, $9.95
Everything® Groom Book, $9.95
Everything® Mother of the Bride Book, $9.95
Everything® Outdoor Wedding Book
Everything® Wedding Book, 3rd Ed.
Everything® Wedding Checklist, $9.95
Everything® Wedding Etiquette Book, $9.95
Everything® Wedding Organizer, 2nd Ed., $16.95
Everything® Wedding Shower Book, $9.95
Everything® Wedding Vows Book, $9.95
Everything® Wedding Workout Book
Everything® Weddings on a Budget Book, 2nd Ed., $9.95

WRITING

Everything® Creative Writing Book
Everything® Get Published Book, 2nd Ed.
Everything® Grammar and Style Book, 2nd Ed.
Everything® Guide to Magazine Writing
Everything® Guide to Writing a Book Proposal
Everything® Guide to Writing a Novel
Everything® Guide to Writing Children's Books
Everything® Guide to Writing Copy
Everything® Guide to Writing Graphic Novels
Everything® Guide to Writing Research Papers
Everything® Improve Your Writing Book, 2nd Ed.
Everything® Writing Poetry Book